ADVANCED
CREATIVE
DRAPING

LAURENCE KING

First published in Great Britain in 2022 by

Laurence King Student & Professional
An imprint of Quercus Editions Ltd
Carmelite House
50 Victoria Embankment
London EC4Y 0DZ

An Hachette UK company

A CIP catalogue record for this book is available from the British Library

ISBN 978-1-91394-772-9

10 9 8 7 6 5 4 3 2 1

Design by The Urban Ant Ltd

Printed and bound in China by C & C Offset Printing Co., Ltd.

Papers used by Quercus are from well-managed forests and other responsible sources.

ADVANCED
CREATIVE
DRAPING

KAROLYN KIISEL

LAURENCE KING PUBLISHING

Contents

Introduction: Creative Inspiration
through Draping 6

Stages of Creative Draping 8

Draping Today's Heirloom Designs 23

Chapter 1: Experimental Draping

Experimental Draping 26

The Skill of Visualization...................................27

Beginning a Collection: Setting the mood
with fabric choices 30

Exercise 1: First Impressions....................................32

Exercise 2: Studying Grainlines 36

Exercise 3: Testing Design Elements......................42

Exercise 4: Construction Testing............................46

Exercise 5: Special Effects and Embellishments 48

Project: Experimental Draping from
Inspiration Boards 50

Chapter 2: Improvisational Draping

Improvisational Draping 56

Working Intuitively 57

Self-Awareness...57

Draping Preparation 58

Exercise 1: Earth's Heritage Studies......................60

Exercise 2: Ikebana Studies 62

Exercise 3: Dark Radiance Studies...........................65

Exercise 4: Upcycle Study 68

Project: The Improvisational Drape 71

Chapter 3: The Block-to-Drape Method

The Block-to-Drape Method.......................................78

Recognizing Templates for Blocks 79

Using Reference Garments...80

Draping and Drafting Methods.................................80

Exercise 1: Draping a Block
from a Reference Garment.....................................81

Exercise 2: Block-to-Drape: the Bodice Block 86

Exercise 3: Block-to-Drape: the Pant Block............90

Exercise 4: Block-to-Drape: the Two-Piece
Sleeve Block...94

Project: Block-to-Drape: the Tailored Jacket 96

Chapter 4: Draping on the Half-Scale Form

Draping on the Half-Scale Form 106

Improvisational Draping on
the Half-Scale Form 108

Exercise 1: Modernizing the Cut of
a Traditional Ethnic Design.............................. 110

Exercise 2: Half-Scale Experimental and
Improvisational Draping 114

Exercise 3: Zero-Waste Cutting 118

Project: Design Development on
the Half-Scale Form 120

Chapter 5: Draping from an Illustration

Draping from an Illustration 128

Design Sketches... 129

Fashion Illustration 131

Technical Flat Sketches.. 132

Exercise: Draping from a Costume Design
Illustration and Flat Sketch 133

Project: Draping from a Fashion Illustration........ 137

Chapter 6: Draping with the use of Two-Dimensional Surface Design

Creative Draping with Two-Dimensional
   Surface Design 148
Maximizing the Impact of a Two-Dimensional
   Surface Design 149
Understanding the Power of Color 150
Creative Draping Techniques to Use with
   Two-Dimensional Surface Design 151
Exercise 1: Ombré, Airbrushing, and the use of
   Novelty Dyeing Techniques 152
Exercise 2: Artisanally Crafted
   Two-Dimensional Design 154
Project: Draping using a Digital Print 157

Chapter 7: Draping with the use of Three-Dimensional Embellishment

Draping with the use of Three-Dimensional
   Embellishment 164
Purpose and Origin of Embellishment 165
Categories of Embellishment 167
Creative Draping and Developing
   Embellishments 170
Exercise 1: Integration of Technology
   in Draping 171
Exercise 2: Embellishment Mock-Up Tests 174
Project: Embellishment Development 180

Chapter 8: Draping for Costume Design

Draping for Costume Design 190
Building a Costume 190
The Stages of Costume Design 192
Exercise 1: Half-Scale Design Development 195
Exercise 2: Experimental Draping 196
Exercise 3: Improvisational Draping 198
Project 1: The Minuet Dancer Costume 200
Project 2: The Beaumarchais Costume 210

Chapter 9: Draping the Heirloom Design

Draping the Heirloom Design 220
Modern Heirloom Garments 221
Exercise: Heirloom Design Development 225
Project: Draping the Modern Heirloom Design .. 228

Glossary 246
Videos 248
Resources 249
Index 250
Credits 254
Acknowledgments 256

Creative Inspiration through Draping

Where does creative inspiration come from? How does it arise in designers and how is it expressed in their work? *Advanced Creative Draping* explores how fashion and costume designers' imaginations can be stimulated in the exercise of their craft—specifically, through the hands-on practice of draping.

The goal is to design from a conceptual base, drawing from your own ground of aesthetic experience to produce clothes that are rich, meaningful, and artfully made. Creative draping nurtures originality and enables an individual signature style to develop.

The draping approaches presented here are intended to stimulate creative inspiration and generate design concepts while also providing instruction in a variety of specific techniques and skills for realizing those ideas. In the first seven chapters of this book, different draping techniques will be systematically explored through visual examples, studies, exercises, and projects. The final two chapters, "Draping for Costume Design" and "Draping the Heirloom Design," draw on all of these methods.

The insights of our community of designers are included in stories and quotations. We build on a wealth of experience. Clothing design and construction have evolved over centuries, and many designs and techniques used long ago are still valid.

Research informs creativity. Use of cultural and historical references gives us a sense of how the old interacts with the new, enabling us to forge new territory. Deepening awareness of one's own context is also research; it illuminates the way you, personally, fit into the creative progression of your design path.

Understanding ergonomics, the study of fit and movement, is an essential element of high-quality design. Included here are sections on fitting and self-assessment. Couture-quality workmanship takes much experience to master, but an understanding and appreciation of the depth of skill involved in superior craftsmanship is a good beginning.

Because draping is intuitive, the designer's personal aesthetic emerges organically.

Projects here present theories and principles of advanced construction such as advanced tailoring techniques, draping with textural embellishments, and the use of support understructures. An understanding of these will help you translate your drapes into working patterns and finished apparel of quality. While some of the exercises are intended to be followed closely, others are simply guideposts to help you while doing an original design project in parallel.

Eye, hand, and heart

Mastering the designer's essential skill of draping requires schooling your eye to recognize balance and good composition, training your hand to dexterity in cutting, pinning and combining complex curves, and using your heart to strengthen individual expression.

Developing what is often called a "good eye" in design takes practice, study, and analytical skills. Thoughtful and critical observation can cultivate a discerning eye and a refined taste level. Draping has the great advantage of giving immediate visual feedback, as the contours of a garment can be seen taking shape during the process.

Training the "hand" can be compared to practicing a musical instrument. The aim is to reach the point where technical skills become so natural that their importance recedes, and creative, subconscious decision-making emerges.

For a contemporary designer, finding the "heart" of your creativity is of utmost importance. To work successfully in this highly competitive field, a designer must have a unique, individual style. New fashion students may feel they must define their personal style right away, but it can take time and patience to develop. The freedom that draping allows nurtures this process in a natural, organic way.

The skill of draping is invaluable for discovering this personal aesthetic, as refining a drape and arriving at a balance is a very personal process. Working hands-on with fabrics to convey an

Madame Alix Grès was formally trained as a sculptor. She opened her first couture house in Paris in 1932, applying sculpting techniques to her fabric forms. Her signature pleated goddess gowns were all done by hand, typically on live models, draping the cloth so the body shaped the dress. Here, a dress for *Images de France* in 1942 is being draped with silk jersey. This drape was lightly held together by a few pins, then vanished like a dream after being captured in this photograph.

emotion, mood, or concept allows your personal style to take flight, expressing itself in a continuous stream of decisions about proportion, scale, and volume. Observing the subtleties of line, shape, and silhouette strengthens visualization skills.

Draping intuitively, and developing the ability to lose yourself in a creative flow is essential to accessing the deepest well of inspiration, helping you as a designer to find your own voice.

Draping with muslin

A simple length of natural muslin, the most humble but fundamental of tools, is our blank canvas, our starting point. A swirling collage of inspirations comes into focus, an idea begins to crystallize, and as the draping begins, a concept becomes physical.

The designers' medium is textiles, but while draping, muslin is our medium. There is a purity to muslin that allows for a focus and concentration on the forms, shapes, and silhouettes being created, the lines and curves being defined.

The simplicity of that blank canvas—the beginning of the muslin drape—is the moment of creative inception.

We are designing when we start to create a shape, and everything is important; we need to find the balance. It is not just technique; there have to be reasons to make a seam here or there. The seam of the shoulder—if it's a little up or down, or out a bit further, this means she is stronger, or softer; the look is changed right away. It's about imagination, sensation, desire, how a woman feels in that dress. Imagine everything. Signify something.

Bastide Rey, modéliste, former head of atelier for Alexander McQueen, Dior, and Lanvin, currently with Elber Albaz. Interview with the author, 2017.

Stages of Creative Draping

Creative draping and design can be nurtured. Muslin is the blank canvas, and draping refines shape and silhouette. Color creates the emotional tenor, while textures, treatments, and ornamentation add emotional impact and refine the energy of the design.

Find your focus
Identify an inspiration

The very first step in design is the inspiration. The designer must discover something they want or feel compelled to communicate, and then articulate that through their design work.

Inspiration can come from something as simple and universal as a beautiful sunset. Feel free to move beyond the familiar and consider natural and unnatural forms in architecture, travel, personal interests, spiritual beliefs, photography, packaging design, cultural influences, even found objects.

Many designers begin by creating an inspiration journal or mood board of ideas they are exploring. The inspiration can be visual images or text. Since the quest for inspiration is about evoking a mood or tone, find reference images that render some essence of that feeling.

Inspiration at the simplest level is just noticing things that attract you, personally. Give physical form to that attraction by creating an assemblage of fabrics, bits of vintage clothing or trims, photos, and artifacts such as pieces of jewelry and tools.

It can be helpful to add written words or descriptive phrases to your inspiration board. Words are powerful—they can spark creativity and also help to define the mood, tone, and the visual style of your work. Your inspiration board can also be very helpful in creating a guardrail that will keep you on track during the creative process. Sometimes when you are deep into the design or construction of a collection, ideas start overflowing. That is when it is good to have a reminder of what you were trying to achieve in the first place. Going back to the board helps keep you stay focused.

Alexander McQueen, Savage Beauty collection, 2011. McQueen drew riches of inspiration from a broad spectrum, his profound symbolism painting emotional landscapes of great intensity and depth, his juxtapositions of color and texture giving the punctuation to his design.

- Dark Radiance is connecting to the cosmic, space exploration of the galaxies.
- The darkness implies the vastness,.
- "The wildness of the night, with the sweetness of the heart" (from the Chinese mystical text the *I Ching*).
- Passionate, romantic love, glamorous nights, mirrors and neon, rich Baroque embellishments.
- Los Angeles and Las Vegas.

The Dark Radiance inspiration board is a fall/winter color palette, with jewel tones and metallic, bronzed finishes.

Define your visual style

Now that you have your inspiration, how you will express it? Consider what you want your visual style to be: formal, and orderly? Wild and disordered?

If the fashion industry can be likened to a conversation, each designer must offer his or her own, unique point of view in order to be part of it. When you speak, you must know what to say, and how to infuse your voice with emotion and color, punctuation and depth.

Many acclaimed designers tell stories through their collections. Note how the two verbal descriptions (right) create very specific, graphic visions of what those stories will be.

That's my thing, making cocoons. Very severe and gray and soundproofed cocoons.

Rick Owens, on commissioning a matte-black Airstream trailer for his road trips through Southern California, quoted in the L.A. Times, July 20, 2015

They were lost and now they were on their way. It feels like they were walking forever on those highways. And the clothes are tripping and falling and fainting, and I think that's a beautiful mood.

Haider Ackermann on Fashionisers.com, describing "handsome women" and the mood and tone of his Spring/Summer 2014 collection

IKEBANA

- Ikebana: a garden both in flower and in decay.
- Butterflies, flowers, the patterns of nature, delicate, airy.
- The life force of the bloom, the lushness of the peony and the delicate edges of the iris.
- The fragility of life; impermanence.
- The poignant beauty of flower petals becoming thin and papery, then turning to dust.

Ikebana: The Japanese spiritual practice of flower arranging according to the principles of Heaven, Earth, and Human. The Ikebana inspiration board is a spring/summer color palette.

Incorporate research

Incorporating research into your work means finding connections to the past, then using your own experience to enrich those connections to create something truly new for today's world. Designers must be up to date. View collections, observe street style, research how other designers are expressing similar ideas to yours, Stay informed about technology: its influence on fashion is woven into every aspect of a designer's world. Cutting-edge technologies may be incorporated as tools in a designer's skill set. Social media is powerful, making it easy to connect, promote, advertise, and sell to new markets globally.

Designer's Aims and Aspirations

- **Find your focus:** Identify your inspiration; determine your visual style.
- **Incorporate research:** Find the connective tissue between past and present, cultural and historical, and be aware of your own personal context.
- **Recognize the principles of good design:** Keep in mind that design principles transcend fashion and apply to all disciplines.
- **Establish your ergonomics:** Ask yourself whether your style of fit and movement is classic, romantic, or non-traditional.
- **Acknowledge the ethics of slow fashion:** Consult your conscience regarding carbon footprint; aspire to integrity.
- **Apply quality of craftsmanship:** Know your craft; be familiar with the essential skills of couture.

Earth's Heritage

- Earth's Heritage is a mystical oasis, centered around the ancient "Rhythm of Nature" diagram.
- Highlights the beauty of nature; the primitive.
- My design inspiration draws on timeless silhouettes; ancient nomads and Biblical times.
- Heirloom-quality, artisanal craftsmanship, hand-worked details.
- The Earth's elements, glaciers, gemstones, shells.

The color palette of the Earth's Heritage collage is seasonless, and the fabric swatches on the board are all of natural fibers .

Find the connective tissue between past and present

The more you know about what has gone before, the easier you will find it to build on it. Knowledge of fashion history is essential.

Wisdom is transmitted and valued in fashion, just as in other creative fields. Whether it be an artisan passing on the secrets of a craft, a chef the techniques of the kitchen, or a teacher the principles and practices of a particular subject, all embody and nourish inspiration. They communicate the authenticity of something that works.

This wisdom is not static. We can absorb the essence of an experience, embrace the living quality that is still there, and decide where and how we can apply those principles again, enriching them with the freshness of today. The goal is to internalize the research, then create the new. The capacity to adapt and innovate is the essence of informed creativity.

Key to Classic Research Methods

- Search by source: internet, library books and periodicals, cultural observation.
- Make a historical timeline.
- Write definitions.
- Classify: How has this thing or concept mainly been used?
- Recognize parts and label them.
- Experiential: What is it like?
- Compare and contrast: How are things the same? How are they different?
- Summarize: Venn diagrams.
- Teach it! You will learn more if you start teaching more.

For the designer, research is more than reading about the past; images are central to receive, absorb, bounce your own ideas against while you construct new meaning. This dynamic is thousands of years old, taking the form of "schools" of art that still thrive today. Be aware of your contemporaries; is someone else is saying the same thing as you? How are they expressing it? Emotion and memory are research as well—such as when you feel the sweetness of a Victorian puffed sleeve, or the tough protectiveness of a heavy leather motorcycle jacket.

We research to learn from the past, but we also borrow directly from it. The trench coat was invented many years ago, but is timeless. This familiar historical reference creates prejudicial bias. I like a trench coat—it makes me feel like Sherlock Holmes or Columbo. So, when I design a new one, I will research its history, list its design elements, and the fabrics from which it has traditionally been made. I will include elements to connect the trench coat to its past, yet feel modern.

As another example of prejudicial bias, imagine a collection referencing a cinematic mood – the romance of old-fashioned Hollywood glamour, a reimagined 1940s' vibe that gives women an aura of mystery, makes them feel attractive, and slightly dangerous or daring. The familiarity of that reference adds a level of comfort and makes it easier for someone to fantasize a positive experience of that era and hence, buy into that collection.

Cultural appropriation or appreciation?

In fashion design, we are all influenced by what has gone before, Historical or cultural cross-pollination enriches fashion, enabling the designer to go beyond the boundaries of a single tradition. However, care must be taken to clearly acknowledge the references, reinterpret respectfully, and offer our own contemporary version. Research is critical to determining the difference between cultural appropriation vs. appreciation, as it can be confusing.

An example is the Chinese cheongsam, a close-fitting, high-necked dress popularized in Shanghai in the 1920s. It was descended from the fitted robes worn by men in the years of Manchu rule, beginning in 1644. At the beginning of the Republican period, in 1912, Manchu style was adopted by women as a form of liberation from their traditional roles. Then, as Chinese women looked to Western fashion in the 1930s, they transformed the cheongsam from a long jacket worn with trousers to a close-fitting high-collared dress worn with stockings and heels, combining the sensibilities of both cultures. So, when a woman, Chinese or Western, wears a modern cheongsam, is that cultural appropriation or appreciation?

Tribalism can be very divisive to our global culture. However, a respectful and authentic interpretation that expresses something new, enriches whatever cultures that inspired it.

Above: Contemporary Sami dress. The cultural crisis of the Sami is not having a structure to support their original identity. Their challenge: to hold onto their values while adapting to urban life.

Left: AALTO, by Tuomas Merikoski, Fall/Winter 2016. Note how the graphic color-blocking echoes that of the Sami design.

Below left: Hellsinki Collection by Tuomas Merikoski, AALTO, Fall/Winter 2016. The low-slung belt echoes the low-belted structure of the Sami coat.

Below right: Forest green coat and hat, AALTO, by Tuomas Merikoski, Fall/Winter 2015. The height and proportion echo the look of the traditional Sami hat.

> My collections are the link between two worlds; the original Sami identity and a new one that reflects their evolving culture and style as it intertwines with the modern world.
>
> *Tuomas Merikoski*

Tuomas Merikoski
Self Awareness

Research includes cultivating an awareness of personal context. A designer who creates by drawing from their own heritage, as Finnish designer Tuomas Merikoski has done, offers riches of depth and authenticity to their statement. He has worked for Givenchy and Louis Vuitton, but with AALTO, his own brand, he takes inspiration from his Sami background, the Laplanders of northern Scandinavia, and this is clearly reflected in his color balance, line, silhouette, and attitude.

Taking self-knowledge further, consider whether you aspire to be original or avant-garde, whether you are making a socio-political statement about society, or about reality, or if you want to use fashion as your art.

What is originality?

"Original" fashion designs are those that are very different from anything seen before. To create original work, the designer must research what has gone before with an inquiring mind and a sense of curiosity, gained a deep understanding of the material, and critically assessed what they have seen. They can then create a new iteration, one informed by their own personal experience. Design that integrates original concepts into a familiar structure is certainly original.

The jumpsuit worn by David Bowie is clearly a highly original piece, because it pushed the boundaries of fashion at the time. The silhouette is distinctive and the fabric innovative, making it visually compelling in a way that original art must be.

David Bowie wearing a jumpsuit by Kansai Yamamoto, 1973.

What is avant-garde?

Avant-garde is the extension of originality from the individual to the group. It arises from people that are the most advanced in any field, whose works are daring, characterized by unorthodox, experimental methods and aesthetic innovation, or which connect with forward thinking in technology, philosophy, psychology etc. It offers new, radical material informed by a questioning of society and culture.

Avant-garde movements are groups of people building on one another's ideas and creativity. Iris van Herpen is an avant-garde designer because not only is her work very forward-thinking and groundbreaking in design, but her work is collaborative with others in the forefront of various technologies and in the scientific field.

In our modern era, and in most cultures worldwide, clothing inherently incorporates a sense of fashion, and to be fashionable in our modern sense means wearing clothes that are just right for the time and the place—aligning with the spirit of the age. Because the fashion industry is so focused on the zeitgeist, it is often in the most innovative, experimental, avant-garde looks that a designer can stand out with and be recognized for their own unique style.

Iris van Herpen: feather dress, 2013 "Wilderness Embodied" collection, a collaboration with several architects and artists using three-dimensional printing and laser cutting.

Paul Poiret, *Les Modes*, 1912.

Paul Poiret was considered avant-garde, part of an early twentieth-century artistic and cultural movement that encompassed illustration, architecture, interior, and furniture design. The diverse members of this movement, including the legendary Erté (Romain de Tirtoff), inspired each other and pushed each other toward new ground.

It is a matter of debate whether Poiret or his contemporary Madeleine Vionnet first dressed women without corsets, but both were avant-garde. Poiret's designs were so shocking that women literally fainted on the streets when his models appeared in his latest creations.

In 1912 the avant-garde group to which Poiret belonged created the *Gazette du Bon Ton*, a publication that featured Art Nouveau concepts, and the style known as Orientalism, employing many of the most famous Art Deco artists and illustrators of the day. Rather than simply drawing models in clothes, these artists went in a new direction, depicting them in various dramatic and narrative situations.

Fashion as a socio-political statement

Fashion has long been an instrument of change because it can create images and attitudes that shift consciousness. It has galvanized numerous social or political movements

In 1968–69 the Beatles went from young men in black suits to superstars wearing pink and orange faux-military jackets, practicing transcendental meditation, and being photographed with the guru Maharishi Mahesh Yogi. These images attuned mass consciousness towards counter-culture values such as the embracing of Eastern religions, and the "Make Love Not War" movement.

In the 1970s, Punk emerged. This socio-political movement was energized by fashion and music, namely the radical designs of Vivienne Westwood and Malcolm McLaren, made in their provocative and edgy boutique, SEX, on Kings Road in London.

Images have the power to shift our perception of reality, to uplift us, or to spur us into action. Fashion is a powerful medium with which to express a message.

The Beatles' *Sgt. Pepper's Lonely Hearts Club Band* album cover. Images can change consciousness.

Is fashion art?

If fashion shares the avant-garde with art, then is fashion itself art? The infusion of art into clothing—painted leathers, or intricately beaded fabrics—has been universal in indigenous cultures throughout human history. High craft—exhibiting beauty, meaning, and originality in clothing—is seen in historical clothing in museums worldwide.

It is an interesting debate to consider what truly brings clothing into the realm of art. Designers such as Paco Rabanne and Courrèges in the 1960s, and into the following decades, Jean-Paul Gaultier, Viktor & Rolf, Hussein Chalayan, Alexander McQueen, and currently, Libertine and Christelle Kocher are clearly exploring artistic, conceptual themes beyond making decorative or practical clothing.

Two of the most successful designers of our times, Rei Kawakubo and Karl Lagerfeld, both claim that their work was not "art." Kawakubo's designs with their compelling shapes and and visceral imagery resonate deeply. Lagerfeld's use of color and innovative materials in his embellishment combined with the highest possible level of craftsmanship, surely transcends the nature of craft and takes some of his pieces into art.

Janelle Monae at the 2019 Met Gala wearing Christian Siriano's "Blinking Eye" dress. If your design makes the person who wears it a work of art, perhaps that makes you both artists.

It's marvelous to appreciate paintings but [...] why not create a whole esthetic ambience? Be your own living work of art?

Truman Capote, interviewed by Gloria Steinem, 1967

Perhaps the women who wear the fashion garments are the art themselves: Countess Greffulhe, who presided over the chicest Parisian salons during the belle époque; the iconic artist Frieda Kahlo; the fashion editor Anna Piaggi, a colorful, unique fixture in fashion circles for decades; the singers Bjork and Lady Gaga, who have continuously pushed boundaries combining their music with art and fashion.

The Ten Principles of Good Design

1. Form Follows Function
Have clarity on where the design will be worn, and why.

2. Awareness of Historical or Cultural Context
Are these design references recreating the design in a new way?

3. Ergonomics
Design for optimal efficiency in fit and movement

4. Visual Interest:
Is it a new and contemporary shape, proportion, and balance?

5. Visual Harmony
Repeated shapes, design forms such as tucks, darts, gathers, and detailing need to agree in style and proportion, mood, and tone.

6. Visual Energy
Identify focal points. Be deliberate with visual repetition and contrast in pattern, texture, and details. Be decisive on tone, whether magnetic or dynamic.

7. Textural Interest
Remember "form follows function" with ornamentation. Use it for a reason.

8. Emphasis
Be clear on the main point of the design.

9. Color
Be familiar with basic color theory and what your choices are communicating.

10. Depth of Content
Good design elements should communicate an emotional impact or philosophical stance.

Recognize the principles of good design

There are specific design principles that have been distilled over time and apply to all disciplines. Analyzing composition, color balance, or textural interest in areas such as cuisine, architecture, or graphics will help you to assess what good design actually is, and learn how to recognize it in your own work and that of others.

Cut in dressmaking is like grammar in a language. A good design should be like a well-made sentence, and it should express one idea at a time.

Charles James

An example of excellence in graphic design, this logo developed by Carm Goode in the 1980s is still used today. It functions both as a logo in isolation and as an exploration of superimposition.

Establish your ergonomics

> Ergonomics: methods of design that optimize human well-being and overall system performance.
> *International Ergonomics Association Executive Council, August 2000*

In fashion, ergonomics relates to fit and movement, and how clothing affects the attitude, psychological outlook, and emotional tenor created by the wearing of that design. The ergonomics, or "system performance," of a garment is the extent to which the garment is draped with a sensitivity to human shape and musculature, and how it exhibits an understanding of the body and its physical needs.

In the study of historical clothing, you can see the ever-changing ergonomics of fashion—for instance, the evolution from loosely fitting togas and tunics to centuries of tightly fitted bodices. Ergonomics shifted in the early twentieth century with the corset-less revolution, and Christian Dior established a totally different silhouette and fit again when his New Look premiered in 1947. The emergence of the Japanese designers Issey Miyake, Rei Kawakubo, and Kansai Yamamoto in 1980s Paris heralded an era of avant garde ergonomics. The silhouettes were new and unusual shapes, the fit oversized with large shoulder pads.

Flawless fit is essential to high-quality fashion, but first the designer must be clear on what kind of ergonomics he or she wants to create, and then understand how that style of fit relates to the body in garment designs—whether it be classic, romantic, avant-garde, or non-traditional.

Above: Traditional fit in a classic coat, this Chanel Haute Couture Spring/Summer 2017 exhibits a high level of formality.

Right: Gareth Pugh's ergonomics are in a romantic, non-traditional mode, as opposed to a classical style, here highlighting the sense of the body in motion. ready-to-wear Fall/Winter, 2011.

Worldwide damage caused by industrial systems, including those of the fashion industry, have contributed greatly to global warming and disasters such as this river being destroyed by algae blooms.

Acknowledge the ethics of slow fashion

Consult your conscience regarding your carbon footprint, and aspire to integrity in your actions. Fashion is one of the world's most polluting and exploitative industries, so today's fashion designers must have a sense of their own "butterfly effect," an understanding of the sociological and environmental impact of their products.

It is essential to cultivate a global perspective, to understand how your work fits into the fashion industry. Your daily decisions concerning fabric sourcing and garment production will have far-reaching consequences for the environment, the well-being of factory workers, and the long-term sustainability of the fibers and processes that go into the garment's creation.

A growing "slow fashion" movement has emerged to address these ethical concerns. While fast fashion is based on high speed, planned obsolescence, and trend-driven, disposable, low-quality clothing from supply chains that are environmentally draining, slow fashion encourages traceability and transparency during the entire life cycle of the garment. It promotes the philosophy that making deliberate, thoughtful garment choices, rather than decisions based on convenience, can change the world and the clothing industry for the better.

Slow fashion aims for long-term sustainability; its goals and objectives to have minimal impact on the planet, with a return to artisanal, crafted products that are created with attention to fair working practices. It is to uphold appropriate pricing, to trade in fine-quality products and to promote integrity in all phases of production practices. Simply stated, the philosophy is "produce less, create more."

To implement sustainable, slow-fashion principles, a designer must learn what questions to ask of fabric suppliers and garment contractors before committing to using any materials or labor. For example:

1. what makes this fabric ethical and eco-friendly? Is it organic, renewable, recyclable, biodegradable, compostable?
2. How is the fabric dyed and finished? What chemicals are used in the process?
3. How many times is it shipped from one plant to another?
4. For contracted garment production, where are the garments cut and sewn? Do the mills have fair-trade pay, child labor laws, and safe working conditions?
5. What is the shipping footprint?
6. As a garment manufacturer, do you invest in community development in the areas where you produce?

Today's fashion industry must be about quality, not quantity. As designers we must promote respect for the integrity of fine materials, such as organic cotton, which is certainly more costly than that produced with standard methods, but can be used with pride in having made a choice for fair trade labor and for our planet.

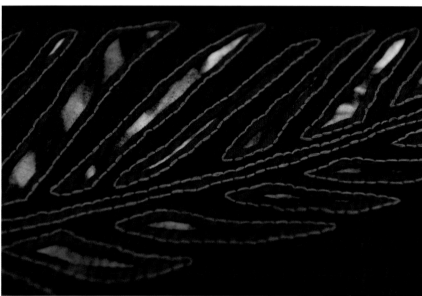

Creating marketable fashion that is 100% sustainable is challenging, The process includes constantly reviewing materials and labor resources, but is also in the realm of public education. It is up to the designer and the fashion firms to present high-quality clothing at reasonable prices so that the public can more easily understand how their purchasing power can help the environment. Consumers need to understand that the better choice is in purchasing just one jacket of high quality which will last for years, rather than five that will go into landfill after a few washings.

There are many successful, responsible fashion brands that aspire to sustainability in the manufacturing of their garments. Some may be by using only fair trade-certified products, upholding standards of animal welfare, or avoiding dangerous chemicals. Others are experimenting with design processes such as zero-waste pattern cutting, or are implementing another major aspiration in slow fashion, that of recycling or repurposing previously worn clothing and materials.

One such exemplary firm is Natalie Chanin's groundbreaking company Alabama Chanin. In 2000, she began by creating clothing from recycled cotton jersey T-shirts, sewn together in a unique and beautiful way using a combination of patchwork and reverse appliqué (see above). Based on a cottage-industry business model, she used her available local labor source, generations of hand-stitchers in Florence, Alabama. While most of Alabama Chanin's techniques are those of the Depression-era South, others have been practiced by generations of sewers.

The Ten Essentials of Couture

1. Quality of design
The work must start with a solid foundation, a strong design that is timeless, appropriate for the culture, and for the client, see The Ten Principles of Good Design (page 17).

2. Draping, marking, and patterning
Advanced draping, marking, truing, and pattern drafting techniques will ensure that integrity of the design is upheld, the emotional content delivered, and all practical aspects of fit and function are covered.

3. Use of the toile for flawless fit
The muslin "toile," or fitting sample is a very important step. Accommodations can be made on this muslin for physical imbalances to achieve an exact fit as well as fine tune proportion and shape.

4. Choosing the highest-quality fabric and trims
Learn to appreciate high-quality textiles.

5. Support system for the fabric *(the Three "S's")*
Have a plan so that a high quality fabric may exhibit its finest assets.
- Surface Integrity: most fabrics will benefit from "flat lining" or "underlining."
- Support structure: engineer the appropriate plan to anchor the fabric in place.
- Stability: identify areas of a design where the fabric needs to be controlled through support elements.

6. Unassailable quality of workmanship
The proper stitching style will determine what areas will be done by hand and what by machine, and whether the work will be done with a firm or light touch.

Utilize advanced construction techniques as needed to uphold design integrity.

7. Expert pressing
Expert pressing is key to couture. Each seam must be underpressed during the sewing process so that the final press is ever so slight. Overpressing can fatally damage fabric.

8. Impeccable ornamentation and embellishment
Any three-dimensional elements must be done for a reason and applied with the highest level of craftsmanship.

9. Aspirational construction
- Be up to date with technology, advances in machinery, and new construction and handwork techniques.
- Experiment with your own new ideas.

10. Finishing touches
Final details will define the emphasis and flow. The twist of the bow or lift of a hem must be done with an eye for the energetic configuration of the client and dress foremost in the mind's eye.

Apply quality of craftsmanship

From the hand-stitched garments of indigenous tribes to the couture salons, it is important at whatever level we are working to take pride in using craftsmanship of the highest quality possible. Of course it is difficult to be an expert in all areas of craft, but as fashion and costume designers, we can strive to know as much as possible. The key is to know how a particular art feels, rather than to master all the skills involved. To be able to recognize and feel the quality of couture, the excellence in embroidery, or the perfect press of an organza hem—that is our aspiration. It will put us in a position to inspire, direct, and then trust the expert craftspeople who make clothes of high value and quality.

Coco Chanel adjusting a sleeve before a fashion show, 1962. The designer who knows her craft has ultimate control.

Know your craft, learn your trade!

This is the constant refrain from Rita Watnick of Lily et Cie to students and her secret to success from working in the fashion industry for decades.

Karl Lagerfeld's knowledge and experience with the artisans at Lemarié brought the brilliance of his embellished designs to full fruition.

Draping Today's Heirloom Designs

Heirloom quality falls into its own special category. It can combine simple hand-stitching with the most complex of techniques. It is different from couture in that it is not necessarily made by a syndicated couture house, and it has deeper significance than decorative beauty. Heirloom-quality clothing is coveted and collectible because it embodies a sense of authenticity and conveys a story or sacred quality.

Typically, a family heirloom is a precious artifact that is passed down from generation to generation: perhaps a special piece of crystal, an embroidered linen tablecloth, a valuable necklace, or a book. Often an heirloom will come with a story about how it was acquired, memories of which grandmother wore it on her wedding day, or details of a journey it took during its early life.

An heirloom piece of clothing is therefore one that is meant to last indefinitely, possibly to be passed on from generation to generation. It is clothing that is thoughtfully and beautifully made, with the deliberate intention that it last a very long time. As consumers become more conscious of quality and sustainability, they will seek these authentic garments that will endure, serve their lifestyle in many different ways, and become part of their own personal heirloom collections.

Advanced Creative Draping lights the path for designers to become industry leaders and innovators. Practicing the draping techniques presented here, from the basic to the most complex, and embracing the concepts within the Designer's Aims and Aspirations described on page 31, will ensure that you are a designer prepared to create the heirloom clothes of the future.

This silk christening gown has been worn by newborn members of my family for three generations.

How to Use This Book

The reader is recommended to have a beginner's knowledge of draping, and some experience of truing and pattern drafting. However, during the truing process of developing the drape into a pattern, drafting skills necessarily improve, and you will come to understand why the curves and angles of patterns are shaped in their particular ways. Draping and pattern drafting skills go hand in hand and are best learned simultaneously.

CHAPTER 1
Experimental Draping

OBJECTIVES

The Skill of Visualization: Train the eye to visualize finished design using a system of fabric evaluation.

—

Beginning a Collection: Evaluate which fabric convey the intended design direction.

Exercise 1: First Impressions

Analyze a fabric's visual and tactile qualities, assess scale and volume.

Exercise 2: Studying Grainlines

Distinguish and mark the three different grainlines.

Exercise 3: Testing Design Elements

Match appropriate design elements with a given fabric.

Exercise 4: Construction Testing

Appraise construction techniques and support materials.

Exercise 5: Special Effects and Embellishments

Discover the possibilities of a fabric by experimenting with color, texture, layering, embellishments, and various crafting treatments.

Project: Experimental Draping from Inspiration Boards

Drawing from a specific inspiration, develop and sketch experimental drapes using a variety of materials and trims.

Which comes first, the inspiration or the fabric?

Experimental Draping

For the painter, watercolors and oils are the medium.
For the designer of clothing or costumes, it is fabric.
A deep understanding of the capabilities of this medium
is essential to manifesting high-quality design.

Experimental draping is a design development technique: draping textiles free form on a mannequin, and pinning, but not cutting into the fabrics. It is often used as a way to gain direction at the very beginning of the design process, stimulating imagination, creativity, and even specific designs. It can also be done after a collection or production is designed, to help you discover how a specific fabric can help to define the vision you want to communicate.

Studying the visual impact and specific qualities of a particular textile through experimental draping will often illuminate how your abstract concepts can be translated into physical three-dimensional form.

Exercises aimed at recognizing grainlines help you to see how even a subtle shift in grain placement can alter the mood and tenor of a garment. Construction exercises show how fabrics perform; some need sharply tailored construction and others seem to sing with just a simple, lightly sewn touch. Observing the way a fabric moves and reacts to various design elements can help you to visualize construction details and, most importantly, how a finished design will look in a specific fabric.

Experimental draping exercises nurture the designer's process of finding their own forms of expression. Many designers find a fabric that matches their signature style and then becomes their own personal medium. Using it consistently and understanding how it will react in various situations enables the designer to stretch its limits and truly make it their own. For instance, Coco Chanel was famous for using Linton tweeds, which then became a signature look for her brand. Another example is the inception of the classic blue jean: Mr. Levi Strauss took advantage of his surplus of blue serge from the French city of Nîmes ("serge de Nîmes"—denim) to start developing an effective work pant (trouser) for the California gold miners.

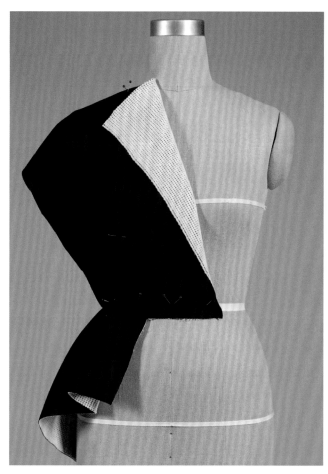

An experimental drape testing design elements for a laminated fabric: black neoprene and cream mesh.

The Skill of Visualization

The skill of visualization entails training the mind's eye to see how a finished design will look when executed in a particular fabric. This crucial skill takes a lot of practice and experience, but the ability to visualize the outcome of a design is a great measure of a designer's chances of success, as it will save valuable time and money in what can otherwise take a lot of experimentation.

Research, strategic exploration, and close study of the drape of the textiles with reflective judgment will help you to develop this skill. Any designer must have a relationship with their fabrics—one that encompasses the visual, the tactile, and the intuitive—as well as an understanding of the range of possibilities with construction, embellishment, and color. Taking the time to get to know a textile makes it possible for the best possible design to emerge.

Getting to Know your Medium

- Shake hands firmly.
- Address them with their proper name.
- Take them out to lunch.
- Wash and wear them.
- Fold and drape them.
- Stitch and fuse them.
- Bathe them in different-colored dyes.

Above: Christian Lacroix experimentally draping fabric on a model, 1987.

Fabric evaluation checklist

When experimentally draping to evaluate textiles, it is helpful to follow a systematic approach. Use the criteria listed below to appraise the fabrics, taking notes or photographs.

1. Visual quality of drape

- First impression: Note how the fabric drapes, and find words to describe its qualities, such as "a heavy, but liquid drape," "flat and impenetrable," "light and airy," "bold and exuberant."
- Note how the fabric relates to the physical body. Does it work for close fitting, or is it better worn with some space? Visualize volume: How much of the fabric would be comfortable to wear on the body at once? Consider the scale; Does the fabric needs a design with broad strokes or delicate looks?
- Observe how the grainlines differ visually. The strong lengthgrain (warp) is usually placed vertically, and the crossgrain (weft) around the body, but consider how a different placement might affect the performance of the fabric. Letting the bias grain of the fabric fall vertically will almost always give a softer, more sensual look. (See pages 36–41 for more about grainlines).

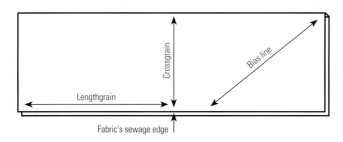

The lengthgrain or warp thread is usually stronger than the crossgrain or weft thread, and used vertically in most garments. The bias grainline gives and stretches as the threads pull open on the diagonal.

2. Tactile quality of the fabric

- Feel the textile's "hand." Find words to describe its weight and body: light, soft, smooth; heavy, grainy. Find out whether it stretches, and determine whether it would be best for innerwear or outerwear.
- Note surface interest: loft, nap, weave, and pattern or print.

3. Mood and tone

- Consider the fabric's sensory, emotional quality—the "story," personality, and attitude in its tactile and visual characteristics.
- Research its historical or cultural references, and note what biases they might give to a garment made from it.
- Imagine a "muse," be it a real or fictional person, in a particular situation to visualize how the fabric will work in a finished garment.

4. Design elements and construction details

- Design elements: Test whether the fabric reacts more naturally with gathers, darts, or pleats.
- Construction details: Note which grainline directions work best, and whether the fabric will need pre-washing, fusing, or underlining.
- Note whether the fabric lends itself to a general construction style with a firm or light touch. It may be light and sheer, and need French seams, or so heavy that it needs flat-fell seams and topstitching.

5. Embellishment

- Consider how adding a three-dimensional element— beading, embroidery, a trim, or a "treatment" (a piece of the self-fabric used to create a trim or special effect)— to the surface of the textile might act as punctuation.

6. Color

- Coordinate the right mix of colors and shades for each garment that will enable it to fit into the group for your collection or production.

Crepe is perfection. It flows on the body. It's smooth as glass, and it's very Cartesian.

Stéphane Rolland

Mini exercise

Study two images of garments that you are taking as inspiration. Using the criteria in the Fabric Evaluation Checklist, note the differences of mood and tone, as I have done with the images opposite.

How fabric color and texture evoke mood and tone

Color and texture create an atmosphere. The tone (think musical tones) is about levels of intensity on a spectra; ranging from light to rich, from sweet to dark. The tone evokes an emotional state, creating "mood": playful and joyous, or passionate and serious. Your fabric choices build an imaginary world with tone informing the mood.

Here, the tone of the earthy, sheer linen of the Danaides is soft and lyrical; the mood that this tone encourages is meditative, languid. The green silk of the *Atonement* costume has a tone of higher pitch; it is edgy and tense, the mood is aggressive.

John William Waterhouse,
***The Danaïdes*, 1903.**

In *The Danaïdes*, by the English Pre-Raphaelite painter John William Waterhouse, the first impression of the fabric is gentleness. It looks soft and fine, and follows the curves of the women's shapes in great detail, giving a feeling of intimacy. You can almost feel the lightness of the hand of the fabric—the drape has a very sensual quality. The mood and tone are demure and innocent, not at all self-conscious, and the sheerness evokes a sense of virginal vulnerability. The light touch of the construction, with its loosely draped pieces, adds to the mood of relaxed freedom. Areas that are gathered create very tiny folds, adding delicacy and femininity. The fabric looks like a natural fiber in a pastoral setting, and, given the date, it is probably a fine linen or wool. The colors are soft and earthy, adding to the women's gently magnetic quality.

Silk charmeuse dress designed by Jacqueline Durran and worn by Keira Knightley in the movie *Atonement* (2007).

In this photograph of a film costume, the general impression of the silk charmeuse fabric is strength and intensity. One can see that it drapes more heavily than the dresses of *The Danaïdes*. It is draped on the bias, falling very sharply to the floor, signifying the bold decisiveness of the character. The hand is soft, with a satin finish; it has a sensual quality, but in a very different way from *The Danaïdes*. This drape, with its shine, matches the assertive presence of the woman. The emotional quality of the sleek, satiny garment suggests polish and sophistication, but shine deflects, so does that mean her character is hiding something? Green can represent the balance of nature, but also in extremes, envy or jealousy.

Beginning a Collection: Setting the mood with fabric choices

Which comes first, the design or the fabric? Some designers start with a strong concept, then find fabrics to match it. Others approach it the other way around, finding first a fabric with a texture or print that inspires them or perhaps reminds them of a feeling or attitude they would like to express.

Study how a fabric with a specific historical usage could translate into something contemporary. For example, wool flannel has been traditionally used for suits. A design that is loose and comfortable, such as a hoodie, with the addition of a few tailoring touches such as welt pockets, would be a way of connecting the past to the present.

It is important to experiment with fabric pairings and groupings. Individually, a fabric can be strong and interesting, and when paired with another its personality becomes even more powerful. Conversely, perhaps a fabric needs another to tone it down, or soften its affects.

Left: Male and female energy combines in this design from Antonio Marras's ready-to-wear Fall/Winter 2019 collection.

Opposite: Karolyn Kiisel's studio. Assembling fabrics to evaluate for a collection.

I am very attracted by opposites, from menswear fabrics—very structured and thick, almost impossible to penetrate, like a classic example of masculine energy—to the light, fluid, soft, transparent, and ethereal fabrics of the feminine. I love to mix, overlap, and drape them and watch them become one thing, unexpected and mysterious like two lovers.

Antonio Marras, 2017

The Designer's Aims and Aspirations: Fabric Choices

Find your focus
Aspirational design tells a story. The inspiration board is a work in progress, so continue to add to it and refer back to it for details:
- Reference garments, vintage or new, help clarify design decisions.
- Physical objects as reminders of texture or theme.
- Words—a poem, phrases, synonyms plucked from a thesaurus.
- Look at the work of other artists which seems to parallel the message or attitude you want to express: fine art, films, social media.
- Use a muse to ground the feeling of the collection.

Incorporate research
Investigate historical, cultural, or contemporary usages of a fabric through reference garments or in print. Knowing how it has been traditionally used, will help you to see what silhouettes, garment types, and construction methods have worked well.

Use research classification techniques:
- Make a timeline of the fabric from historical uses to present day.
- Find current examples of garments in that fabric.
- List areas where the fabric is used most often, (activewear, sportswear, or eveningwear?).

Study its composition by comparing and contrasting:
- Describe the "hand" (the "feel" of the fabric), and try to recognize its composition. Describe the feel of different fibers.
- If it is a blend, describe the attributes of the constituent parts.
- Compare and contrast by weight, sheerness, or body. For example, check the sheer quality of three lightweight silks.

Recognize the principles of good design
Choose the right fabric for your design: Review The Ten Principles of Good Design (page 17) especially "Form follows function." Evaluate first whether the fabric is appropriate for its function.

Establish your ergonomics
Consider how each fabric will perform in movement. Will it be worn close to the body, or as an outer layer? Does it lend itself to a fitted construction technique? If a knit, how much of the stretch will be utilized?

Acknowledge the ethics of slow fashion
Ask the right questions: educate yourself about the fabric's carbon footprint (see page 19).

Apply quality of craftsmanship
Consider the context and price point of the garment for which the fabric will be used. Identify the quality of fabric and level of detail you can afford.

EXERCISE 1:
First Impressions

Experimental draping needs to feel relaxed and intuitive. Here, I am exploring those that may fit into my Ikebana, Earth's Heritage, or Dark Radiance groupings. Use whatever fabrics you are able to source for these exercises, and follow a systematic approach. I have roughly followed the Fabric Evaluation Checklist as a guide, beginning with broad impressions, then mood and tone, the visual and tactile qualities, design and construction elements, etc. Journal notes as you work so you can refer back to them.

Then, before you begin evaluating your fabric, have your inspiration board in front of you and take a moment to breathe. Let the ideas you want to communicate wash over you.

These two different types of red silk—a chiffon, and a peau de soie, are being considered for the Dark Radiance group. Red is a signature color of that group, which gives me a positive bias, but for now I will evaluate the quality of the drape, the hand, and the sensory, emotional qualities of each fabric.

Handle your Fabric with Care

Before beginning your experimental draping:
- Check that your pins are not so heavy as to damage the fabric; check needles also if you are thread-tracing grainlines.
- To avoid snags or pulls in a very delicate fabric, it may be necessary to wear gloves while you drape.
- Try not to cut the fabric while you are studying it; let the excess fall to the back or onto the floor.

Record:

- Photos of the grainline drapes
- Grainline schematic sketches
- Favorite darts, tucks, or gathers
- Successful support element tests (crinoline, net, or wire)
- Stitch tests, maybe an edge finish
- Experiementing with embellishments

Silk chiffon: The first impression is that of a soft, airy drape that feels ethereal in its transparency, the attitude is soft and magnetic.
- Volume: A lot would be required to make a big statement; even 6 yards (5.5 m) of silk chiffon may not be enough for a dress with sleeves.
- Scale: The small, fine gathers seen here seem right for a, delicate piece with fine stitching and details.
- The hand is very soft and sensual, almost weightless.
- Historically, it has been used most often for scarves, overlays for bridal or eveningwear, or light blouses. It feels appropriate for something loosely draped that shows off the beauty of the sheerness.
- The color is strong, but the fabric will not work in the Dark Radiance group; it is too light and unobtrusive, for this group's powerful energy.

Visuals: Scale and Volume

Remember that scale and proportion have a lot to do with individual design sensibilities—they will set you apart as a designer. Be original; you can create your own look through interesting use of scale and volume.

Silk chiffon.

Silk peau de soie.

Silk peau de soie: An initial impression is that it exhibits a strong, substantial silhouette. The gathers create a lot of body, and it stands out crisply, retaining its shape with no support.

- Volume: The 3 yards (2.75 m) draped here is the most I would want to wear at a time—unless I were Lady Gaga at the Met Gala.
- Scale: This fabric takes up a lot of space both physically and psychologically. It lends itself to broad strokes, and a larger piece.
- When testing the grainlines with gathers, the lengthgrain makes rougher gathers and the crossgrain finer gathers, so the weft thread must be stronger than the warp in this fabric.
- The hand is thick and crisp, yet malleable, and it has a very soft satin finish, which gives it a sensuality.
- Historically, silk peau de soie has been used for eveningwear and large skirts, so the prejudicial bias here is that it would always appear dressy.
- This is a sexy fabric, soft on the surface, but with inherent strength. The attitude is overt and aggressive; it will draw attention in a crowd.
- This fabric feels appropriate for the Dark Radiance group.

The next two fabrics, both in Spring/Summer color palette, are being tested for inclusion in the Ikebana group.

Silk satin organza: The first impression is that this is the ultimate in lusciousness, light and airy, yet full and substantial, like a big marshmallow.

- Volume, scale: very fluid drape, like I'm chasing it as it falls through my hands. A larger scale design with a full, generous cut, worn away from the body, would show off its crisp, light quality and sense of movement.
- Gathers smoother on the lengthgrain than the crossgrain, and has a definite softer flow on the bias.
- The hand is soft and cool, almost weightless. The texture is matte on one side, but has an intriguing sheen on the face (right side).
- Its "story": elusive, fast-moving, yet light and flirtatious, an attitude of soft, feminine energy; it moves gracefully and almost shimmers.
- The shade of blue fits into the sky of the Ikebana board.

Silk satin organza.

Silk matelassé: The first impression is that this silk matelassé has loft and is substantial, yet surprisingly light and crisp. It holds its shape in a perky way.

- Scale and volume: It is oversized in perception and reality; it would attract attention, lending itself to broad strokes, and calling for a design that is large and grand.
- The hand is weightless, but stiff, slightly scratchy, and dry. It feels as though it would be best for a garment worn away from the body, perhaps a jacket or gown.
- The matelassé floral weave has a rich texture and surface interest; the variegated color tones give it a lot of depth.
- It evokes a light cheerfulness, playfulness, springtime, gardens, blue skies, and fluffy clouds. The attitude is playful, but its rich and complex texture is elegant.
- This shade of green is not widely worn, so it needs someone with a sense of distinction; perhaps a fashionable celebrity at a showy wedding.
- The spring color palette and interesting texture make it suitable for the Ikebana group.

This fabric is being tested for visual scale of the print. Both colorways will be included in the Dark Radiance collection, but in only one scale.

Silk charmeuse: The first impression is of a very soft, fluid drape. It is thin but opaque, and has weightiness to it; the print adds sharp definition.

- The fabric drapes quite close to the body. Gathering would create some volume, but a modest-sized silhouette seems most appropriate.
- Length- and crossgrain seem to drape about the same, but the bias grain falls and stretches quite heavily.
- The silk is soft but has a slightly grainy feel. The attitude is soft but complex.
- Silk charmeuse, a staple of the silk trade, has been used most often for blouses, dresses, full skirts, and light jackets.
- Our historical reference is the 1980s. This fabric looks quite similar to prints that were popular at that time, and that reference would be emphasized if used in a garment featuring strong shoulders with pads.
- Assessment of scale: It seems the smaller proportion will work better with the type of fit and volume needed for the Dark Radiance group.

Spring green silk matelassé.

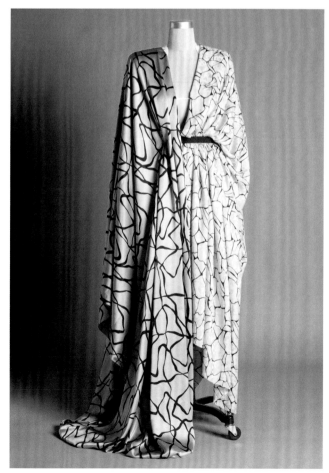

Silk charmeuse prints, in two colorways.

Close-fitting drapes

The following fabrics will be analyzed in terms of ergonomics. They will all be worn close to the body, so they must be checked for qualities of stretch and ease.

With woven/non-stretch fabrics, a certain amount of ease is needed for a comfortable fit. A general guide for classic fit is to allow 2" (5 cm) total around the bust, 1" (2.5 cm) total around the waist, and 2" (5 cm) total around the hips.

Note: For non-traditional ergonomics, there are no set guidelines.

Silk matelassé: The first impression of this silk matelasse is of delicate strength.

- The fabric reacts well to the design elements, such as the underbust tuck.
- It is crisp, but soft enough to be worn close to the body.
- The perkiness of the peplum flare matches the attitude of the fabric very well.
- The ease looks perfect. It has been checked by pinning at the side seam.
- This amount of ease is about right for the intended garment (see above guide). It is snug, yet comfortable.

Rose pink variegated silk matelassé.

- **Rayon modal knit**: The first impression is of a soft stretch with a very fluid drape, so would be appropriate for use next to the skin; as a T-shirt or undergarment.
- The fabric will be tested for utilization of stretch. There will be an optimum point where it will feel comfortably snug, then beyond which it does not work to pull it tighter.
- Draping freely, it creates a smooth, clean look, so would also lend itself to a design with volume where the fabric could be gathered or cut to fall vertically.
- Note: For knit fabrcs, no ease is necessary. However, always test fabrics for optimum utilization of stretch to allow their best performance. They will look strained if pulled too tightly.

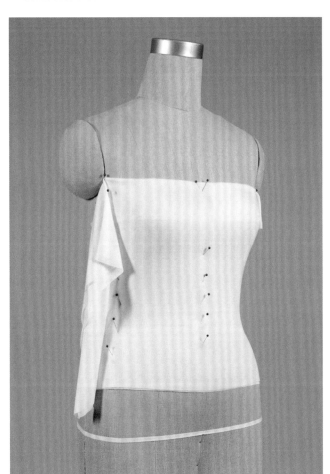

Lightweight rayon/modal knit fabric.

Studying Grainlines

The knowledgeable use of grainline position is the designer's secret weapon. Conscious control of the grainlines can alter the look of a design, changing its look, attitude, and mood. You can accomplish a lot through different juxtapositions, or the use of the bias. Prepare the fabrics before draping by carefully marking the grainlines; this will enable you to easily see the results of the grainline placements during the draping tests.

Studying the differences in the way a fabric drapes on lengthgrain, crossgrain, and bias will help you to visualize the outcome you want and make decisions about design features. Be sure to take photos or sketch the results of your experimental draping, and use words to describe the effects that you see.

Locating the grainlines
Testing fabric tension

Step 1
- Grasp the fabric on the selvage edge and about 12" (30.5 cm) inward.
- Pull firmly to test the tension.
- Test by grasping the fabric a few inches up or down, and pull again.

Step 2
- Continue moving the pulled area up and down until you find the "sweet spot" with the most tension, which will be the true length- or crossgrain.
- Mark with a pin.

Observation and Assessment

Begin the assessment and evaluation process as soon as you start working with a fabric. Even when doing something as simple as a thread-trace line, the qualities of a fabric begin to emerge, and its tactility becomes familiar.

The pick-and-pull method
- For use when exact grainline placement is of utmost importance, such as with a corset, a very fitted garment, or a fabric where the grainline is extremely pronounced.
- Clip into the fabric about ½" (1.3 cm).
- Isolate one thread in the weave, and begin pulling it gently so that it creates a "run" in the fabric or gathers up the fabric.
- Mark this run with a pencil or chalk. While this method is good for finding a cross- or lengthgrain edge, note that it will permanently mark those lines.

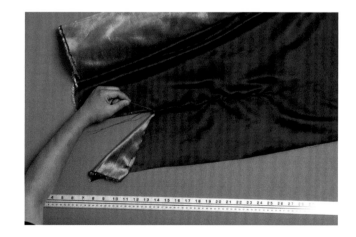

Marking the grainlines

The basic "measure and mark" method—finding the grainline by measuring from a torn edge or selvage edge—can be used. However, consider carefully what to use to mark the grainline if you are using final design fabrics. Chalk, or invisible-ink marking pens are options, but always test first to see if they can be safely removed later.

Thread-tracing

This technique is used on final design fabrics. First, locate the grainline. This will be the selvage edge (lengthgrain) for an uncut piece of fabric. If it is a cut piece, use one of the above methods to confirm the length or crossgrain. Then decide where you would like your thread-traced grainline to be positioned. For an experimental drape, this will be arbitrary, and approximately 12" (30.5 cm) will be sufficient for testing.

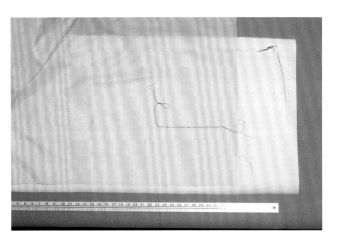

Using a ruler or yardstick, measure in from the selvage edge and mark it with a pin line or tailor tacks. Place the pins perpendicular to the sew line, and use the entry point of the pin as your line demarcation.

Leaving the fabric on the table, pull the needle and thread through it along the pin line, using very large stitches. It can be helpful to place weights on the ruler or yardstick to keep the fabric from moving while you stitch it.

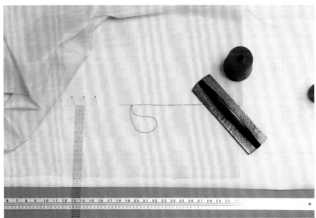

For marking the crossgrain, use a square to find the perpendicular line, and follow instructions as above.

Using draping tape

First, test the tape to make sure it doesn't mark the fabric. Follow the steps above to locate the length and crossgrains, and then center the draping tape along the line instead the thread trace.

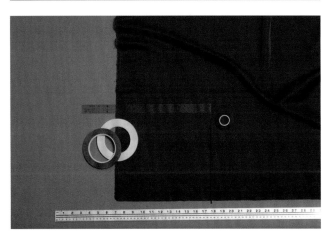

Studying the drape of the grainlines

Most fabrics will have a more harmonious fall when the lengthgrain is placed vertically, giving the garment a longer, leaner look, which tends to be more flattering to the wearer. However, there may be cases where you want the strong lengthgrain going around the body, pushing the fabric out. Also, there are fabrics where the weft thread (crossgrain) is stronger than the lengthgrain (warp thread), giving a vertical crossgrain drape a smoother hang. Always test the bias grainline, which will usually have a softer drape with some stretch.

Studying grainline direction

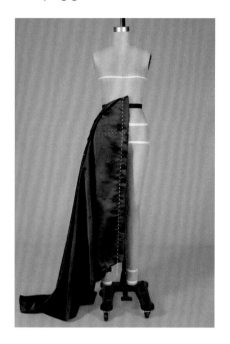   

Here the lengthgrain is horizontal

Here the lengthgrain is vertical

Step 1
- Test the silk peau de soie for grainline direction.
- Pin, with the marked lengthgrain falling vertically.
- Tie a length of ribbon or elastic at the waist, then pull the fabric through the waist tie.

Step 2
- Adjust the gathers evenly, so that the crossgrain is parallel to the ground and the amount of fabric above the elastic is even.
- Analyze the drape of the fabric, and photograph it.
- Repeat the drape so the crossgrain is hanging vertically, then photograph it and compare the two drapes.

Conclusion
The lengthgrain clearly has a smoother hang than the crossgrain, which puffs out at the hip, and also makes a chunkier gathered area.

Here, the difference between the two is even more evident, but interestingly, it is the crossgrain hanging vertically that gives a smoother look (right image). Because this wool/silk blend has a stronger weft than warp thread, the crossgrain/weft thread (left image) is pushing the fabric outward at the hipline.

Wool/silk blend. Lengthgrain vertical.

Crossgrain hanging vertically.

Studying the bias grainline

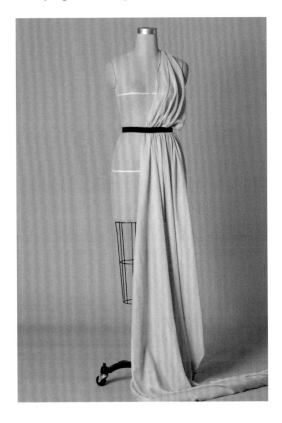

Step 1

- Use the thread-trace method to mark the grainlines of this soft silk mesh fabric, including the bias.
- Pin the marked bias grain at the shoulder, with the bias line hanging vertically.
- Tie a length of ribbon or elastic at the waist, then pull the fabric through the waist tie, adjusting it evenly.
- Here, with the bias grain falling vertically, we can see its soft flow as the threads open and stretch. Note how the bias drape tends to cling to the form, creating a sensuous quality and a soft mood.

Understanding your fabrics and their qualities

The more familiar a designer becomes with all of the different fabrics available to them, the easier it becomes to choose the best one for a design. Also, while draping, you must be able to visualize their qualities as compared to your muslin as you work.

Setting mood and tone with grainline direction

The following drapes were done as research for the for the Dark Radiance, Ikebana, and Earth's Heritage groups, focusing on studying the performance of the three grainlines, and how they influence mood and tone. It is not necessary to follow exactly what has been done here; the point is create a drape where you can view all three grainlines at once, to help you observe their differences. Try working with the grainline schematics (see next page) for inspiration.

Step 1

- Mark the grainlines, including the bias line.
- Drape the fabric first on the lengthgrain, and pin at the waist or shoulders.
- Study the fall of the lengthgrain and describe its visual qualities.

Step 2

- Drape the fabric on the crossgrain, and pin at the waist or shoulders.
- Compare and contrast the different grains. For another perspective, compare and contrast photographs of the drapes.
- Drape the fabric on the bias, for give.
- Record your impressions of scale, volume, ergonomics, and how that relates to what designs would look best in this fabric.
- Make rough sketches or grainline schematics to refer to during the design process.

Assessment

This midnight-blue, double-faced silk for the Dark Radiance group is similar in weight to peau de soie, but has a much softer drape. The bias has some give, and it makes beautiful folds across the bust. The lengthgrain and crossgrain drape comparably.

Mini exercise

Map out the energetic flow of a garment by creating rough grainline schematics to use for direction while draping.

Note how "A" has a lyrical flow and a focal point at the waist. "B" has a downward pull with an interesting shoulder flourish.

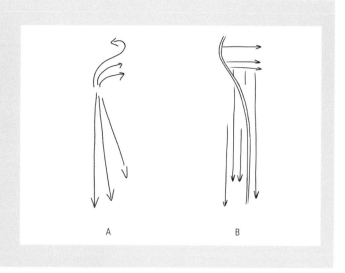

A   B

Gold metallic linen

This fabric for the Ikebana group is a linen laced with a gold metallic thread. It has a lovely shimmery quality, and the metallic thread adds weight to the hand of an already soft and malleable linen. The flat weave would make it easy to sew, and allow for complex construction.

Step 1

- Mark the grainlines, including the bias line.
- Drape the fabric first on the bias, pinning at the shoulders, then smooth over the bust and toward the sides.
- Note how using the bias grainline for this bodice area affects the fit and the ergonomics, because it automatically has some stretch as it shapes over the bust.

Step 2

- Drape the fabric on the lengthgrain by pulling in some pleats at the waist and letting the fabric fall vertically toward the floor.

Step 3

- Drape on the crossgrain by letting the fabric on the right side of the form fall from the shoulders.
- Note the difference between this area (the crossgrain) and the front pleated area (the lengthgrain).

Assessment

- Step back and view the visual impact of the drape from a distance.
- Make notes about the fabric's visual qualities, and jot down words to describe its properties.
- Assess the volume and scale by asking yourself how many yards/meters of this fabric you would want to see used in one garment.

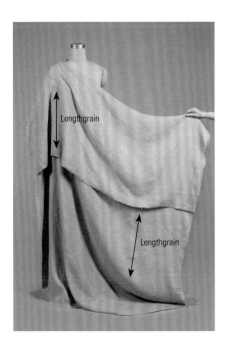

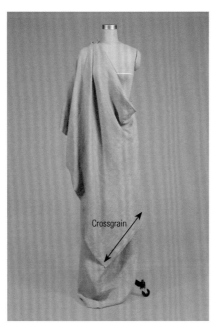

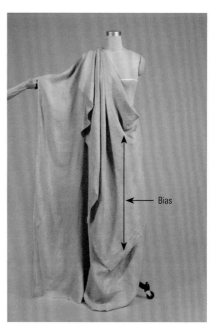

Step 1

- Mark the grainlines, including the bias line.
- With the length of the fabric falling vertically, fold under approximately 40" (101.5 cm) toward the front.
- Pin at the right shoulder, 10–12" (25.5–30.5 cm) in from the edge of the fabric.

Step 2

- Pin the left hip, letting the fabric drape as shown here.
- Bring the right shoulder fabric forward to create a bias drape falling vertically.

Step 3

- Grasp the corner of the outside layer until it is horizontal to the form, pleating toward the center of the form until you are about 10" (25.5 cm) from the selvage and it creates the cascade shown here.

Step 4

- Take the selvage edge from the back area and fold it about 2" (5 cm) inward, toward the center of the form. Pin at the shoulder.
- On the left hip, adjust until the bias is running vertically down the center front, creating the cowl on the hip.
- Pin the excess to the left back to create a clean look.

Assessment

The first impression of this sage-green silk hemp for the Earth's Heritage group is soft, earthy, and comfortable. Observe the difference in the visual qualities of the lengthgrain falling down the front, the bias as it cowls toward the right hip, and the crossgrain drape at the right-hand side.

Testing Design Elements

Experimentally draping to explore design elements makes it easier to visualize how a fabric will look as a finished garment, and how it will react to design elements such as gathers, tucks, pleats, darts, cowls, and cascades. This skill of visualization will be of great help to you when developing your designs. You will find that some fabrics work better than others—for example, that a particular fabric is much more successful with a wide pleat than with gathers.

Remember: You do not have to use unusual fabrics to create original looks. Sometimes an unexpected use, such as gathers in wool or wide pleats in chiffon, will produce an original result. Or, using a traditional fabric in an innovative way, such as washing peau de soie, pleating leather, or using the "wrong" side as the face, will suddenly make a fabric look new and fresh.

Draping to test design elements

Having selected the fabrics you wish to experiment with, drape each one as follows:

- Gathers: Use elastic on the form, pulling the fabric under it and letting the elastic do the work for you as you adjust the fabric. Try gathering on lengthgrain, crossgrain, and bias lines (see page 40).
- Darts: Pin fold along the dart intake, perpendicular to the foldline, for the smoothest look. Try shoulder darts, side bust darts, and French darts.
- Tucks and pleats: Experiment with folding in small (½"/1.3 cm) tucks, then fold larger (1"/2.5 cm) tucks, then try pleats up to 2" (5 cm), to see what works best.
- Inverted pleats: Fold both sides toward a center point.

Analyze your results. Study the fabric as it falls on the form, and take photographs to refer to later. Sketch as your ideas arise, even if it is just liking the way a specific size of pleat looks in a certain fabric. Note which approaches fit the theme or vision of your collection or production.

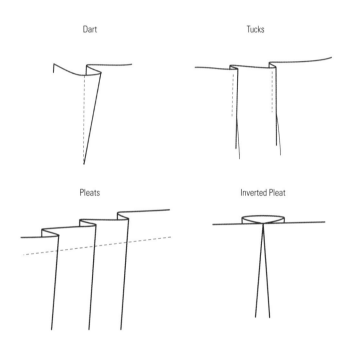

The dart is stitched on the inside and creates almost invisible shaping. "Tucks" are small fitting aids and are often angled. "Pleats" are repeated folds of any width or direction that can be pressed or not, and are sometimes "inverted."

Testing gathers: gold metallic linen

- This linen is being considered for the Ikebana or Earth's Heritage group. It was tested for tucks, pleats, and gathers, and found to be best suited to gathers.
- With the lengthgrain placed vertically, the gathers make small, controlled folds, catching the light and optimizing the delicate feel of the fabric.

Checking pleats, and the "face" preference: grey Italian wool

- Lightweight Italian wool with a metallic thread has been folded into deep pleats.
- It was found that a wider pleat such as this looked better than a small one, because it gave the fabric room to relax into a graceful fold.
- A decision will be made about which side is treated as the face. Note the difference in the two selvage edges and the varying shades of gray the two sides produce.

Gold metallic linen.

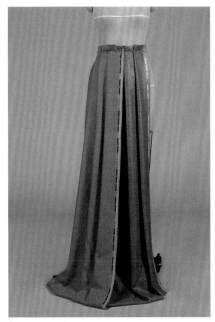
Grey Italian wool.

Navy bouclé and tweed.

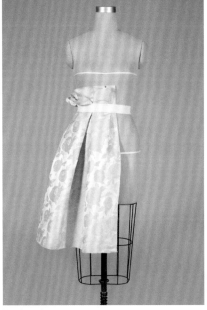
Pink damask.

Pink damask with crinoline underslip.

Coated yellow cotton.

Darts: navy bouclé and tweed

- This blue/black wool tweed harmonizes well with a vertical dart. This approach enables the check pattern that you can see from a distance to flow in a fairly unbroken way.
- On trying a French dart, or shoulder dart, the vertical and horizontal lines go out of alignment, resulting in a dart that looks less smooth and lacks finish.

Inverted pleats: pink damask

- This heavy cotton pink damask has been folded inward, creating an inverted pleat. Because of its weight and thickness, it needed a larger-scale pleat.
- The wide elastic helps to hold the pleated fabric in place during adjustments.

- This fabric fits into the Ikebana collection.
- Here, a piece of crinoline has been added to the "skirt" piece, to gauge the degree of stand it will give.
- Next, the inverted pleats have been directionally angled out at the waistline, to allow them to flare.

Testing tucks: coated yellow cotton

- This is a coated yellow cotton that has been worked into a series of mini inverted pleats. The proportion of the pleats suits the weight of the fabric.
- A tiny origami-folded embellishment is being tested at the waistline, to see how the fabric might fit into the Ikebana collection.

Creating cowls, cascades, and flounces

The cowl drape was popularized in the 1930s, but it dates to at least the draped tunics and togas of Greco-Roman times. A cowl is simply a straight edge (usually on the bias) that is adjusted to create extra fabric in the center. A cascade is a circular cut piece, usually falling vertically. A flounce is a straight or circular piece, usually sewn on to the edge of a skirt.

This silk satin crepe fabric was pinned first at the shoulder and then at the right hip, letting extra fabric fall to the center into the "cowl" drape.

Silk satin crepe

Draping a "half-lock" cowl

Step 1
- Fold the fabric in half diagonally, so that the top, bias-folded edge lies across the form at the shoulders.
- Pin at the shoulders so that the fabric lies smoothly across the front chest.

Step 2
- Release the pin on the left shoulder, and adjust more fabric toward the center, allowing the fabric to drape downward.
- Repeat for the right shoulder.
- Continue adjusting the fabric equally on the right and left sides until you have reached the desired depth of cowl.
- For more volume, fold a 2" (5 cm) tuck upward and pin at the shoulders.

Step 3
Grasp the tucked fabric of either the right or the left shoulder.

Step 4
Turn the fabric outward, flipping it over to create the half-lock drape.

Draping cascades and flounces

To test your fabric for a cascade, cut it in the following shape.

Below: Experiment with different methods of cutting cascades and circular flounces. The tighter the curve, the more flare will result. A simple circle cut (figure "B") will give variation of size and flare.

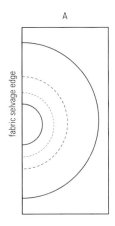
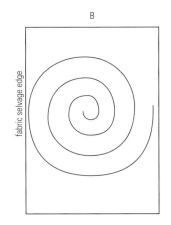

Here we compare silk satin crepe and lightweight peau de soie. Note the subtly different looks of these two cascades, which were cut from the same pattern. On the right-hand side of the form is the satin crepe, and on the left is the peau de soie.

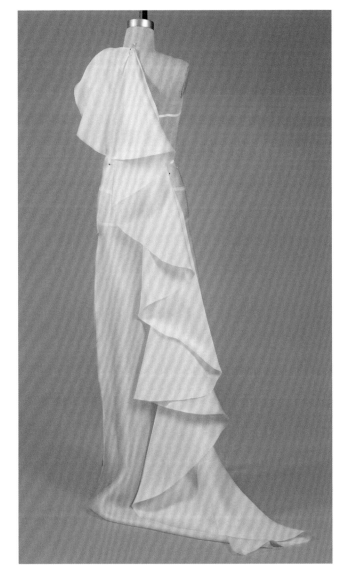

An oversized cascade in white silk taffeta is draped on a diagonal.

These circular flounces in a silk mesh paisley print are baby-hemmed, which makes them stand out slightly.

Construction Testing

The style of construction details—whether they are done with a light or a firm, touch—can alter the look of a design immeasurably. Testing stitches, seam finishes, and support elements to see how a fabric reacts, will also help you to visualize the final outcome.

Review The Ten Essentials of Couture to fully understand how aspirational construction can elevate the quality of a garment (see page 21).

Controlling the hand and surface textures of a fabric

The tactile sense, or "hand," of a fabric provides the sensory, emotional quality. Fusing, underlining, laminating, or laundering, can all produce interesting, and sometimes unexpected results.

Fusing

Fusible interlinings will help to maintain the integrity of the fabric and its surface texture, and give support at pressure points such as waistbands or shoulders.

Compare and contrast the look of these two neckline drapes. Note the crisper neckline edge of the fused silk.

Silk jacquard   Fused silk jacquard

Underlining

Underlining prolongs the life of the fabric, and enhances its integrity. The extra layer of support protects it from damage at stress points, and hides construction details. Most commonly used for underlining are lightweight flat-weave cottons, linens, and organzas that, while adding support to the main fabric, don't take over the style of the drape. If desired, an underlining can change the hand of a fabric, such as this blue Chinese brocade, now quite heavy and soft, paired with a heavy flannel. The rust brocade, now has a light, crisp effect backed with a starched organdy.

Wash tests

All fabrics should be wash tested. Note here the softer, more languorous drape of the washed silk on the right. Washes and dyeing all produce different effects, sometimes transforming a fabric into one that is more unusual or interesting.

Compare and contrast the two hem treatments shown here. It is important to note how the different stitching techniques create totally different looks.

This silk charmeuse dress has cascades of silk mesh ruffles that have been finished with a flat zigzag.

These red silk chiffon ruffles have been baby-hemmed with a filament so they stand out quite strongly, creating what is called a "lettuce-leaf" hem.

Stitching tests

Testing different types of stitching is crucial to achieving the look you want and finding the limits of a fabric's performance. These tests might include: joining, topstitching, seam finishes, hem finishes, closures, elastic shirring, or specialty stitching The style of construction—whether done with a light or heavy touch, controls the mood of a design. Note here various innovative seam and edge finishes.

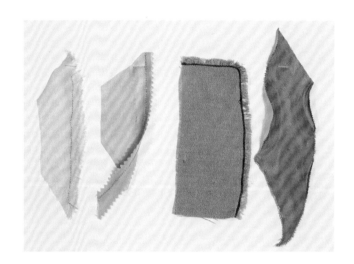

Seam and hem finishes

Because it is sheer, this silk organza has been joined with French seams. The proportion of the baby hem has been coordinated with the French seams, to create a harmonized, graphic look.

Adding support elements

Draping with support elements enables you to see what might be needed for various silhouettes and/or design forms. In addition to fusible and non-fusible interlinings, and the multitude of underlinings, there are many support elements available to help you achieve your goals. Here are just a few:
• Shoulder pads (see page 99)
• Batting (wadding) or padding layers
• Crinoline, tulle, or net petticoat layers
• Horsehair (see page 73)
• Boning
• Millinery wire

The challenge is to match each one with the right fabric. You may need to test a lot of crinolines and horsehairs to get just the right tilt to a full skirt or enough boning in an eveningwear foundation.

Special Effects and Embellishments

When reviewing fabrics for a collection or production, evaluate whether they would be enhanced by a special effect, treatment, or embellishment. These can amplify the emotion of a design, just as the right choice of color can alter the mood of a design.

Layering fabrics

Try creative uses of color, such as layering fabrics together, which can add interesting effects to your work. Create your own composite fabric by layering two or more fabrics. This can create very interesting juxtapositions and tonal affects.

- This silk tissue gazar in deep orange and cream has been layered over both a citrine yellow (right side) and a pink lining (left side), creating an airy, dimensional effect. Each trial side is different in color, but similar in tone.
- This kind of fabric was widely used in the 1950s for full-skirted garden-party dresses, so it carries connotations of slightly dressy formality. The effect is reminiscent of a garden, with sunlight filtering through leaves or flower petals.
- These combinations of fabric and color fit well into the Ikebana color story.

- This layering of an intense turquoise silk under a bold black lace creates a strong visual impact because of the high-contrast color combination. The strength of the two colors matches the boldness of the lace pattern, and the effect of the bright silk glowing from under the lace is captivating.
- The effect is reminiscent of stained glass or the picture on the Dark Radiance inspiration board of the Siena Cathedral interior, with the wrought-iron gates hiding the paintings. The mood is slightly mysterious, giving it a sexy aura.
- This look works in the Dark Radiance color story of rich jewel tones with illuminated accents.

Treatments and Embellishments

Experiment with treatments by using the self-fabric for braiding, twisting, or shredding for decorative additions, or for seam and edge finishes. Experiment with embellishments by adding trims, feathers, beading, found metal objects, and so forth. The right treatment or embellishment can give the design its emotional power, used as an accent to amplify something needed to express.

- Experiment with "treatments" (using the actual fabric of the design) for decorative reasons, or also for seam and edge finishes. It can be braided, twisted, shredded.
- Experiment with "embellishments" by adding elements to the fabric: feathers, beading, found metal objects, etc.

Does that fabric lend itself to that additional element? Is it heavy enough to support it? Where on the garment will it go?

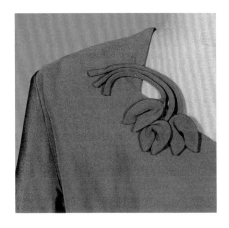

The fabric of this dress is a rayon crepe, and fairly basic. The neckline treatment was made of a bias cord made of the self fabric for the stems, and shaped bias semi-circles for the flowers. The treatment amplifies the focal point at the neckline, which already has a distinctive "sweetheart" shape.

The Minuet Dancer's costume appears in a dream sequence; the costume is light, airy and dreamlike (see page 200). The embellishment here is punctuating the sweet and delicate tone. The chiffon of the skirt was used, first sewing a bias "tube," and then gathering it in tightly to form the "poofs." The flower petal trim was made with tiny pieces of brocade sewn into miniature bows.

The waistline treatment here fits with the Ikebana inspiration board, the self fabric twisted origami style, and tacked into intricate, delicate flowers.

The "Napa Valley Almond Blossoms in the Rain" project conjured a specific visual image and this embellishment helped convey the sense of lightness; the petals soft and whimsically shaped, the crystals hinting a drops of rain. Various fabrics were tested for the petals. Different sizes and shapes were cut, then edged finished/melted with a heat gun to get just the right curl on the edges, feathers added to suggest a floating object.

An embellishment is needed for the lapel (see full drape on page 172). Here, a group of jewel-toned chiffon and organzas are twisted into rosettes as an experiment.

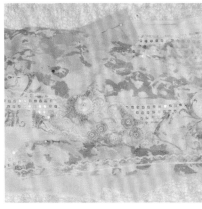

Here, a group of Ikebana fabrics have been sewn onto a piece of abstract lace, then tulle overlaid and topstitched to experiment with creating a "new fabric" with bits of scrap fabric.

Experimental Draping from Inspiration Boards

Once you have chosen fabrics for a collection or production, experiment with draping a few of them together, exploring how different combinations work. The fabrics may eventually be used together in one garment, or just as part of the same collection. Try adding trims or embellishment ideas to see if this amplifies the theme.

Inspired by the J.T. Burke artwork at the top right of the Ikebana board, this drape is joyous and lively, and the yellow brings an uplifted perkiness with its crisp hand. The vintage jewelry embellishment adds sparkle, like dewdrops in the garden.

Above: Artwork by J.T. Burke—
Beautiful Mask II (2009) from
the series *Beautiful Again*—has
inspired this drape in silk tissue
faille.

Documenting the drapes

Photographing the experimental draping will help you to focus. Studying it later can provide you with design material, or ways to communicate the design concepts to others:

• Sketch and photograph different areas of the drape, and the overall drape.

• Photograph accessories with it, and observe how the mood and tone of the fabric changes when styled or accessorized in different ways.

• Describe the changes in mood and tone that occur.

• Add this research to your inspiration boards; they are works in progress that evolve as the collection or production is developed.

Above: The inspiration for this Ikebana drape is taken from the dying flower image, *Tiger Lily*, a tintype by Gerard Walsh, 2019.

This drape has been inspired by a different part of the Ikebana mood board. The bodice is draped with the crisp silk matelassé, seen on page 35. The crinoline underskirt seen on page 43, has been pulled into a bubble shape by gathering the pink damask along the hem. To maintain that shape in a finished garment, it would then be attached to a lining piece.

The part of the inspiration board that informs this drape is the dying flower (lower center of the board).

Part of the beauty of flowers is the way they look as they fade; the petals fall like fragments of silk or feathers, and the colors become softer and more muted. Here, a piece of taupe/gray fine silk tulle has been draped over the cotton damask, to create that soft, muted look. The embellishment of dried roses provides a color accent as well as emotional punctuation for the theme of impermanence.

The Dark Radiance theme sets a tone of deep notes with its multi-dimensional layers and rich colors. The resulting mood is one of mystery, yet elegance, reflected in the graceful figure at the lower left of this inset.

Included here are three jewel-toned fabrics from the Dark Radiance group. They are all different weights, as shown in the bias pleating above the waist. The gathers at the waist mirror the Big Bang cosmic explosion. The fishnet bodice evokes the look of stained glass, the embellishments create depth, the sequins glitter in the sky. A designer could develop many designs from studying this one drape.

What is Meant by Mood and Tone?

These refer to the frame of mind and emotional state induced through choice of fabrics, the colors and textures, the cut of your draped design, style of construction, and ergonomics.

Tone is the timbre, the pitch, the intensity—a point along a spectrum ranging from light and ethereal to sepia toned, to dark and saturated. It can be very specific. Was her speech "passionate," or "condescending," or "tender"?

Mood is how that tone makes you feel, it is the atmosphere being created within you. In draping, you are evoking a mood by the shapes, contours, and proportions you choose. For example, does a freely draped caftan feel expansive and relaxed? Does a sharp-edged, fitted dress feel powerful and aggressive? Do those fussy construction details make you feel constricted?

The Earth's Heritage theme incorporates the colors of nature, the grounding earth tones, the sky blues, and the sensory textures of animal fur, rope, and wood.

The Earth's Heritage fabrics say to me: "Earth below, sky above." The left-hand side of the form has the raw silk and hemp silk in earth tones, falling quite heavily. It would feel grounding, and hence be comfortable to wear. The trim is a heavy bronze sequin that would complement this feeling.

The tones of the right-hand side of the form evoke a different mood. The sky-blue linen is light and feels airy, so would lend itself to more open garments such as a blouse with the open collar. The flutter of the hem created by a bias fall adds to this feeling of graceful lyricism. The gold trim provides a shimmer that is hardly noticeable, but accents the emotional tenor of the drape.

CHAPTER 2

Improvisational Draping

OBJECTIVES
Work intuitively.

—

Cultivate self-awareness.

—

Assemble and prepare draping tools and materials.

—

Learn assessment protocols, implement a systematic
approach to self-assess work.

Exercise 1: Earth's Heritage Studies
Create a series of improvisational muslin bodice drapes
inspired by a single theme.

Exercise 2: Ikebana Studies
Interpret the mood and tone of an inspiration for improvisational
drapes that aspire to the principles of good design.

Exercise 3: Dark Radiance Studies
Examine the qualities of a reference garment,
use said qualities to guide an improvisational drape.

Exercise 4: Upcycle Study
Use improvisational draping to devise a new design by
repurposing an existing garment.

Project: The Improvisational Drape
Execute a full improvisational drape that reflects the
form and emotional tenor of your inspiration.

Free-form draping inspired by the fabrics.

Improvisational Draping

Improvisational draping is a freehand, intuitive, design development technique. It involves experimenting with ideas and inspiration on the dress form, cutting and pinning muslin without a preconceived design. It can be used to develop something new, refine a specific area of a design concept that is in progress, or redesign or re-purpose an existing garment. The goal is to develop original and innovative work. Improvisational draping will stretch your imagination and improve your technical draping skills.

Use muslin for this technique, rather than final design fabrics. While studying the contours of your forms and shapes, it is easier to focus without the emotional aspects of color and texture.

Just as an artist sketches one figure that might appear in the corner of a larger painting, before executing the final work of art, we can make studies in our medium of muslin, working on the drape of a single element, such as a sleeve or collar. Improvisational draping is a way to explore complex construction details, unusual seaming, or to work three-dimensionally on ideas that are difficult to sketch out on paper.

Although this technique is a free-form draping style, it is always helpful to have decided on your inspiration and done your research first, to internalize your intent. Preparation is key to getting the best results.

Jazz musicians often improvise, as do writers—such as Dylan Thomas, or James Joyce in his stream-of-consciousness style—and comedians who do "improv." But in each case, preparation is done to enable the free-form creativity to flow.

Designer Rick Owens' complex looks seem effortless and improvised. However, before the execution, he has laid the groundwork. He has a strong and unique design identity and a clearly defined aesthetic that guides his creative process.

Tips for Improvisational Design Research

- Review your inspiration board to find clues to what and where to research.
- Determine some areas that you want to explore; an interesting sleeve or a specific type of drape for a collar, or a detail that you want to explore.
- Catalogue the clothing of the historical periods that interest you.
- Find a cultural milieu that reflects your mood, or that has silhouettes or details which you want to interpret in your own way.
- Collect reference garments with design elements that inspire you.
- Explore what other designers have done with a particular look or concept.

A Rick Owens' design in cotton jersey that has the appearance of being draped improvisationally.

Working Intuitively

Being intuitive means to access the subconscious, discover what you love, follow your passion. Preparation for the intuitive process of improvisational draping involves internalizing your inspiration, so that you can hold that inspiration or abstract concept (or several at the same time) in your mind as you work.

Draping from sketches may start to feel routine. With improvisational draping, the outcome is open-ended, so the imagination is free to explore new pathways. As a multitude of decisions are made about shape, silhouette, and form, your personal vision emerges organically. Follow what you like, what feels good to you. Then the contours and shapes that emerge inevitably echo your chosen attitude or concept.

Take your theme from an idea on your inspiration boards, or perhaps one that you developed while experimentally draping with an interesting fabric. Because the choices and process are so personal, they lead you very directly to a uniquely individual and often very original result, which is, of course, always the ultimate goal. Draping improvisationally nourishes the development of a personal, signature style.

Self-Awareness

Are you "classic" or "romantic"?

Understanding ourselves is another aspect of research. Geographically, or economically—we usually know where we stand. But how can we know that the work we've done reflects our own passions, and not someone else's? Gaining self-awareness as an artist is a hard path to navigate. Defining your own style is a process that can take time.

One very broad generalization is to understand whether you tend toward the classic or the romantic, categories that pertain to all disciplines.

Romantic style and classical style both have their place in understanding how to build a garment. "Romantic" can be understood as focusing on and believing in the power of inspiration and instinct, whereas "classical" designers are more aesthetically retrained and more practical, and prefer to stay closer to traditional forms. Do you like to break the rules, or do you value form and structure over creative versatility? The way you balance the two in creating your design is an important element of your personal style. We need both logic and intuition; we need instruction manuals and we need poetry. It is helpful as a designer to know where you stand in this balance.

Hussein Chalayan's "Medea," intuitively draped in the romantic mode. The strands of fabric falling freely from the garment capture and release energy.

Draping Preparation

Draping with muslin is recommended for this method. It is your blank canvas, undistracted by color and texture. It is an important moment in the inception of design, so see this as a meditative process, enabling your intuitive side to emerge as you contour your silhouettes and play with various shapes and cuts.

White wood, raw cotton, coarse canvas: waiting for color. In process. The work is in progress, caught halfway between its origin and destination. Behind their apparent blankness, these bare objects or states teem with possibilities. Non-color is this precious and fleeting moment where colors are still to come, have not yet solidified. Colors in the mind's eye. We project and imagine, combine and foresee. Pure potentiality radiates.

Li Edelkoort, trend forecaster, "View on Color" 02/20

Preparation
Inspiration
- Study your inspiration boards for ideas and experimental draping work for fabrics you feel compelled to work with.

Research
- An essential part of the preparation, its goal is to synthesize data and impressions so that you can add something new to the conversation.

Fabrics
- Review your experimental drapes and photographs.
- Focus on the fabric swatches that feel right for your current designs.
- Note what design elements (such as darts or gathers) worked well on those fabrics.
- If you have already chosen a specific fabric, drape with it in view, to help you visualize the result.

Muslin preparation
- First, determine what kind of muslin to use, comparing choices to the tactile and visual qualities of your fabric, then select the one that most closely aligns with the hand of your final fabric.
- Estimate how much muslin you will need, then tear, block, and press it, and mark the appropriate grainlines.

Flat sketches
- In improvisational draping, sketches are not necessary. However, it can be helpful to make a grainline schematic (see below) that reflects the energy you would like to express, or sketch something quite rough to just get you started.

Preparing the dress form
- Apply any support elements you need (shoulder pad, stuffed arm, crinoline ruffles, etc.)
- In addition to bust, waist and hip, twill tape any areas that will help to determine parameters.

The pink damask used in the Ikebana drape (page 51) was cut in a petal shape, given loft with an underlining, and draped nearby as inspiration.

Preparing a dress form by using paper to sculpt the target shape of the finished skirt (page 75). It will act as a support while the skirt is being draped improvisationally.

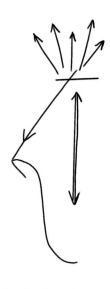

Grainline schematic used for experimental drape

First impressions:

1. Perspective:
a. Get some distance from the drape and look at it from all angles.
b. A mirror will be helpful to see the shape and silhouette from multiple angles as well as from varying distances.
c. Try it on a model if possible; observe how it moves and whether your ergonomics are working as intended.

2. The overview:
a. What is it that you wanted to express?
b. Is it conveying the concept with enough of an emotional punctuation?

3. Review the vision of the original inspiration or mood board
a. Does it fit the mood of the inspiration board?
b. Visualize the muse to see if it still fits the situation you imagined.

4. Fabrication:
a. Is it helping or preventing the concept to be expressed?
b. Are there other fabrics that might work better?

5. Embellishments and trims:
a. Do they seem integrated with the design?
b. Are they contributing to the emotional power or statement of the piece?

Detailed Analysis:

1. Good design
a. Does it have visual energy, harmony, and interest: Is the design compe
?
b. Review The Ten Principles of Good Design (page 17) to help you assess the separate elements.
c. If it has historical or cultural references, does it have enough of those references to make it clear, and yet different enough to have been brought new and modernized?

2. Ergonomic quality
a. Assess fit and ease.
b. Is it comfortable and appropriate?
c. Is it the style of fit that you intended?

3. Balance and stability
a. How are grainlines working together?
b. The seaming and dart angles should be balanced (symmetrical or asymmetrically) and purposeful.

4. Construction quality
a. Review The Ten Essentials of Couture (page 21).
   a. Is it crafted with as much artisal excellence as possible?
   b. Can this drape be realistically translated into a working pattern?
a. Will it make sense to the wearer? Where do closures go?
b. Review the three S's: surface integrity, support structure, stability.
c. Detail scan:
   i. Start at the top and work down, looking at necklines, armholes, any specific areas that might need correction.
   ii. Find areas of it that you like, and perhaps adjust areas that you don't like as well.
d. Mark any corrections with red chalk or pencil.

Earth's Heritage Studies

The series of improvisational drapes here were inspired by my Earth's Heritage board. Follow the steps as I have carried them out here, change and adapt the bodices to your own aesthetic, or choose one of your inspiration board themes and do a group of bodices inspired by a single theme.

Bodice variations
Preparation
Inspiration

- The inspiration for the drape on the following page is the origami section of my Ikebana board, and also some elements of the Butterfly drape shown here.

Fabric

- Raw silk will be used for the bodices, silk taffeta and silk dupioni for the leaves.

Muslin preparation

- Heavy muslin twill in combination with a standard muslin has been used for these drapes.
- Tear, block, and press muslin pieces as for a standard bodice block (sloper).

Executing the Improvisational Drape

1. Ground yourself with your inspiration; think of the story of your muse, and keep nearby the fabric you envision for your design.
2. Choose your grainline angles.
3. Drape the muslin, cutting and pinning as needed.
4. Review volume and silhouette, and make final adjustments.
5. Add any embellishment or treatment ideas.

Why Drape in Muslin?

- It is an industry standard used for draping and fitting toiles.
- It has a stable, visible grainline, and does not give or stretch easily.
- It maintains its shape while draping, and does not lose consistency.
- It is light and easy to handle.
- It can be creased, folded, and cut easily on the form.
- The light but crisp hand makes it clear to see how pieces are fitting together and when they are balanced.
- It is easily obtained and relatively inexpensive.
- Its smooth surface makes it easy to mark and transfer to a pattern.
- Most importantly, its absence of color creates a neutrality that helps you to see the silhouette you are sculpting, providing a blank canvas on which to create a design.

⊤ The drape

Working with negative space.

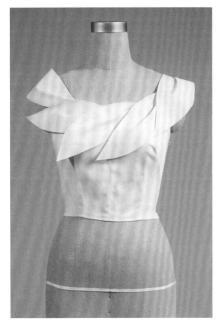

Adding repeated shapes.

The two bodices with cut-out treatments would work really well with laser cutting to make permanently clean edges.

Use of contrasting fabrics.

Adding a sleeve to the bodice.

Working with negative space

- Drape a standard bodice, darting to fit.
- Cut out shapes relating to your inspiration. Here, leaf shapes have been cut and then twisted into an exterior three-dimensional treatment.

Use of contrasting fabrics

- Drape a bodice with a contrasting fabric; here, a dark-brown was used.
- Drape the muslin bodice over the contrast bodice. Chalk in lines inspired by nature—here, tree branches—and stitch down.
- Slice out the lines on the muslin to show contrast.

Adding repeated shapes

- Drape the muslin bodice using a French dart and waistline dart.
- Keep the neckline wide and bateau and the sleeve slightly off the shoulder to hide the neckline edge with the leaves.
- Create the leaf shapes with a different piece of muslin, and drape them around the neckline.

Adding a sleeve to the bodice

- Drape a darted bodice with a wide scoop neck and narrow shoulder seam.
- Use a waist dart to pull in the hem at the lower edge.
- Cut the muslin along the neckline to create a buttonhole-style opening, then insert the first leaf and tie it to hold it in place.
- Drape the cowl sleeve. (Follow the instructions for draping a cowl, page 44.)
- Pin an additional tuck upward at the pin point to create more volume in the sleeve, then drape the underarm sleeve and pin to the bodice.
- Finish the blouse by adding a few more leaf ties along the neckline, then adjust all proportions until you are happy with the result.

Ikebana Studies

The following improvisational drapes are inspired by my Ikebana inspiration board. As I reference the Japanese culture and their arts of Ikebana and Origami, I will follow their sense of structure, order, and precision. My own interpretation has an enhanced sense of wildness and freedom, especially in the embellishment. Do your own version, perhaps using the information recorded during the fabric evaluation. For example, if deep pleats looked particularly good in a given fabric, drape something using similar deep pleats; and if you liked the way a cowl drape looked in a particular fabric, try to capture the look of that cowl.

Origami bodice

Preparation

Inspiration

- The inspiration for this bodice is the Origami section of the Ikebana board.

Research

- Practice origami paper-folding techniques to prepare for this drape, which is informed by the precision and beauty of this Japanese art.

Fabric

- Taffeta feels very crisp and paper-like, but is also soft and delicate, like flower petals. The sequin fabric is evocative of flower stalks, or sparkles like dewdrops.

Muslin preparation

- Mark grainlines, including bias lines on the muslin.

Dress form preparation

- Attach stuffed arm.

Sky blue metallic silk organza was the inspiration for this Ikebana Butterfly drape.

Working with historical or cultural references

- First discern what it is about the reference which speaks to you, pinpointing the three-dimensional representation of that. For example, if it is a Victorian-era garment, is it the bustled back, the puff of the sleeve, the delicacy of detail?
- Figure out how to interpret those elements in your own way, with your own style, while still maintaining the feel of those expressions.
- As you assess the finished drape, determine whether you have connected the past with the present in a relevant way.

The drape

Note: Although following these draping steps will
result in something similar to what I have draped, it is
best if you experiment with doing your own version.
Follow your intuition to arrive at something that
satisfies you.

Step 1

- Do some experimental draping with
  different fabrics to inspire you.
- The drape will need a base/bodice fabric
  and a contrasting collar and/or
  embellishment fabric.

Step 2

- The fabric was tested to see which
  grainline worked best for the neckline
  tucks. It was determined the best position
  for the grainline was for the bias line to
  fall straight down the princessline area.
- Fold tucks toward the center front.
- Slash at the armhole area to wrap it
  toward the side.

Step 3

- Use the extra fabric as it goes toward the
  back neckline to create an embellishment.
- Here, it is manipulated into origami-type
  folds to create clusters that look like
  flower petals.

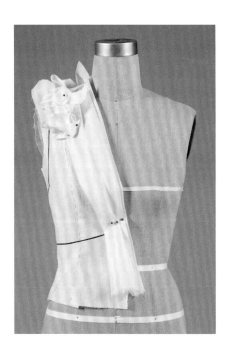

Step 4

- Trim the front below the high hip area so
  that the fabric will lie flat as it is
  smoothed toward the side seam.
- Cut away for the armhole.
- Create fit with a waist dart or princess
  seam.
- Tape the armhole and high waist style
  lines.
- Adjust the embellishment until it feels
  balanced with the rest of the design.

Ikebana dress

Preparation
Inspiration:

- This Sogetsu-style Ikebana, by Guy Blume, which is always comprised of the elements of Heaven, Earth, and Humanity.
- Heaven is represented by the green branch that reaches upward, Humanity by the complex, busy white and orange floral pieces in the middle, and Earth by the lowest part, which opens out and supports the other two elements.

Research:

- The Japanese art of Ikebana is a spiritual practice. It is followed as a discipline, and also creates great beauty.
- Review other examples of this style of Ikebana to familiarize yourself with the concept.

Fabric:

- Pink damask (see page 58) works well with deep inverted pleats, which help form the petal shapes While draping, keep the final design fabrics nearby to help you visualize the result.

Muslin preparation:

- Estimate the size of the leaf shapes, and prepare several for the skirt sections.
  - Mark grainlines lengthgrains.
- Prepare muslin for a bodice.
  - Mark grainlines
- These measurements and grainline positions can be approximate since it is an improvisational drape and a specific outcome is not planned.

The drape

Improvisational draping calls for following your intuition, so drape your own interpretation of the Ikebana.

Step 1

- Begin with the bodice grainline placement. Here, the strong lengthgrain is positioned from left princess point to shoulder.
- The muslin is stabilized at the waist with tucks.
- The section at the shoulder has been manipulated to get as much height as possible, to symbolize the heaven element.

Step 2

- Drape the skirt by creating several of the petals and pinning the centers into inverted pleats, which will look like real lily petals.
- Place the petals around the body from the waist, being careful to strike the right balance with the hem length.

Step 3

- Finish the drape by making final adjustments to the three elements, creating a finish at the waist wrap that completes the look.

Assessment

- Assess how it relates to the Ikebana. Identify the three elements, heaven, Earth, and humanity, and evaluate their balance.

EXERCISE 3:
Dark Radiance Studies

Improvisational draping inspired by my Dark Radiance board felt very fabric-dependent, but working in muslin, I tried to find shapes that reflected the mood of the board. Here, do your own version using an inspiration of your own, or working from the spirit of this mood.

Dark Radiance drape
Preparation
Inspiration
- The NASA starry sky image from the Dark Radiance inspiration board.

Fabric
- Two-faced heavy silk taffeta, which is malleable and holds its shape, reminiscent of the undulating, pulsating mood of the dark skies.

Flat sketches
- Design development sketches.

Muslin preparation
- Cut pieces for the bodice and collar, and mark the grainlines.

The drape

Step 1
- Drape the bodice, using any type of darting that feels right.
- Keep the neckline wide as a bateau, but leave enough width in the shoulder to support the collar piece.

Step 2
- Study the look of the midnight-blue silk, and drape it roughly on the left shoulder of the form to remind you of its qualities.
- Working intuitively, create tucks and twists that move around the neckline.

Step 3
- Finalize the collar drape by going back to the starry sky inspiration and translating the feeling of that image into your final drape. Pin in place.

Assessment
- See Assessment Protocols (page 59).

Assess your improvisational drape

- Take some photographs to study and compare to the drape.
- Journal some notes.
- Sketch any other ideas that are generated from this look.
- Review the Assessment Protocols on page 59.

"Starry Sky" drape
Preparation
Inspiration

• The NASA images on the Dark Radiance board inspire me to drape billowy, expanding shapes.

Research

• A study of galaxy formations and destructions, finding lines and drawing contours that trace the curvature of space..

Fabric

• Dark, patterned, or glittery chiffons.

This silk metallic chiffon inspires visions of glittering starry night skies.

Muslin Preparation

• Visualize the volume you want for the final design fabric and prepare the same amount of muslin. Mark length, cross, and bias grains, so that you can observe how the grainline placement affects the energy of the drape.

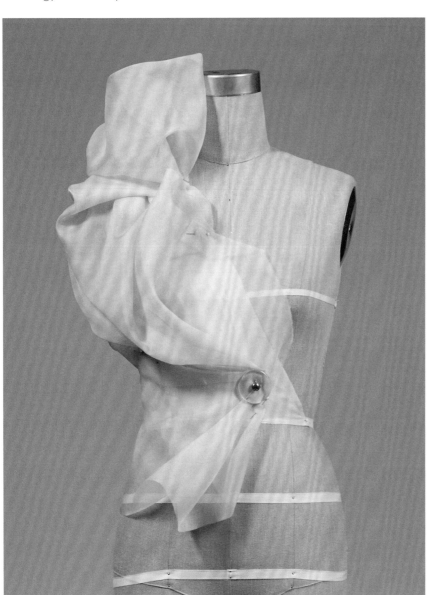

The drape

This drape is an example of my own improvisational techniques. Study the fabric and the inspiration, and drape something that reflects your own individual aesthetic. Treat this process as a meditation. Don't be distracted, focus on the project, and let it draw you in. Practice letting your intuitive side come to the fore.

Step 1

Begin the bodice drape by positioning the length grain vertically. Here, it feels as though it wants to follow the unfurling folds along the neckline.

Step 2

• Work the bodice area with darts or tucks. The organza is light and crisp, but tricky to control because it is slippery and bouncy, so be ready with pins when you hit the shape you want.

• Focus on the sense of the expanding star cluster.

Assessment

• See Assessment Protocols (page 59).
• Review The Ten Essentials of Couture (page 21).

The glamour of four-ply silk crepe
Preparation
Inspiration

• This reference garment, a Stéphane Rolland design using four-ply silk crepe, fits the Dark Radiance mood, hitting the sweet spot between glamour—which feels stylish, flirtatious, and sometimes even humorous—and a tone of sexiness, which can feel intense and serious.

Research

• Study historical and contemporary design to see how four-ply crepe has been used. It is a very luxurious silk but can be tricky to execute well with detailed construction.

The drape

Review what qualities of the reference garment you are attracted by, and let your imagination take flight. Before beginning the drape, steep yourself in the mood of your inspiration and relax your mind.

Music and muses

Accessing the intuitive or subconscious works differently for everyone. However, a relaxed mind is a good start.

> I listen to the music of the production while I sketch; this inspires me and invites in the rhythm of the characters I am working on.
>
> *Dominique Lemieux, on designing for Cirque du Soleil, interview with the author in 2018*

If what you are trying to communicate is hard to put into words, using a muse may help to stimulate your imagination. Develop the story for the muse: who they are, where they are going, what their mood is, how they are feeling. Think about how much space they take up, whether physically, kinetically, or emotionally, and why they have made that particular design choice.

> Find the story of the dress, the story of the woman, [and] focus on how you want her to feel.
> It is about sensation, dreams, creation.
>
> *Bastide Rey, modéliste, former head of atelier for Alexander McQueen, Dior, and Lanvin; currently with Elber Albaz. Interview with the author, 2017.*

A Dark Radiance reference garment: Stéphane Rolland Haute Couture Fall/Winter 2019 show as part of Paris Fashion Week

EXERCISE 4:
Upcycle Study

Repurposing an unusable piece of clothing is a very worthy project, since so much cast-off clothing goes into landfills. Here, a classic Japanese kimono is improvisationally draped into a contemporary dress. Do this exercise with a kimono, or follow the general steps with any garment you would like to upcycle.

Study the original design carefully on the dress form and identify which elements you like and want to retain: the fullness of a sleeve, the trim at a neckline, and so on. Then work improvisationally to restructure the garment, trying different proportions and silhouettes as you go.

Repurposed vintage kimono
Preparation
Inspiration
- An authentic vintage kimono, manufactured in Japan toward the end of the twentieth century or at the start of the twenty-first century.

Research
- Study the construction of a classic kimono.
- "Flat sketch" of your original garment to help you understand the structure that you will be working with.
- Study the kimono and think about how it might be updated. The sleeves and shoulders are always an important consideration with a kimono, since their volume makes it harder to move the arms freely. One idea would be to remove the sleeves, add that fabric to the width of the skirt, and belt the kimono into a dress.

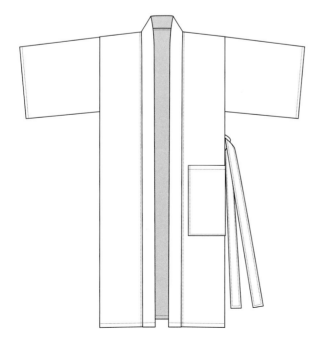

After you have taken apart and started working with the kimono, do a flat sketch of the new design. Once you are fairly certain what direction you are going in, it will help to map out your construction, especially if you are short of fabric. Here, I used every inch of the original kimono, even using the neckbands ends as the pocket.

Step 1

- Remove the sleeves.
- Open the side seams and shoulder seams to the neckband, which is not cut. (If there are no shoulder seams, which is common in classic kimonos, find the center point between the front and back hems, and cut the shoulder seam there.)

Step 2

- Fold a tuck at the shoulder to bring the edge of the fabric in to the shoulder point.
- Slash the side horizontally at the waist, to about the princess seam point.
- Pin the upper (bodice) sides together, front over back, fitting with a minimum of 2" (5 cm) total body/bust ease.
- Fit the bodice at the lower edge to create a fairly close fit.

Step 3

- Attach the sleeves to the open side seams. Here, the sleeve is sewn to the front part of the kimono.
- Sew the other side of the sleeve to the back part of the kimono.

Step 4

- Join the sides.

Step 5

- Use the old kimono belt to form a waistband for the dress.
- Pin the belt at waist from princess front to princess back, letting the excess become the tie ends of the belt.
- Make final adjustments to the design.
- Mark and true the drape.

Step 6

- Front pattern layout. Note the chalked seam allowances that have been added, and the chalk marks for the back shoulder dart and front shoulder tuck, as well as the notches for the waist tucks.

Step 7

- Back pattern layout. Note the square armholes and sew-line chalk marks, as on the front.
- The side panels are shorter than the front and back, but that construction problem will be solved by adding a "facing" piece of matching blue to the sides which will even them out after hemming.
- Sew the dress and assess the project on the dress form or model.

Step 8

- The finished front, with a pocket made of scrap fabric added at the left-hand side. Buttons have been added at center front along the neckband.
- The finished back. The belt was set into the bodice from the front princess to back princessline, and then the excess left to create the tie ends of the belt.

Assessment

- See Assessment Protocols (page 59).

The Improvisational Drape

Birth of the Cosmos skirt

Inspired by the Big Bang image from my Dark Radiance board, this skirt must be improvisationally draped to echo the asymetricality of the starbursts. . Follow the steps here to create a similar skirt, or adapt it to your own aesthetic. Alternatively, choose one of your own inspiration board themes and do a full improvisational drape following the basic guidelines from this chapter.

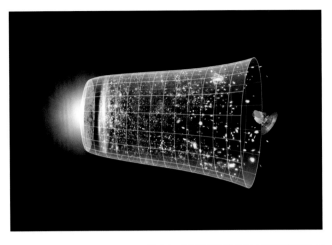

Preparation
Inspiration
- The shape of the Big Bang Diagram is the shape that I want for this skirt. It has a sense of the vastness of the universe; the shape is beautiful and compelling, a bell that expands to infinity.

Fabric
- Midnight-blue, double-faced silk satin has been chosen, inspired by the experimental drape on page 39. Shown here, studying the two different sides, and grainline placement.

Research
- Working on the darting and embellishment samples to explore creating various textures of light and shadow. Sourcing different sizes and shapes of crystals to evoke a night sky.

Flat sketches or rough sketches
- Since the final construction will be developed while improvisational draping, no flat sketch is needed. However, this rough sketch done for my Dark Radiance inspiration board provides a starting point.

Right: Experimenting on muslin with darting and crystals.

Muslin preparation:
Draw bias lines on a roll of muslin about 15" (38 cm) apart down the length of the fabric.

Dress form preparation:
This skirt will be improvisationally draped, but will try to capture the silhouette of the bell-shaped inspiration photo. Because the fabric will be difficult to handle during draping, it is helpful to create the desired shape first using a support element, and then drape over it. Paper can be an alternative to muslin for draping a difficult shape, since it has a crisp body and can be easily cut and taped together. Because it is cheap and ubiquitous, it can be used to experiment with the shape of a skirt, or to create a large cascade (see page 45), without wasting muslin. The yoke is draped first as a preparatory step so that there is something to anchor the skirt into place.

The drape

Note: Although following these draping steps will result in something similar to what I have draped, feel free to do your own version of it. Make changes as you go, following your intuition to arrive at something you like.

Step 1

- Check the grainline of the fabric and make sure the bias is straight down the center front.
- Experiment with the darting treatment, starting from the top edge and pinning to the yokes.

Step 2

- Determine the volume for the back at the hem by letting the fabric flare out at the sides.
- The bell shape of the skirt will need volume at the hem, but that cannot be determined until some of the darting is completed.
- Begin the back drape by pinning to the back yoke.

Step 3

- Drape and dart the skirt front, following the shape of the paper bell.
- Determine the dart spacing: smaller at the top and becoming wider toward the hem.

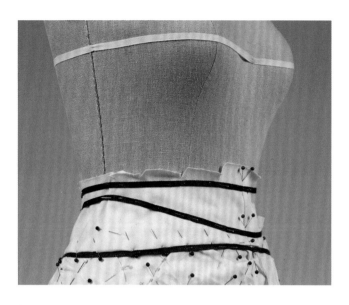

Step 4

- Note how the shape of the inspiration photo informs the shape of the waistband.
- Figure out how the silver (reverse) side of the fabric might be incorporated into the seaming of the yoke perhaps as a piping inserted into the seams.

Step 5

- Continue darting the skirt toward the hem, making the darts longer and the spaces wider.
- Complete the darting on the skirt, then turn up the hem.
- Review the waist yoke curved lines, and determine the closure area.

Step 6

- Because we are aiming for a very specific shape for the skirt, the hem will need some control. Horsehair braid will work well to create a more beautiful, evenly shaped hemline.
- The skirt is bell shaped, so the top edge of the horsehair braid will need to be narrower than the lower edge.
- Pin it around the hem with the "cord" edge on top.
- Find the string (see arrow) and gently pull until the braid conforms to the shape of the skirt.
- This is a delicate, time-consuming process, but must be done.

Marking and Truing the drape

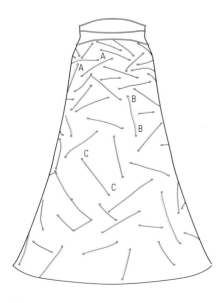

Step 1

- Mark the drape, following the checklist opposite. Darts must all be carefully marked before you remove the pins. Make sure to mark on both edges of the pinned darts, as well as both points of the dart. Because there are so many, you will need a coding system; here, I have used an alphabetical system, where "A" at one end of the dart matches "A" at the other end, and so on.
- True up the drape, following the steps in Truing Fundamentals (see box right).
- Before cutting, make sure you have decided on the support fabric, since you may want to cut both together. For this skirt, a black lightweight, woven cotton was used as a support.

Truing Fundamentals

"Truing" the drape means to make it into a pattern from which a fitting muslin can be cut.

1. Remove all pins, and press the creases gently if necessary. Be aware that heavy pressing may cause unwanted shrinkage and crinkling.
2. Smooth and blend the marked dotted lines, using a clear graph ruler for straight lines and a hip curve or small French curve for all curved lines.
3. "Walk" the seams to match each other, using your crossmarks as guideposts.
4. Establish a final, corrected system of notches (using crossmarks from the drape) to help you match the pieces up during stitching. Note that not all crossmarks need to be used for notches.
5. Add seam allowances.

Be aware that there are sometimes stray marks which don't fall in line with the others as you blend the lines. Make a decision based on your knowledge of pattern drafting, either to smooth them out and disregard the marks outside the lines, or to re-pin the muslin and set it back on the form to determine whether those marks indicate a subtlety of draping that you want to incorporate.

Step 2

- The underlining has been diagonal-basted (tacked) to the self-fabric. The stitches are in rows, quite close together, since the darts must pick up both layers of fabric during stitching.

Step 3

- Darts can be marked in several ways:
- With an awl, punching through the fabric.
- With carbon paper and a tracing wheel, marking the ends and lines of the darts.
- With tailor tacking (technique used here).
- Darts must be sewn with careful attention to the ends, tapering them gradually.

Step 4

- The waistband will hold considerable weight, so it has been reinforced with fusing and a light padding as an underlining.
- The piping has been made from the reverse side of the self-fabric, and the bias binding finishes the inner yoke edge, which will lie over the skirt lining to finish the inside of the skirt beautifully.

Step 5

- Before embellishing the skirt with the crystals, check the final shape.
- Are the darts nicely sewn, with no unevenness in texture? (Shown here are the darts being corrected with pins.)
- Also check the seam at the yoke. The skirt should balance perfectly all the way round. If there is a custom fit, a smaller or larger hip might require this seam to be adjusted. Even a very small adjustment will allow the skirt to balance perfectly.
- Review how the hem is working: is the horsehair on the hem creating the right lift? If it is too stiff, it will move in an artificial way; we want it to look soft and organic, yet still hold the shape of the silhouette.

Assessment

- See Assessment Protocols (page 59).
- Compare the skirt to the image of the Big Bang Diagram. Is it close enough to match the reference/inspiration?
- The fabric choice works well, holding the silhouette and its feeling of luxury and depth pique the imagination as it should.
- The crystal embellishment could be more pronounced, either with larger crystals or more of them.

CHAPTER 3
The Block-to-Drape Method

OBJECTIVES
Recognize design templates that can be
converted into blocks (slopers).

—

Identify reference garments that can be used to
establish proportion, volume, and scale of detail.

Exercise 1: Draping a Block from a Reference Garment
Apply basic draping methods to create an original block
from an existing garment.

Exercise 2: Block-to-Drape: the Bodice Block
Modify an existing block into a new bodice block design.

Exercise 3: Block-to-Drape: the Pant Block
Design a high-waisted, fitted pant (trouser) using an
existing block and a reference garment.

Exercise 4: Block-to-Drape: the Two-Piece Sleeve Block
Differentiate between the armhole and sleeve curves of a classic
two-piece sleeve and an angled equestrian-style sleeve.

Project: Block-to-Drape: the Tailored Jacket
Use the block-to-drape method and a reference garment to develop
a classic tailored jacket design, applying techniques of advanced
tailoring to create a finely tailored fit.

A tailored jacket block provides a starting point for a new jacket drape.

The Block-to-Drape Method

The "block-to-drape" method consists of using pattern blocks (slopers) of existing styles as a starting point to create an original design. The block and its grainlines are traced on to the muslin before draping, giving basic guidelines for shape, volume, and fit. The measurements of reference garments can be used to define specific proportions.

"Block" ("sloper" in the UK) is the term used in the fashion industry for a basic master pattern that has been tested and found to have good balance and fit. Once a block has been found reliable, it is used as the basis for extrapolating new styles. In draping and pattern drafting, using a block is more than a time-saving tool, it gives the designer the security of knowing exactly what to expect in terms of look and fit. For example, if the designer is creating a new shape for a two-piece sleeve, it can be helpful to start with an already tested two-piece sleeve block and then expand, reduce, or change the shape, while maintaining the elements that give it the right fit.

Fashion firms develop blocks with measurements that work well for their customer. A youth brand's bodice block will have very different measurements and proportions from one that markets to the mature buyer. Blocks used in professional situations go through many fittings, not only to perfect the fit, but also to arrive at the right attitude for the label.

Using blocks and reference garments gives the designer a starting point from which to build their own looks. Blocks are often best if they are basic and generic, so that the new designs exhibit their own unique look rather than the attitude of a previous design or trend.

Even though more than one designer can use the same template, the subtleties with which it is interpreted will give the resulting pieces their unique personality, helping the designer to define their own personal aesthetic.

Alexander McQueen, Dante jacket, Fall/Winter 1996. Trained as a tailor on Saville Row in London, McQueen produced clothing with a consistent excellence of fit and style that is remarkable and difficult to achieve without the use of blocks.

Recognizing Templates for Blocks

A template is a design that is standard enough in its shape and fit to be used as a block from which new designs can be developed. Classic silhouettes and basic, familiar garment types are templates that make good blocks because people are attracted to the familiar, and that familiarity creates a positive prejudicial bias.

The classic bomber jacket first appeared in World War II. It was so comfortable and practical that after the war new versions continued to crop up over several decades. The historical thread runs from that inception point to motorcycle jackets, the classic Levi jacket, the college "Letterman" jacket, and all the way to the contemporary teenage girl's satin bomber. Making a pattern block out of a recognizable template such as this creates that prejudicial bias, an automatic level of comfort with the resulting new designs. Other examples of templates that would translate into good blocks are the Chanel Tyrolean-inspired, three-panel jacket; 1960s' sheath dress, a classic riding jacket, a trench coat, a perfectly cut trouser, and a classic swimsuit.

Imprinting your personal style onto a template

Remember that, if you are referencing an iconic piece such as this World War II bomber jacket, in a design, aim to express your own take on it. It is in the interpretation of the template that the designer's individuality emerges.

Above: This World War II bomber jacket incorporates the elements that made it a classic: cropped shape, wide shoulders, ample collar, and protective feeling front pockets.

Left and below: This Harley-Davidson jacket is an evolution of the World War II bomber jacket.

Using Reference Garments

A companion method to using pattern blocks is the use of reference garments. Designers commonly collect vintage examples of favorite pieces so that when they need to, they can measure the sweep of a skirt hem or the width of a pant (trouser) cuff to pinpoint an exact proportion that they would like to duplicate.

After a pattern block is traced on to the muslin, relevant measurements from the reference garment can be marked on the muslin before draping starts, to provide additional parameters for volume and proportion. Sometimes the very specific scale of a collar or sleeve will capture the feeling or look of that reference garment exactly.

For example, to design a jacket that expresses equestrian formality and fit, create a block from an actual riding jacket, then use reference riding jackets to check measurements of their details, using the block-to-drape method to create the new design. These methods will help the stylistic subtleties and essence of the riding jacket to emerge. Then the designer can determine how to make it into something new and original.

Studying reference garments raises awareness of the details of fit. Understanding why an armhole looks so flattering, or why a pant fits so well, trains the designer to recognize the shapes and proportions they want to implement.

Taking measurements from a reference garment can also save time. An experienced designer knows that on a shirt front, there is a big difference between a 1" (2.5 cm) placket and a 1¼" (3 cm) placket, but it is expedient to have a shirt to refer to when confirming a proportion.

Keep your own collection of favorite garments so that you can use their measurements for reference. Not only does using a block from a classic garment or the familiar proportions of a reference piece create a particular desired attitude, it also helps to produce concrete results the designer can rely on.

Draping and Drafting Methods

After identifying a garment that fits the guidelines for a good template or block, determine which method of creating the pattern block will work best: drafting or draping. Perhaps there are some areas of the garment that can be easily traced off, or mathematically drafted, such as cuffs, collar, or plackets. Situations in which the draping method is preferable would be if the fabric is too delicate to stretch out on a table and pin or use the tracing wheel, or if the design has elements that are easier to work with on the form, such as directional pleats or tucks. Also, if ease and stretch have been used in the construction—in a tailored jacket, for example—the drape can accommodate that. Sometimes the shape is simply more easily understood on the form rather than lying flat. The block may also be a combination of the two methods, using the techniques and following the basic order outlined below.

1. "Ease" is sleeve cap.

2. Roll line taping for fit and shaping purposes.

3. Outer lapel edge tape to align edge to hug jacket body.

EXERCISE 1:
Draping a Block from a Reference Garment

This classic 1940s' rayon dress is being copied for use as a block because it displays the distinctive elements of that era: the strong shoulders, with pad, and the pronounced waistline. The cut of the bodice and skirt reflect a common silhouette of that era.

This will be draped, because the fabric is faded and worn, and could be easily damaged. Also, the directional tucks on the skirt will be easier to drape than to draft on the table.

Developing a Block from a Drape

Step 1 Drape the Block
Step 2 Mark and true the drape
Step 3 The Re-Pin
  Re-pin and position on form to check the truing.
  Mark and adjust for corrections
Step 4 Transfer the drape to a paper pattern
Step 5 Cut, sew, and fit a toile, correct as needed

1940s dress
Preparation
Flat sketches and grainlines

- Mark the grainlines on the dress
- Locate the grainline positions on the dress using the testing fabric tension method on page 36.
- If thread-tracing, check that the needle and thread are fine enough not to damage the fabric, and if using sticky tailoring tape, make sure that it will not damage the fabric when you remove it.
- Mark length- and crossgrains on all pieces. Seen here are the bodice at center front and bustline; the skirt at hipline (center front of the skirt is not necessary, because there is a center front seam); on the back, the skirt and bodice crossgrains (center back not necessary because there are seams); and the sleeve center and crossgrain at bicep line.
- Prepare flat sketches of the front and back, accurately recording all seam positions and construction details.

Muslin preparation

- Determine type of muslin to use by assessing which is most similar to the final fabric.
- Prepare a muslin preparation diagram to aid in economy of cutting the muslin pieces.
- Tear, block, and press.
- Mark the grain lines on the muslin that correspond with the thread traced lines on the dress.

Dress and dress form preparation

- Select a dress form with as close as possible sizing as the dress.
- Pad dress form to size if necessary.
- Apply support elements: shoulder pad, stuffed arm.
- Balance the dress onto the form by aligning center fronts and center backs of dress and form.
- Balance the shoulder seams of the dress so that it is not swinging toward front or back, then secure into place with pins.

Muslin Preparation

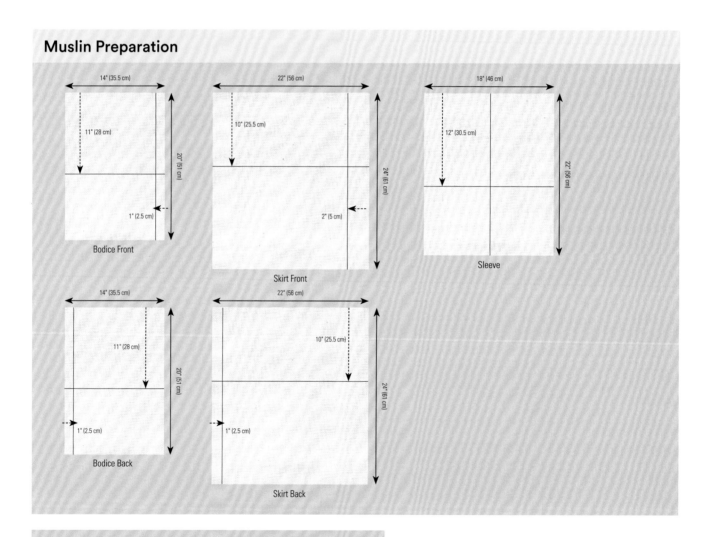

Muslin Preparation Diagrams in this Book:

- Indicate the dimensions of the muslin pieces for the style to be draped/
- Feature grainline markings that help position the muslin on the form.
- Are oriented with the lengthgrain vertically, and crossgrain horizontally.

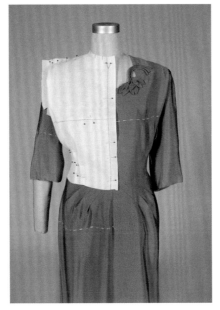
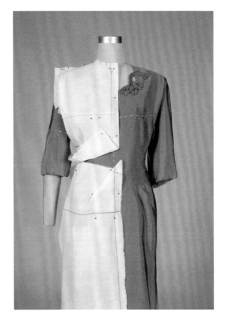

Step 1

- Begin at center front and pin the muslin on to the dress along the center front thread-traced line and the crossgrain at the bustline.
- Clip and trim at the neckline.
- Measure and mark the position of the waist tuck.

Step 2

- Trim away the excess muslin at the side seam and armhole to enables the muslin to lie against the dress fabric, smoothing it toward the side and shoulder.
- Use the measurements of the dress waist tuck to create the waist tucks on the muslin, and use the measurements of the shoulder tuck to create the shoulder tuck.
- Pin the shoulder seam down to the dress and the side muslin to the side seam of the dress.
- Repeat for the back bodice, draping the back neck and waist darts (not shown).

Step 3

- Gently lift the bodice muslin and pin it out of the way to begin the skirt drape.
- Pin the skirt down the center front, aligning the marked lengthgrain of the muslin with the center front thread-traced line of the dress.
- Pin across the hiplines, but only for the first few inches, since the large tucks will pull the side seam fabric quite a bit.
- Pin the first tuck by folding the tuck intake downward, using the measurement on the dress tucks as a reference.

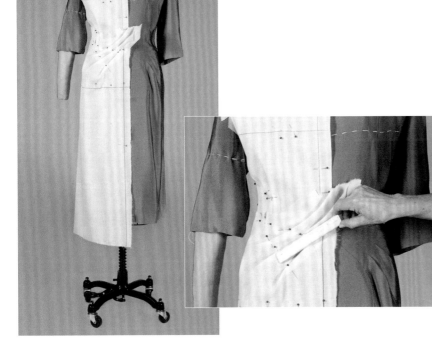

Step 4

- Pin the second and third tucks.
- Clip and trim the top edge of the skirt to allow it to lie smoothly along the waistline.
- Use a ruler to check the depth of the tucks and their length and spacing against the tucks of the reference dress.
- Drape the back skirt, aligning the center back of the muslin with the center back of the skirt, and creating a dart at the back princessline.

Sleeve Draping Order

This draping order works for many different styles of sleeve. Work alternately from the cap area to the wrist and back, working down the armhole and up the underarm seam, ending at the underarm point.

1. Set the correct angle of the sleeve, with the lengthgrain slightly toward the front, as the natural hang of the arm.
2. Pin the cap at the shoulder.
3. Set the wrist and pin circumference. Match the crossgrains.
4. Set the pivot/notch points.
5. Work the underarm seam from wrist to elbow.
6. Trim the excess and refine the upper half of the sleeve cap.
7. Move up the underarm seam, turning the excess to the inside and finalizing the sleeve width in the bicep area.
8. Work the lower sleeve curves from pivot points to underarm point.
9. Finish the underarm seam, joining it with the underarm point of the sleeve.

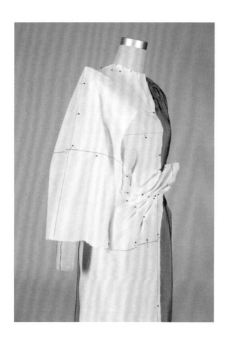 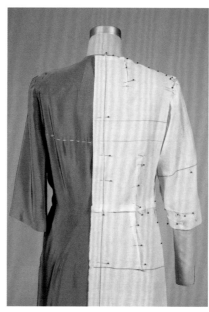 

Step 5

- Begin draping the sleeve by aligning the lengthgrain of the marked muslin with the lengthgrain of the sleeve.
- Pin the lengthgrains and crossgrains together.
- Follow the classic sleeve draping order (see box), trimming away at the cap, adding ease where the sleeve fits into the armhole, and double-checking the sleeve length and hem against the actual dress.

Step 6

- Repeat steps 1–4 to complete the back of the dress.
- Be sure to include the darts on the back of the sleeve, near the elbow.
- Pin the side seams front over back, smoothing toward the side to make sure the muslin lies smoothly on the fabric.

Step 7

- Trim the top edge of the skirt, leaving a 1" (2.5 cm) seam allowance.
- Fold the bodice over the skirt.
- Trim the neckline, clipping at the square cut and turning under to match the dress neckline.
- Finish the drape by checking all measurements of the muslin drape against the dress.
- Mark the floral embellishment on the muslin by tracing with a pencil or chalk.

Step 8

Before moving on to the marking and truing, check your drape carefully:

- Confirm that you have captured the look of the original design.
- Review each piece to make sure that all seams are smooth and matching.
- Check that the muslin is lying smoothly on each piece.

Marking and Truing

Carefully mark all muslin pieces. See the Checklist for Marking the Drape and Truing Fundamentals (page 74).

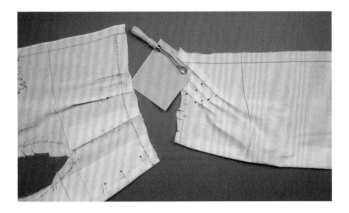

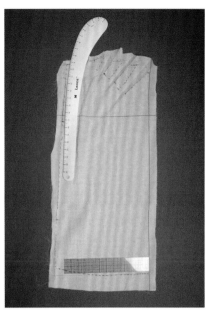

Step 1

- Use carbon paper and a tracing wheel to mark the finished angles of the tucks.
- Before removing the pins from the skirt, walk the waist seam with the bodice waist seam and make sure the side seams and center front/center back seams match.

Step 2

- Use the hip curve to smooth out the side seams. Note: The front and back side-seam curves will match below the hipline, but not from there to the waist, because the deep tucks will create a different angle in the front.
- The hems of the front and back skirts should make a right angle to the center front and center back, and be perpendicular to the side seams.

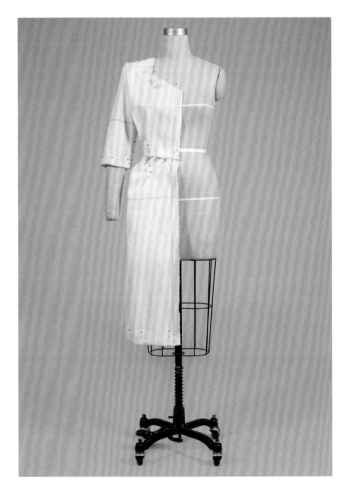

Step 3

- Re-pin all the dress seams together in the order in which they were draped. Pin fronts over backs, bodice over skirt.
- Reposition the muslin on the dress form and check the re-pinned drape for corrections.
- Mark any corrections with red pencil or chalk.

Assessment

- See Assessment Protocols (page 59).
- Perspective: Check the drape from a distance and from various angles to make sure it is balanced and all seam connections are precise.
- Take photographs to study; you may see issues in the two-dimensional photo which you do not notice on the three-dimensional draped piece.
- Use your skill of visualization to note the difference between how the muslin dress drapes in comparison to the 1940s' rayon crepe.

EXERCISE 2:
Block-to-Drape: the Bodice Block

1930s-style "Dubarry" blouse

This exercise uses the balance and proportion of a classic bodice block to drape the design of a 1930s-inspired blouse. Balancing the shoulder seams and side seams of a bodice, jacket, or coat takes time and experience. Once a successful result has been achieved, using the carefully calibrated balance of those pattern pieces saves time. The classic bodice block used here has been through a careful fitting process, so we can be confident that the balance and proportion of the new draped bodice will work well.

Preparation
Inspiration

- The attitude of this Dubarry pattern illustration is conservative, but very sweet, and has a vintage charm to it that I will aim to capture in the design.

Research

- Choose a block by checking muslin choices on the form. Compare elements such as seaming, silhouette, armhole height with the inspiration for the design.
- This basic bodice with a side bust and front waist dart will work perfectly, because it has a good, easy fit and the armhole is the right shape and height.

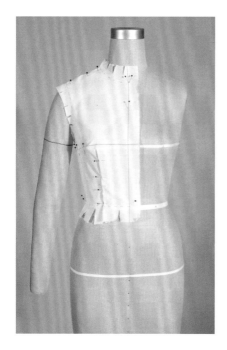

5287

Flat sketches

Muslin preparation

- For front and back bodice: Use the measurements of the front, back, and sleeve bodice blocks, adding 2" (5 cm) around each piece.
- Tear, block, and press the muslin, and mark grainlines with pencil or chalk to correspond with the grainline on the pattern block.

Draping preparation chart

1. Tear and block the Muslin	2. Press the Muslin	3. Mark the grainlines—use pencil or chalk
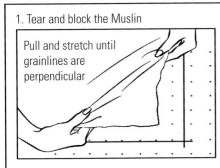	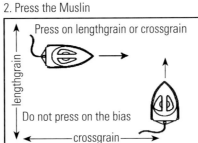	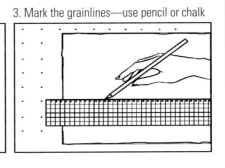

1. Tear and block the Muslin

Pull and stretch until grainlines are perpendicular

2. Press the Muslin

Press on lengthgrain or crossgrain

lengthgrain

Do not press on the bias

crossgrain

3. Mark the grainlines—use pencil or chalk

Block-to-drape preparation

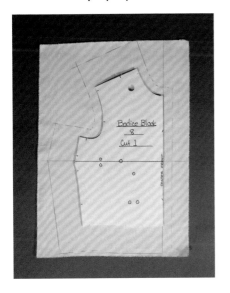

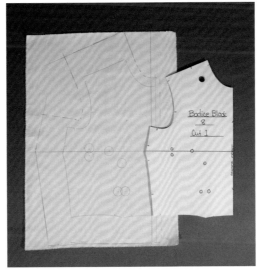

Tracing the block onto the muslin and marking important reference measurements

- Aligning the grainlines, place the block on the muslin.
- Trace around all edges lightly with pencil or chalk. All marks should be made lightly, so that they aren't too distracting while you drape.
- Remove the block and add 2–3" (5–7.5 cm) to all edges.

Dress form preparation

- Add the stuffed arm and a small shoulder pad, which will help to create the 1930s/1940s' look.

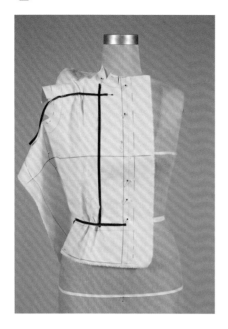

Step 1

- Start with the front bodice drape by aligning the center front grainlines with the center front of the form, and the crossgrain with the bust line.
- Check the sketch and determine where the gathers will be placed. Here, the gathers from the side bust dart and waist dart will be moved to the shoulder yoke and waist.
- To create the balance of those gathers, pin the side seams, starting at about the middle and letting most of the dart intake go into the armhole, which will pivot fullness/gathers into the yoke.
- Tape the style lines: neckline, yoke, front panel seam, and waistline. Here, sticky tape is used to mark the vertical panel seam near the center front, but non-stick twill is used for the other two horizontal lines so that the gathers can be adjusted underneath it.
- Repeat for the back bodice, keeping the shoulder dart intact and letting the waist dart release and create gathers.

Step 2

- Join the shoulder seams. Pin to the outside first, pinning at the original line of the neck. On the outer (sleeve) edge, allow extra for the shoulder pad.
- Finalizing the volume and shape, pin the shoulders and sides, turning front over back, seam allowances to the inside.
- Add mock-up buttons and belt to the drape. This will help to finesse the exact proportions of this drape, which are important, because there are many elements to coordinate. Adjust the button spacing as it relates to the exact position of the neckline.

Step 3

- Mark the center front piece of the bodice along the tape lines, and mark the position of the buttons.
- Mark the side front piece, making sure to notch at the "yoke" point for the seam.
- Mark the yoke piece, notching with the back at the neckline.
- Mark the waistline at the belt, and note the measurement of the finished gathers at the waist.
- Mark the depth of the neckline and the armholes.
- True the lines and notch.

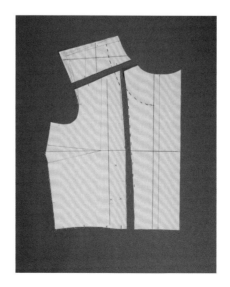

Step 4

- Cut the front muslin into three separate sections: center front piece, side front section, and front yoke. These pieces now have no seam allowances. The new trued lines are marked in red.

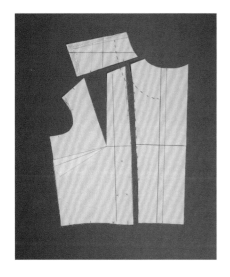

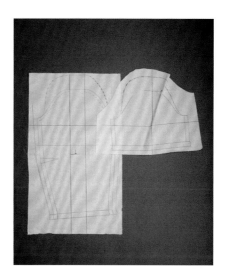

Step 5

- Pivot the side bust dart into the yoke seam:
  - Cut the side bust dart to the apex point.
  - Cut the yoke seam to the apex point from the center of the seam, as shown.
  - Pivot the side bust dart to the yoke seam area.
- Make sure the crossmarks are clear to rejoin the seams.
- Add crossmarks for the shirring placement at waist and yoke.

Note: If during draping you have added more gathers to the waist than is provided by the waist dart, pivot some of the fullness into the waist from the bust dart.

Step 6

- Cut new muslin fronts with seam allowances as follows:
  - Center front: Leave an extra 2" (5 cm) to allow for the button closure overlap.
  - Side front: Add a 1" (2.5 cm) seam allowance all the way round.
  - Yoke: Add a 1" (2.5 cm) seam allowance all the way round.

Step 7

- To prepare for sleeve drape:
  - Trace the sleeve block on to muslin, matching the grainlines.
  - Approximate the amount of extra fabric needed at the cap (2–3"/5–7.5 cm).
  - Approximate the length (ending at the elbow).
  - Cut the sleeve muslin to the correct length, leaving extra for the hem (the muslin is on the right of the photo).
- Fold in the sleeve tuck, as in the sketch.

Step 8

- Drape the bodice pieces front and back, and pin along the new marked sew lines.
- Drape the sleeve prepared in Step 7.
- Make final adjustments.

Step 9:

- True up the sleeve and trim the seam allowances.

Assessment

- See Assessment Protocols (page 59).
- Photograph the drape, and compare it to the inspiration image. Make corrections as necessary.
- Sketch any other ideas that are generated from the drape.

EXERCISE 3:
Block-to-Drape: the Pant Block

High-waisted, fitted pant

A basic, well fitting pant block is a valuable asset to a designer. Here, a reliable block has been selected from which to extrapolate a new design. Subtle changes in style lines and silhouette will give it sleeker lines and an edgier attitude. The block has been adjusted and improved through many fittings, so can be used with high confidence of a great fit.

Preparation

Inspiration

- The Ungaro velvet pant provides inspiration that matches the look and attitude of the Dark Radiance group.

Research

- Studying similar pant designs and reference garments will help focus on what changes need to be made.
- The Ungaro velvet pant will be used as Reference Garment 1, providing specification measurements for the high waist.
- In addition, Reference Garment 2 (gray striped pant, see page 91) will be used for crotch depth measurements and style lines. This piece has an ideal crotch depth for a good fit ending right at the waistline. The seam that runs down the center back leg will allow for a close, shaped fit.

Fabrics/Trims

- The pant block was made for a "stretch woven" fabric with exact specification at 96% cotton, 4% spandex. Draping in standard muslin will work because utlilization of stretch is not for fit, but for movement and comfort.

Flat sketches

- Flat sketches show a seam down the center of the back leg as seen in Reference Garment 2.

Muslin preparation

- Tear, block, and press the muslin. Prepare one piece for the front and two pieces for the back, to allow for a two-piece back leg. Mark the grainlines.

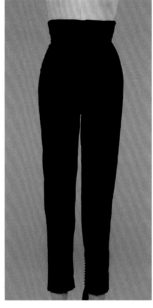

Emmanuel Ungaro black velvet pant, circa 1980, as Reference Garment 1.

Block-to-drape preparation

- For the pant front, first draw length- and crossgrains on the muslin. Align the length- and crossgrains of the front pant pattern block with the muslin, and trace it.
- Measure the waist height (crotch to top edge of pant) of Reference Garment 1, and note that on the muslin.
- From Reference Garment 2, measure from the crotch seam to the pant waist and mark on the muslin.

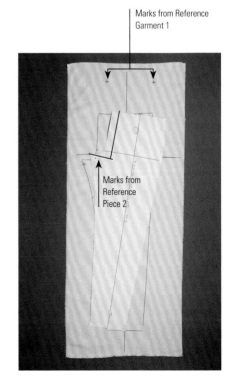

Tracing the block onto the muslin and marking important reference measurements

Marks from Reference Garment 1

Marks from Reference Piece 2

- The pant will be draped in two sections, a side section and the center back section.
- For the back pant, align and trace the front, block, but separate the pant at the lengthgrain line by about 4–5" (10–12.5 cm). That way, the striped pant can be traced over this block to use the pattern shape of the two backs.
- Use carbon paper and a tracing wheel to mark the reference pant sections carefully.

- Before beginning the drape, pin the inseams together on the table. This will be far easier than doing it on the form. Pin front over back, leaving a little open at the crotch for adjustment.
- The two back pant sections will be sliced apart during draping to create fit along the length of the back leg.

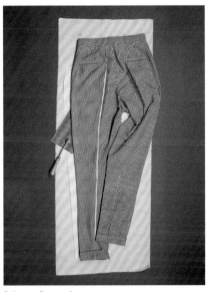
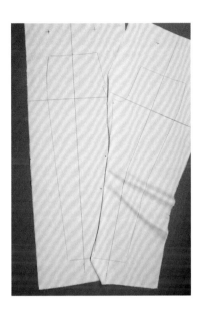

Reference Garment 2.

Dress form preparation
Tape the center back of the leg on the dress form to guide the drape of the two back pant sections.

The drape

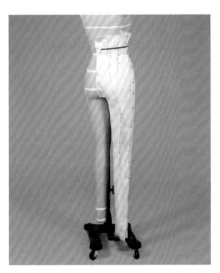

Step 1
- Drape the front pant, clipping at the crotch seam.
- Pin a dart at the princessline.

Step 2
- Pin the two back seams together, following the carbon/tracing-wheel line on the muslin.
- Add a back dart to the side back piece, because it needs the fit at the waist.
- Pin the side seams outward and check the fit, then turn front over back to pin the raw edges to the inside.

Step 3
- Tape the top edge of the pant. Let the front curve into a gentle arc, and tape the back lower for comfort and a better fit.
- Check the hem by comparing the measurement to that of the pant block, and turn under the excess.

Prepare the pant toile

Follow steps to Developing a Block from a Drape (page 81). To prepare a fitting toile, use a stretch woven fabric for cutting the fitting sample, since this was what the original pant block was made for and what the final pant will be cut in.

- After the pant has been cut and the pieces machine-basted together, it will be checked on the pant form for corrections before being fitted on a live model.
- The front of the pant fits well and the height of the waistline seems correct, so there will be no corrections to the front.

The fitting problems seem to be only in the back: There is extra fabric on the center back section at the thigh and crotch, and the waist is big at the side back area.

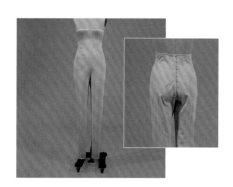

Pattern Correction Technique when Pinning at a Seam is Difficult

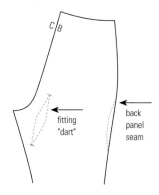

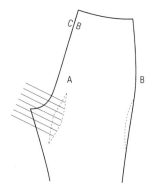

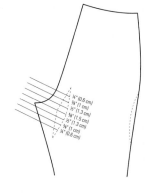

1. Pin a dart shape to remove unwanted, excess fabric from the area in question.
2. Thread-trace or chalk mark both sides of the dart "legs," and the ends of the dart shape.
3. Un-pin. Study where best to remove the fabric and adjust the pattern shape. Here the dart closest to the crotch area (A) will work well by taking it out of the crotch curve and inseam. The vertical dart (B) can simply be smoothed out of the back pant seam at the princessline.

4. First, draw a series of lines about ½" (1.5 cm) apart along the dart, toward the area where you will shift the pattern line.

5. Measure the dart intake of each of those lines.

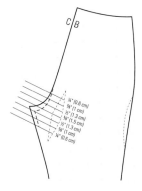

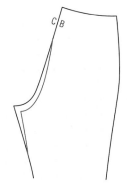

6. Transfer those measurements to the outside line of the pattern.

7. Use a curve to connect those marks, creating the new pattern line.

Note: The amount of fabric taken out by the dart is removed from the outside edge of the pattern without affecting the fit of the rest of the pant.

- The extra fabric can be removed to improve the fit.
- Because there is a seam in the center of the leg, that seam can be used to pull out a little more fabric under the derriere (see pinned area).
- The other area where fabric can be removed is at the crotch, so a small diagonal dart has been pinned out there.
- In addition to the fit of the pant leg, extra fabric will be taken out of the darts at the waist to create a slightly tighter fit at the back waist.

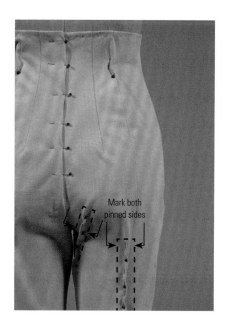

Mark both pinned sides

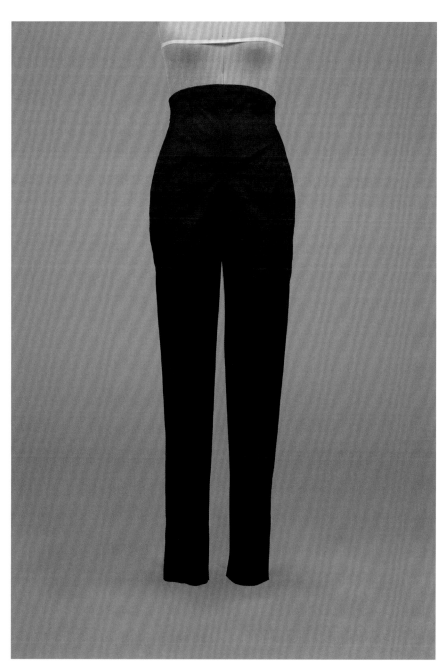

Corrections have been made, and the finished pant sample is seen here in the final design fabric.

Assessment

- See Assessment Protocols (page 59).
- Remember to step back, view the pant from a 360-degree perspective, assessing the visual impact from a distance. The overview: Does it feel like it captures the mood of the inspiration pant? Is the fabrication working as far as conveying the sleek, modern tone of the Dark Radiance group? Does it have enough stretch?

EXERCISE 4:

Block-to-Drape: the Two-Piece Sleeve Block

Equestrian jacket

When horseback riding, the arms are outstretched forward, so riding jackets must be cut to accommodate that. A classic two-piece sleeve pattern block will be used to shift the angle of the sleeve toward the front for a riding jacket fit. The block-to-drape method is helpful when making small, subtle changes to a pattern that already has a good fit and balance.

Sleeves and armholes fit together in a complex combination of curves that are notoriously difficult to perfect.

Preparation
Inspiration

- Make a timeline study of sleeves and armhole shapes/depths to further your understanding of the importance of this part of a jacket.

Muslin preparation

- Prepare two pieces of muslin, for the top and under sleeve, leaving at least 3" (7.5 cm) on each dimenion for the block-to-drape method.
- Tear, block, and press the pieces, and mark the grainlines to correspond with the grainlines on the block.

Block-to-drape preparation

- Trace the two sections of the sleeve block pattern on to the muslin pieces, aligning the grainlines on the muslin with those on the pattern.
- Trim around the pieces, leaving a small amount extra all the way around. (See undersleeve piece.)

Dress form preparation

- Add the shoulder pad and stuffed arm.

Flat sketches

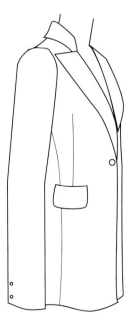

Classic jacket with two-piece sleeve, side view.

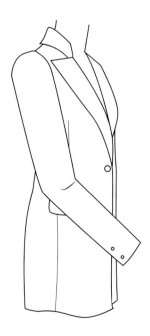

Equestrian jacket with two-piece sleeve, side view.

Below: Tracing the block onto the muslin and marking important reference measurements

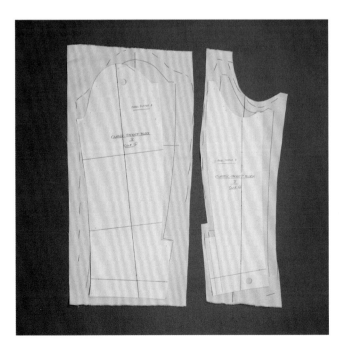

94

Step 1

- Pin the two sleeve sections together, with seam allowances toward the outside.
- Fit the sleeve on to the stuffed arm and pin roughly at the cap.
- Study the shape of the sleeve and armhole.
- Note that the sleeve hangs straight down, with only a slight forward tilt. The object is to angle that sleeve forward, cant it outward just a small amount, and perhaps slim down the volume while keeping the look of the sleeve, and the shape and size of the armhole, intact.

Step 2

- Experiment with moving the arm forward and outward.
- Observe the additional fabric needed in the back sleeve to allow for those movements.
- Pin around the cap area while keeping the arm angled forward and outward.
- Start at the cap area, then work toward the underarm, adding more fabric to the back and underarm as needed and experimenting with how much to move the sleeve forward.
- Adjust the shape of the sleeve itself, slimming it down as desired. The inside seam at the elbow will need less fabric, and the back elbow will need a little more.

Step 3

- Observe the finished sleeve and compare it to the sleeve on the classic jacket.
- Mark and true the sleeve.
- Refer to the Steps to Developing a Block from a Drape (page 81) to create the new sleeve block.

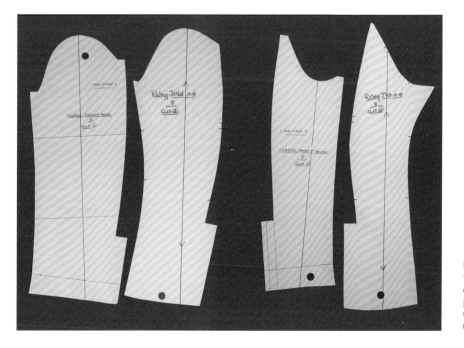

Left: The two pattern pieces on the left are the classic jacket; the two on the right are the "riding jacket." Note the more exaggerated curve of the riding jacket bicep area. The classic jacket, while still curved, is much straighter. Note the undersleeve inside curve. Again, the riding jacket curve is much more pronounced.

Block-to-Drape: the Tailored Jacket

Alexander McQueen tailored jacket

The tailored jacket is to the fashion student what the study of anatomy is to the fine-art student. There is much to be learned in the construction of a fitted jacket. Alexander McQueen was a master tailor, and his jackets were a compelling combination of classic fit and innovative design.

The block-to-drape method will be used to develop a fitting muslin for this jacket. After studying available blocks for general shape, seaming, fit, and type of armhole, a block has been chosen to work as a springboard for the project.

Using a classic three-panel tailored jacket block will give:
• Three body pattern sections that have been balanced and will allow enough seams to adjust the shape to match the McQueen jacket.
• A pattern that already has some fit/shaping at the waist.
• Shoulder seams that are well positioned and balanced.
• A two-piece sleeve that has a good proportion.

Note: Advanced tailoring techniques will be needed to achieve this look.

Alexander McQueen, La Poupée jacket, Fall/Winter 1997.

Preparation
Research
• Study jacket silhouettes and compare and contrast the shoulder height, shaped waist, and lapel shapes. Especially note the exaggerated shoulder shapes of the 1980s and late 1990s.
• Find reference garments to use for measurements and study.

Flat sketches

A reference jacket (c.1980 Charles Gallay wool tailored jacket) helps to set shoulder height and width.

The chosen pattern block cut and basted in muslin.

Guide for taping the roll line.

- The block has been chosen, then cut and sewn in muslin.
- Set the machine-basted muslin of the pattern block onto the dress form and carefully study the proportions of the machine-basted muslin.
- It has the basic body seaming needed.
- The shoulder is not as high or pronounced as in the McQueen jacket, but has similar strength.
- Importantly, the armhole height is correct. The complex curves of the sleeve and armhole are very hard to perfect, so using these to begin with is a big advantage.
- Measurements can be taken from this muslin block to set some of the parameters for the drape:
  - Measure the shoulder angle: Hold a ruler straight out from the neckline, then measure the distance from the top edge to the straight angle to gauge how high to make the shoulder.
  - Measure the shoulder width: Measure at the top of the shoulders from sleeve seam to sleeve seam.
  - Measure the width of the lapel: Measure from the roll line to the outside edge at the largest point.

- Following the proportions of the photograph or flat sketch, mark the:
  - Roll lines
  - Both left and right outer lapel shapes
  - Collar notch
  - Fold-under point on the right-hand side
  - Hem
- Pin the waist, but do only minimal fitting until you actually drape the jacket.
- On the right front here, note the pin at the bust, indicating that the roll line must be taped to create that fit.
- Having this cut and sewn muslin of the pattern block will enable you to mark freely on the jacket. Alternatively, use thread-tracing on the actual jacket, first making sure the fabric will not be damaged by your needle and thread.

Refer to The Ten Essentials of Couture (page 21) during the making of this jacket, for hints about how to make it the best possible quality. This step of easing in the front of the lapel will make a remarkable difference to the fit of the front jacket.

- On the left front here, the pin also means taping at the roll line, but because this roll line is a severe concave curve, it will be necessary to cut the lapel as a separate piece.

Muslin preparation

- Be very thorough and careful when preparing the muslin for this jacket. The fit is very exacting, and the lines will be subtle. See Draping preparation chart (page 87).
- Prepare the muslin pieces by measuring each piece of the block, then adding at least 3" (7.5 cm) all around to allow for draping the new shape.
- Mark with grainlines corresponding to the grainlines on the block.

Block-to-drape preparation

- Align the marked grainlines of the muslin and the block, and trace around the edges of the original block (see below, left).
- Transfer all inside lines with a tracing wheel and carbon paper. Include the darts and roll lines.
- Transfer the "research" information from the muslin block and the reference jacket on to these muslin pieces before beginning the drape:
- First take the measurements from the red jacket,

and mark on to the muslin as follows: shoulder height; shoulder width (from back sleeve seam to sleeve seam); and lapel width.

- Next, align the marked muslin sample with the grainlines on the pattern and carefully mark as follows: roll lines; the outer lapel shape; the collar notch; the fold-under point on the right side. Use a tracing wheel for inside marks, and pencil or chalk for outer edges.
- Note: These measurements are guidelines only. Once the piece is back on the dress form for draping, you will have to create the proportions with a good eye for balance and silhouette, not by following strict measurements.
- Repeat the above for the back section (see below, right).

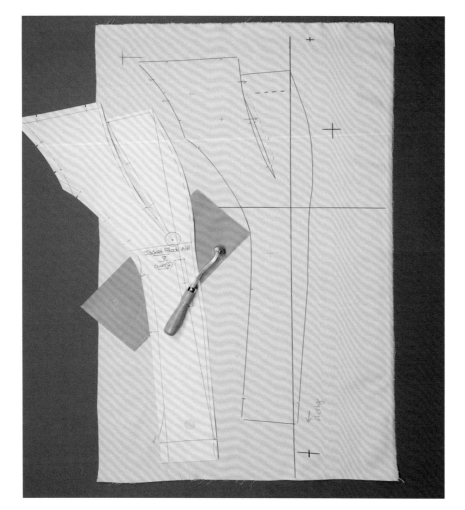

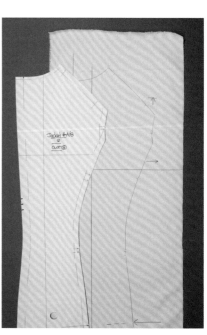

Tracing the block onto the muslin and marking important reference measurements. See left, for center front section, above, for center back.

Dress form preparation

- Add the stuffed arm, add shoulder pads to both sides (since it is asymmetrical), and tape the lapel lines.
- Note: It is not normally recommended to do a lot of taping of style lines before draping, but here, the lapel roll lines have subtle curves that must be duplicated, so it is useful to set them up ahead of time.
- Finally, display the photograph of the McQueen jacket where you can see it while you are draping. This will help to keep you on track as you fine-tune the complex angles and curves of the jacket silhouette.

- Set the shoulder pads, estimating the height of the finished shoulder, minus the thickness of the fabric, hymo underlining, and lining.
- Here, two pads have been used to achieve the right height.
- Custom pads may have to be built by layering the padded sections.

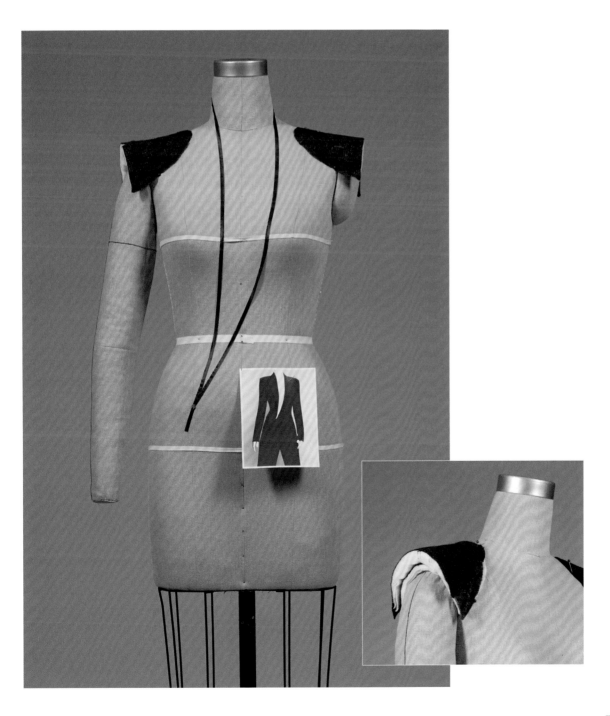

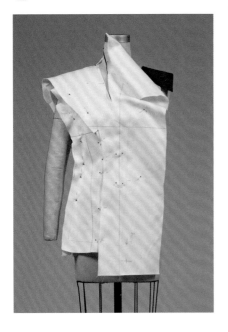
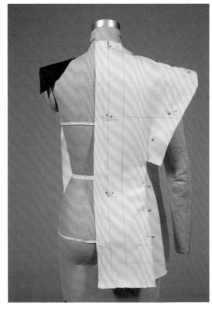

Step 1

- Begin the drape with the center front section, aligning the center front grainline on the muslin with the center front of the form, and smoothing upward.
- Set the side front, finding the correct position by matching the notches.

Step 2

- Set the back, again pinning with the side front by matching the notches.
- Turn the shoulder seams to the inside.

Step 3

- Cut the muslin to create a neckline dart. This dart will help to create the roll-line curve.

Hymo is a tailoring canvas that comes in various weights and traditionally has goat hair woven into it for the purpose of adhering to the wools it is used with. Feather-stitched into a jacket lapel, it gives the weight and control needed for the lapel to keep its shape.

Step 4

- Pin the neckline dart and finalize the outer edge of the right lapel.
- While draping the lapel, consider the feather-stitching that will be done on the lapel to help shape and curve it inward (see the jacket front below, with hymo feather-stitched on to the lapel).

- Sometimes a *modéliste* will mock-up this feather stitching during the draping to experiment with the effects it can create.

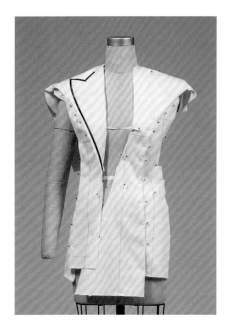

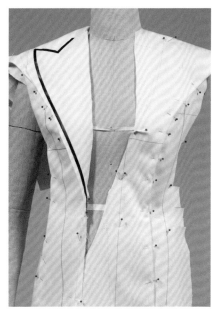

Step 5

- Estimate the notch/collar edge on the right lapel.
- Set the left front of the jacket:
  - Trim away the left front, following the tape line as a guide to create the roll line.
  - The lapel will be cut separately, because this curve is too severe for a foldback lapel.
- Set the side front by matching the notches.

Note: It is not necessary to set the left back, because it is a mirror image of the right back already done. However, if it helps you to gain balance, do it.

Step 6

- Pin a small tuck for ease at the bust, as shown. This will be achieved through taping the roll line, not as an actual dart.
- This tape is usually ¼" (0.6 cm) cotton twill tape, sewn in.
- Taping the roll line will let you control the length of that line, adding support to bias areas, and placing ease where necessary for specific curvatures.

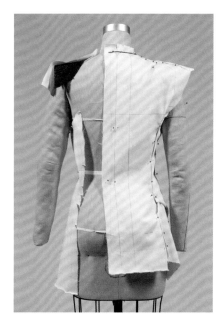

Step 7

- Drape the left front collar.
- Ease at the bust, as in Step 6.
- Tape the outside style line and notch area.
- Compare the two lapels carefully and check the photograph to correct where necessary.

Step 8

- Drape the right front hemline, which is tucked under to create the drape, as seen in the photograph.

Step 9

- Finish the back drape, noting that the center back line flares out below the waist.
- Note the back shoulder dart. This dart will not be sewn, but will be eased with tape.
- Note the tuck at the right hip, which gives shape to the hemline drape.
- Prepare for the collar drape by taping the neckline.

Step 10

- Note here that the shoulder shape is not a straight line but an S curve that follows the shape of the wearer's shoulder, dipping down from the neck and rising again at the outer/arm edge.

- The back neck tape should make a smooth line around to the front to prepare for the collar drape.

- Note the small shoulder dart which will not be sewn, but be eased into the front shoulder with taping.

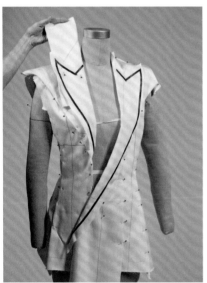

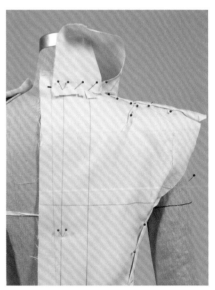

Step 11

Most collar drapes begin at the center back neckline (see Step 13). Here, an alternative method is used because the flow between collar and lapel at the gorge line is critical.

- Prepare for the collar drape with a 12" × 12" (30.5 × 30.5 cm) piece of muslin, with the lengthgrain and bias lines marked.

- Begin the collar drape at the front by folding the muslin piece with the lengthgrain running parallel to that foldline, laying it under the lapel as shown.

- Keep the folded edge on an exact line with the roll line, and pin it to the top part of the lapel.

Step 12

- Wrap the collar piece around the neck toward the back.

- Observe the nature of the fold shown here; it appears crisp and has quite a high stand.

- Test by angling the piece until you arrive at what you feel is the correct height of stand.

- You will have to fold up the "hem" edge of the collar while doing this, since that edge must sit perfectly on the shoulder of the jacket.

Step 13

- Once you are satisfied with the look and proportion of the collar, carefully turn it up and begin pinning it to the back neckline, clipping as you move toward the shoulder.

- The pinning should run straight for the first 1" (2.5 cm), horizontally, perpendicular to the center back. Pin and clip along the neckline.

- Finalize the hem edge of the collar.

- Experiment with the collar by draping it again with the grainline on the bias, which will give a smoother roll and a softer look.

Marking and Truing

- Mark and true the jacket drape.
  See the Checklist for Marking the Drape and
  Truing Fundamentals (page 74).
- Sew the fitting muslin. Follow steps 4–8 of the
  Steps to Developing a Block from a Drape
  (page 83–4).

This menswear suit collar has been backed in the traditional
way with a heavy linen cut on the bias, and feather-stitched to
give it shape. The backing will help the lengthgrain collar not
only to stand well, but also to roll smoothly around the neckline.

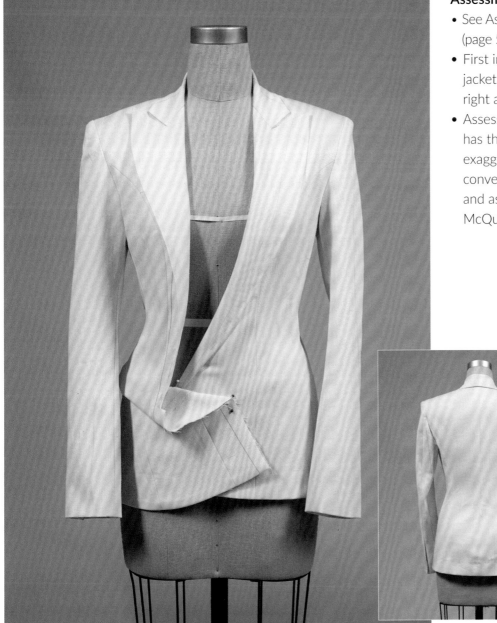

Assessment

- See Assessment Protocols
  (page 59).
- First impressions: Does the
  jacket feel like it has the
  right attitude?
- Assess whether your drape
  has the strong shoulder and
  exaggerated lapel shapes
  conveying the sense of strength
  and assertiveness as the
  McQueen jacket.

CHAPTER 4

Draping on the Half-Scale Form

OBJECTIVES

Apply learned draping techniques to the half-scale form.

–

Determine the best technique for taking half-scale drapes to full size.

Exercise 1: Modernizing the cut of a traditional ethnic design

Reinterpret the seaming of a traditional ethnic coat, draping on the half-scale form. Use the mathematical draft method to scale drape to full size.

Exercise 2: Half-Scale Experimental and Improvisational Draping

Develop a dress design inspired by a found object. Use the "re-drape" method to scale to full size.

Exercise 3: Zero-Waste Cutting

Solve a "zero-waste" cutting challenge by designing improvisationally on the half-scale form.

Project: Design Development on the Half-Scale Form

Breaking down a found inspiration, develop a coordinated ensemble design on the half-scale form. Identify and apply the correct enlargement method to execute a full-scale pattern.

Half-scale form draping as a design development tool.

Draping on the Half-Scale Form

Draping on the half-scale form is a design and pattern development tool that can be both efficient and inspiring. In the same way that a sketching style exhibits individuality, this draping method can help you to develop your personal aesthetic through practice and intuition.

Whether draping from a sketch or working improvisationally, using either muslin or final design fabrics, it is excellent for testing and appraising your own ideas, as a single design concept can be explored quite quickly because of the smaller scale.

Refer to The Ten Principles of Good Design (page 17) as you go, noting especially:
- Visual interest in design: shape, proportion, balance, and silhouette
- Visual harmony: seeing and studying the garment from all angles
- Visual energy: movement and focal points
- Textural interest: treatments and embellishments, and their scale, volume, and placement
- Color balance in final design fabrics

Draping on the half-scale form also has these practical applications:
- Presentations: for a fashion designer, showing a concept for a group or collection; for a costume designer, showing ideas for a production
- Working out construction details: experimenting with and finalizing seaming positions
- Calculating yardage needs
- Exploring various ways to do zero-waste cutting
- Demonstrating a quick mock-up of an idea that can be passed to an assistant to complete
- Digital print scaling tests, allowing visualization of options, saving time and money

Techniques to take Half-Scale Drapes to Full Size

1. Mathematical-draft method to scale up the draped pieces to a full size pattern.
2. Re-drape on the full-size form, using the half-scale drape as a guide.
3. The scan and tile method: using a printer to scale up and then tile the pieces.
4. Use a CAD or Gerber system to digitize the trued pieces and scale up.

Madame Vionnet with her miniature form, circa 1915

There are interesting examples of historical precedence in the use of miniature forms. In early twentieth-century Paris, Madeleine Vionnet used one to drape her signature bias gowns, providing an early example of zero-waste cutting. Because working on the bias entails cutting seams at diagonal angles across the fabric, with the potential to waste a lot of fabric, Madeleine Vionnet cleverly used her half-scale form to fit the pieces together jigsaw puzzle-style, thereby making maximum use of the fabric and leaving the smallest amount of scrap.

After the economic devastation of World War II, there was a shortage of funds and fabric to develop full-scale collections. A group of forward-thinking artists solved the problem by creating miniature sets and wire figures upon which to show the collections.

Sculptor Jean Saint-Martin designed the wire figures and along with his avant-garde group of artists, created Théâtre de la Mode, thereby bringing the couture collections back to life in 1945–6.

A Madame Grès design; black silk organdy long evening dress over a bright green organdy underskirt and shoulder length veil with Tibetan pheasant feathers. It was featured in the 1946 New York/San Francisco edition of the Théâtre de la Mode.

Crafting stuffed arms for the half-scale form

As with full scale draping, it is sometimes imperative to have a stuffed arm to work with. Following is an easy method for making one yourself.

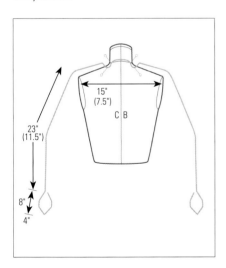

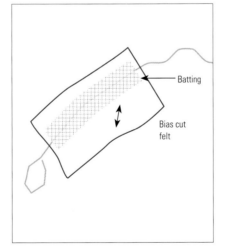

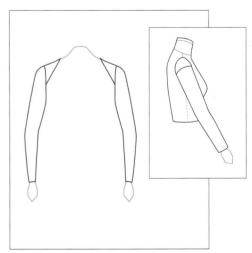

Step 1:
Shape a length of millinery wire to go across the shoulders and the length of both arms. (Note half-scale arm length spec: approx. 22"/56 cm to wrist.)

Step 2:
Cut a layer of batting or felt to underline a muslin rectangle the length of the arm.

Step 3:
Sew the muslin onto the wire arm and create a triangular "cap" to pin onto the form.

Improvisational Draping on the Half-Scale Form

Half-scale draping works well when working improvisationally. Instead of sketching with paper and pencil, the designer "sketches" with fabrics, trims, and colors. Because it entails working with smaller lengths of fabric, it saves both time and resources.

Christelle Kocher, from half-scale drape to runway

The contemporary French designer Christelle Kocher, founder of the Parisian brand Koché, works on a half-scale form, often draping improvisationally, either with muslin or with the final design fabrics and trims. These drapes are her "sketches." Pinned or sometimes hand-sewn together on the form, they are slightly rough, but in the way that a loosely drawn illustration is—not focusing too much on small details, but clearly communicating her creative energy through a specific look. The half-scale drapes provide enough information to hand over to a *modéliste* ("one who drapes") to scale to full size, and make a pattern.

Below are some examples of Kocher's use of the half-scale form, and the corresponding runway shots of the same designs.

Koché: Cube T-shirt.

The interesting shape and silhouette of this design had to be organically draped to form the innovative seaming. You can see that it would have been difficult to sketch it two-dimensionally before having worked out this simple but ingenious pattern. It needed the study of all angles of the garment to arrive at this design, with its asymmetrical and distinctive sense of balance.

Referring to The Ten Principles of Good Design (page 17): It has visual interest because the shape compels the eye to travel all around the design. Even though it has several focal points, it flows harmoniously.

Koché: Lemon layered chiffon dress.

Koché: Navy fly-away coat.

The beauty of this dress is in the intriguing layering of the chiffon. The challenge was to combine the asymmetry with a sense of balance. The drape on the half-scale form enabled a lot of experimentation before arriving at an interesting shape and silhouette.

Draping the navy cotton in sections has resulted in an interesting shape and silhouette, with the panels of fabric creating wildly different angles and cascades, yet with their own asymmetrical sense of balance.

The realization of these half-scale drapes is seen here in Koché's Spring 2017 collection. The surface interest of the lemon layered dress has been amplified with the use of ombré dyeing. The navy fly-away coat, seen here in tan canvas, has been simplified but retains the personality of the original drape. The "Cube" T-shirt has been styled in a way that amplifies its avant-garde look.

Modernizing the Cut of a Traditional Ethnic Design

Sikh prince coat

Traditional ethnic garments were historically made of carefully hand-woven panels of cloth that were constructed without cutting into them, simply pieced together with practicality and economy of cut. In contrast to our contemporary standards, they often are not very fitted, so working with these geometric panels by adding shape to the seams gives them a more modern silhouette.

To reinterpret and update the seaming of this traditionally cut ethnic coat, it will be draped on a half-scale form. The mathematical draft technique will be used to scale the drape to a full size pattern

Preparation
Flat sketches

- Plan the re-drape by doing some flat sketches.
- Because the integrity of the ethnic design is based on square-cut panels, the side/front seams will be straight and the side panels used for fitting and shaping.
- The sleeves will be short instead of full-length.
- The new "dress" will be belted to craft additional fit.

This Sikh prince coat is a good example of a traditional ethnic garment cut from simple woven panels. The artist is the celebrated German ethnographer Max Karl Tilke (1869–1942).

Muslin preparation
- Estimate the size of the pieces needed by measuring approximate dimensions on the half-scale form.
- Map out a muslin preparation diagram to maximize economy of cutting (see page 98).
- Tear, block, and press the muslin, and mark the grainlines.

Dress form preparation
- If you do not have a stuffed arm for your half-scale form, create one either by following the directions for a full-sized stuffed arm, scaling down the measurements by half, or by crafting one from wire and felt (see page 107).
- Measure the distance from waist to floor of your half-scale form and set it at half of your specifications for the full-size waist-to-floor measurement.

Grainline marking guide
Front
- Center front/lengthgrain (leave room for wrap/overlap)
- Bust area crossgrain
- Hip area crossgrain
Side
- Lengthgrain centered on muslin piece
- Crossgrain at bust and hip areas
Back
- Center back lengthgrain (1"/2.5 cm from edge)
- Crossgrain at bust and hip
Sleeve
- Lengthgrain: running down center of arm
- Crossgrain: center of muslin piece
Neckband
- Lengthgrain on length of neckband

 ## The drape

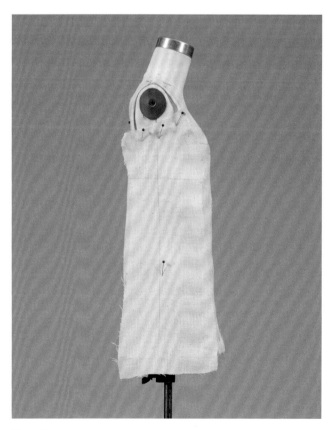

Step 1
- Begin with the center front, aligning the lengthgrain of the muslin with the lengthgrain of the half-scale form, keeping the crossgrain horizontal.
- Repeat for the back piece (not shown).

Step 2
- Set the side panel with the lengthgrain perpendicular to the floor and the crossgrain horizontally balanced.
- Begin pinning to the front and back sections:
  - Add shape (additional muslin) to the bust area.
  - Add flare to the hem, adding to the side panel only.
  - Adjust muslin at the waist by reducing the side panel.

Step 3

- Pin the front and back seam allowance over the side panel.
- Position the waist/belt section slightly below the waist.
- Turn under the side panel for armhole size.

Step 4

- Drape the sleeves: Use rectangular pieces of muslin, and pin starting at the top of the shoulder. Make it slightly longer in the back than the front, and taper the sleeve into the body of the dress at armhole height.
- Drape the front band: Using a rectangular piece of muslin, begin at the center back, pinning along the neckline and creating a curve that opens the neckline slightly and offers additional room over the bust, pulling it to the back to form a tie.
- Pin up the hem.

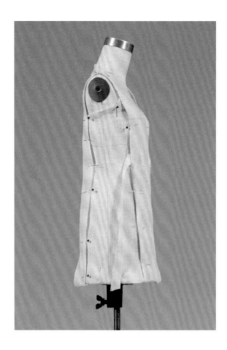
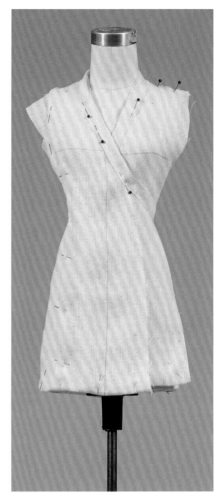

Using the mathematical draft method to scale up the drape to a full size pattern

- Mark and true the half-scale pieces. Scale to a full size pattern (Steps 1–3), which will then be used to cut fresh muslin pieces of the dress.
- Using your muslin preparation diagram as a guide, double the exterior dimensions of each piece
- Then draw out each of the pieces onto graph pattern paper. Check the measurements of the draped and trued pieces and adjust these dimensions accordingly.
- Add 2" (5 cm) extra around each piece to allow for flexibility while re-draping.

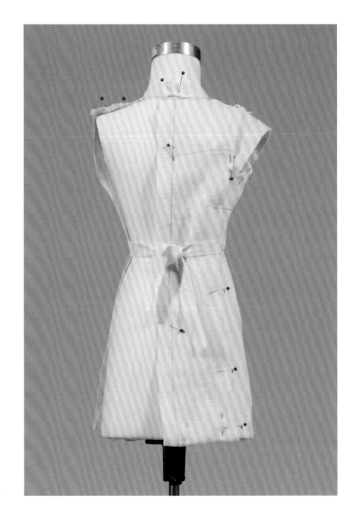

Finished back view on the half-scale form

Step 1

- Add grainlines to correspond with the grainlines on the muslin pieces.
- Create a dot graph system to position important key points
  - Draw a 1" (2.5 cm) grid on the draped half-scale muslin pieces
  - Draw a 2" (5 cm) grid on the pattern paper
  - Label verticals numerically and horizontals alphabetically
- Draw each new pattern piece as follows:
  - Make a series of "key" marks on the half-scale muslin pieces to indicate the important points of the pattern dimensions and a sense of the curves. Include the inner and outer shoulder seams; the front and side dimensions at bust, waist, and hip; and the length from shoulder to hem.
- Using your dot graph system, transfer the key marks on the half-scale muslin pieces to the full-size paper pattern by doubling the measurements on the graph and then locating the positions of each mark on the new pattern.

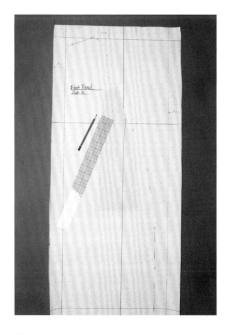
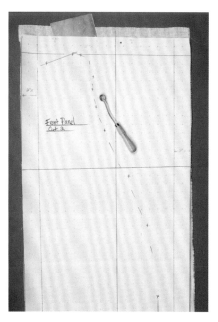

Step 2

- Transfer each paper pattern piece to muslin as follows:
  - Mark grainlines onto the blocked and pressed muslin to correspond to the grainlines on the paper.
  - Lay the paper "pattern" on the new muslin rectangle.
  - Use carbon paper and a tracing wheel to transfer the key marks.
  - Draw in the lines, connecting the marks.
- Lightly add lines 2" (5 cm) around each piece, for adjustability when draping.
- Cut the muslin around the pattern, leaving the 2" (5 cm) margins.

Full-scale drape

- Following the same step as for the half-scale drape, drape the full scale pieces.
- Follow the markings on the muslin, but only as a guide, as now is the time to fine-tune the exact shape and silhouette that you want.

Assessment

- See Assessment Protocols (page 59).
- Compare and contrast the two versions. The full scale has a longer length and fuller side panel.

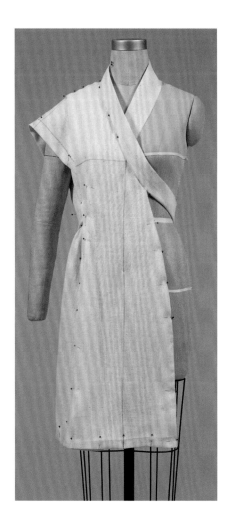
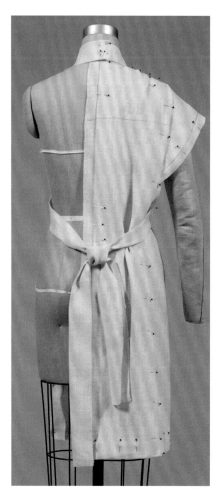

Finished drape: front and back views on the full-scale form.

Half-Scale Experimental and Improvisational Draping

The Dacquoise

Experimental draping is a good way to start this project. Finding the right fabrics that capture the deliciously luxurious mood of the Dacquoise will be the key to its success. Rough sketches can be done for inspiration, then the dress, draped improvisationally, will evolve smoothly and enjoyably.

Preparation (any or all of the below)
Inspiration

- "Dacquoise"—even the name is enchanting. The generous whipped cream is held in by the wall of ladyfingers (sponge fingers), which have a golden crustiness. The berries are nestled charmingly in the center, topped with a sprinkling of gold. The muse: a young ingénue attending a child's christening or an early-summer graduation.

Research

- Photograph uses of chiffon and organza. Compare how they drape and gather. Review designer collections that specialize in this type of dress.
- Also see The Designer's Aims and Aspirations: Fabric Choices (page 31).

Fabrics/trims

- Experimental draping with the colors and textures of the Dacquoise will help you decide on your final design fabrics.

In a bakery near my studio, this dacquoise pastry attracted my attention with its feel of luscious indulgence and the quirky pop of the berry colors.

Editorial Fabric Research

Research and learn to identify the fabrics used in fashion editorial photography or runway shows. You will begin to see what qualities you like about each of them, understand what silhouettes look good, what design elements and construction style works well.

The Designer's Skill of Visualization

Drape a large piece of your final design fabric on a nearby dress form as a reference, to help you visualize how it will drape.

  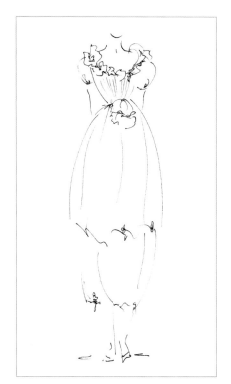

Inspired by experimental draping, these rough sketches were done to simply start some ideas flowing; to get a sense of what silhouette and length I would be working toward as I drape improvisationally.

Sketches

- Because the dress will be draped improvisationally, only very rough sketches will be needed to help you plan your approach. The ladyfingers display a strong vertical, so they call for a lengthgrain configuration using soft fabrics.
- Choose which sketch to focus on by using The Ten Principles of Good Design (page 17) to help your decision-making. Go through this checklist and study each look systematically for points such as:
    - Visual interest: shape, proportion, and balance
    - Visual harmony
    - Visual energy: movement and focal points
- In this case, I will not draw flat "blueprint" sketches, because I want the drape to be improvisational, giving me the option to change and collage the elements together as I work.

Muslin preparation

- On analyzing the elements of the dress and the use of sheer and semi-sheer fabrics, I will work with the final design fabrics to get an accurate drape of the design. The base will be a slip lining, and layers of crinoline will support the layers of chiffon I will use on top.

Dress form preparation

- Attach the half-scale stuffed arm.
- Indicate on the form the empire waist with tape and a target hem length, either by noting the measurement to refer to while draping, or with a pin.

🔲 The drape

Step 1

- Estimate the size of the slip lining piece (the silk or cotton) you will begin with. Here, I have estimated needing a piece measuring 22" × 22" (56 × 56 cm).

  Note: Although I am draping right and left sides, don't worry about draping exact mirror-image pieces. For pieces that are mirrored, only one side will be marked and trued.

- Drape the bodice and underbust area.
- Create the neckline with gathers (as seen).

Step 2

- For the next fabric, experimentally drape some satin organza, a silk satin that can be used for the underskirt to give shape and support. This is the heavier fabric, and it reminds me of the way the ladyfingers make a supporting "wall" for the whipped cream.

  Note: Remember to take photos and notes as you proceed to help easily recreate the look for the re-drape.

Step 3

- The satin organza has been added as an underskirt, its oval shapes echoing the shapes of the ladyfingers.
- Sections of silk crinkle chiffon are gathered into the underbust area.
- The sections are also gathered about two thirds of the way down the sides.
- The hemline is pulled up in a bubble shape.
- The base for the sleeves is formed with crinoline sections.

Step 4

- The skirt is finished on both sides with additional panels of ruffles
- The silk crinkle chiffon is draped over the crinoline base on the sleeves
- The "berries" are added in the form of twisted pieces of the colored silks.

Draping with a Mirror

It is very useful to drape in front of a mirror. When learning how to study silhouette and shape, it becomes important to see it from a distance. With a mirror, it is easy to glance up and observe the drape from 4 to 5 ft (about 1.5 m) away, which is how we usually view clothing on others. A mirror also provides a good perspective check, enabling you to view your drape with fresh eyes, and to compare it to the sketch or photograph you are working from.

Assessment

- See Assessment Protocols (page 59).
- Visualize the muse. Does the look fit the vision of her wearing it to one of these events?
- Are the fabrications successful?
- The silk crinkle chiffon and satin organza are working well to convey the feeling of the inspiration.
- Are there other fabrics that might work better? It is possible that something a little lighter and more sheer than the crinkle chiffon would give a more interesting affect, especially full size. Some experimental draping would help to determine if that is so
- Embellishments: The pop of color at the underbust is the focal point, and as an embellishment, it secures the final punctuation of the mood and tone of the design.

Scaling up: The re-drape method

For the re-drape method, repeated the same steps as the half-scale drape, but in full size. The half-scale drape and the photographs of its progress will serve as a guide.

- Make flat "blueprint" sketches, either from the final drape, or using elements from the rough sketches done before the drape. Detail the understructure elements—the slip/lining/crinoline layer—as well as the overlayers. Don't forget to include the closure construction.
- Determine the muslin, using two or three different weights to represent the different fabrics.
- Map out a muslin preparation diagram.
- Tear, block, and press the muslin pieces, and mark the grainlines.

Re-drape, following the steps of the half-scale draping.
- Use your photos and notes as a guide.

Note: Because this design is symmetrical, it is only necessary to drape half the design as is usually done with mirror image pieces.

- Think about what interesting touch could be used for the sprinkling of gold on top of the berries.

Assessment

- See Assessment Protocols (page 59).
- Assess also how the silhouette and tone may have changed as it transformed into the full-scale drape.

EXERCISE 3:
Zero-Waste Cutting

Original dress design

Zero-waste cutting is an invaluable skill in today's fashion industry. Creating compelling and beautiful designs without having to throw fabric into landfill is a great example of the ethics of slow fashion in practice.

Many designers, including Angelos Bratis and Alber Elbaz, have followed in Madeleine Vionnet's footsteps, draping designs from a single piece of fabric. This takes experience and skill. Draping improvisationally on the half-scale form—saving both time and fabric—is a very efficient way to practice this technique.

Preparation
Inspiration
• The Angelos Bratis dress that I am using for inspiration has a clear focal point, which will inform the new drape.

Research
• Referring to The Ten Principles of Good Design (page 17), note the points on visual energy, movement and focal points.
• Pull some research images of other designers doing zero-waste cutting.

Fabrics/trims
• Select something appropriate: since a clear focal point is important, perhaps something not too textured nor a busy print. Also, since it may need to have some areas with more fullness of drape, something with a soft, light hand will be best.

This simple and elegant design by Angelos Bratis from the Spring/Summer 2015 collection, a dress cut from a single length of fabric, is the inspiration for creating this zero-waste cut design.

Flat sketches
• Not necessary, but doing a grainline schematic might help to focus the design process.

Muslin preparation
• It's important to determine how much of the chosen fabric you will use. A good method is to think about how much of a given fabric you want to see or feel on the body at once.
• Arrive at a specific measurement, then divide it by two. Here, 4 yards (3.7 m) is my target for the finished garment, so for my half-scale drape I will use a 2 yard (1.8 m) square.

Dress form preparation
• I will use a foundation for this design, which will make it easier to construct, because the cowls and ends can be stitched to the foundation.
• Note: This is optional since this design is particular to individual tastes.

Draping on the Half-scale Form with Final Design Fabrics

When using your final design fabrics on the half-scale form, remember that the smaller pieces of fabric may not drape in the same way as the larger pieces. You may find it helpful to keep larger samples of the fabrics draped nearby, to help you visualize the results.

The drape

This exercise is intended to be an original design, so these steps are suggestions as to how to handle the fabric. Try to use your intuition to guide you to a result that satisfies you. Don't be timid about cutting and pinning; have several lengths of the chosen fabric on hand, so you can try multiple variations or different approaches.

Step 1

- Begin the drape, using the foundation to hold the fabric in place.
- Drape the fabric simply by pinning from the left hip to the right top of the corset, letting the extra fabric cowl on the right-hand side.
- Wrap the opposite end of the fabric around the back and pin at the right hip.

Step 2

- Cut the fabric vertically, releasing the pointed piece in the back to fall.

Step 3

- Pick up the point and bring it around to the front, to cover the body under the front drape.
- Turn the triangle at the upper back to the inside, as shown.

Step 4

- Bring the remaining drape to the right hip, creating a cascade, and adjust the top of the bodice, tacking it to the corset to finish. Seen here is the completed front.

Step 5 (inset)

- This image shows the completed back. Document the drapes as you go, then use the re-drape method (see page 117) to recreate your drape at full size.

Assessment

- See Assessment Protocols (page 59).
- Reflect on your design, take some notes, photograph it, and use The Ten Principles of Good Design (page 17) to critique your work.

Design Development on the Half-Scale Form

"Napa Valley Almond Blossoms in the Rain"

The inspiration for this project is from the "Earth" board: the amethysts, the cotton, the skies, and the memories of a lane in Napa lined with almond trees, overflowing with soft white blossoms, and then a light rain. The blossoms fell softly through the branches, on to grass, on to the soft, dark earth.

Preparation
Inspiration

• The "Earth" board details.

Research

• I researched the shape of real almond blossoms ito create my embellishment.

Fabrics/trims

• Experimental draping will be done to test various fabrics and to determine which mood feels right: classic or romantic.

Flat sketches

• Not necessary, but grainline configuration sketches or rough concept sketches are recommended to give the drape some direction, while still keeping it intuitive.

Muslin preparation

• Tear, block, and press the muslin, and mark the grainlines.

Right: Grainline configuration sketch #1: Classic lines.

Far right: Grainline configuration sketch #2: Romantic lines.

Earth board

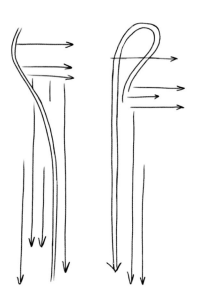

Experimental drape #2

Experimental draping to evaluate fabric choices, their differing moods, and grainline choices.

Experimental drape #1 (opposite)

- This sandwashed silk charmeuse drapes more softly on the bias, following the form more closely.
- The open-weave lace knit is the right mood for the piece, and the amethyst trim provides a focal point and color accent at the underbust.

Experimental drape #2 (right)

The charmeuse is draped on the lengthgrain to play with vertical lines, evoking rain.

- Lace is added, as well as strips of charmeuse and braided embellishment. The ribbons hanging on the left-hand side are not as soft as the rest of the look, but contribute to the vertical impact.
- Shape and silhouette: As long as the dress remains slim and vertical, the round shape of the cocoon wrap will work with it.
- The shape of the cocoon wrap echoes the curved lines in the grainline configuration sketch and has become a nice focal point. The piece flows well, with good visual energy and movement.
- The punctuation of the little braided pieces is reminiscent of a nun's robe, with a rosary hanging at her side.

Experimental drape #2

The first drape is an example of a very standard, classic eveningwear look: a fitted bodice with a long skirt, cut either on the bias, or for a form-fitting look, on lengthgrain. It is a controlled shape and the pieces would sit very comfortably together as a finished ensemble.

The second drape is a more fashion-forward look with the combination of underdress and tabard overdress and the collage style mix of different fabrics. It could be described as romantic as the look is free-form; the improvisationally draped hanging strips imitate the look of falling rain, an emotional reference. Refer to Hussein Chalayan's Medea (page 57), which is a perfect example of emotional romanticism; it feels wild and free, the hanging strips releasing energy and connecting the viewer with the piece.

The drape following will reflect the romantic option. Follow the steps below to recreate the look, or—because this exercise is improvisational—feel free to create your own version.

The Importance of Documenting your Process

When working on the half-scale form drape, take photos and journal notes during the process. That way, when you are scaling up the drape, you will have that additional information as a reference.

The drape

Step 1

- Drape the bodice, using underbust darts and a center front dart to keep the fabric close to the body at the center front.
- Create a wide strap.

Step 2

- Drape the skirt by setting the center front bias grainline at the center front of the form.
- Smooth the fabric over the hip and fit it close to the body by creating an angled French dart from underbust to hip, wrapping it around to the back.

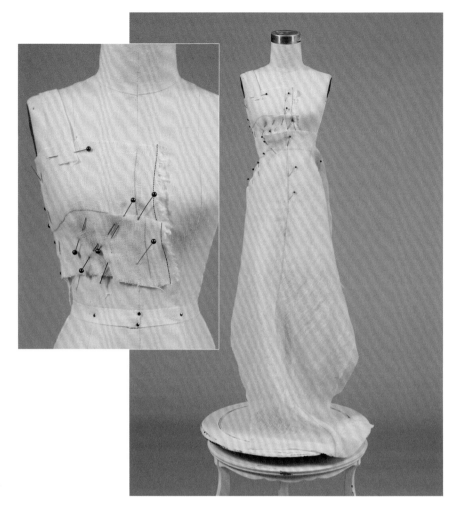

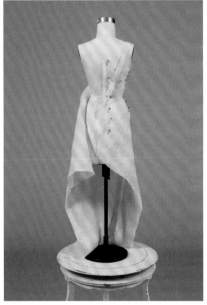

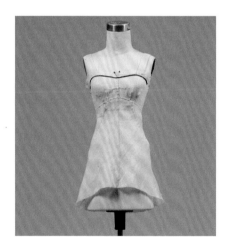

Step 3

- Drape the back underskirt by continuing to wrap the fabric from the front around to the back and smoothing it over the hip area.
- Pin along the top edge.

Step 4

- Tape the top edge.
- Trim the hem shorter at the front than at the back.
- Because so many other layers will be draped over it, remove the pins from the bodice now and hand-sew the pieces together.

Step 5

- Drape the tabard.

Note: This element will be a mirror-image design, but in this case the whole piece must be draped, to help you visualize all the pieces in combination.

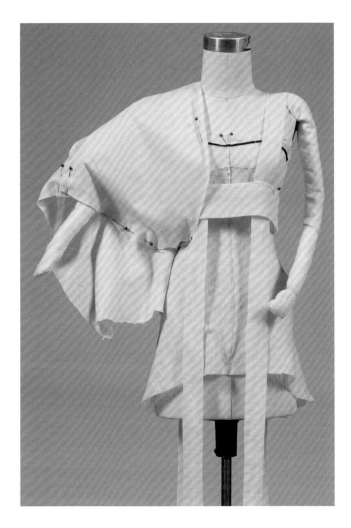

Step 6
- Drape the cocoon wrap, attempting to simulate the volume from the first drape.
- Pin at the underarm and set the neckline.

Step 7
- Adjust the back cocoon to balance with the front cocoon

Scaling up the bodice: the scan and tile method

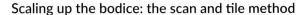

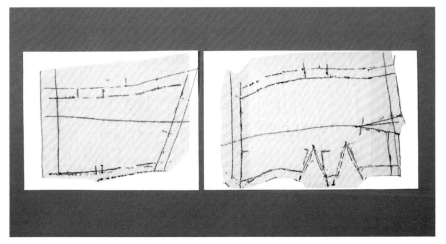

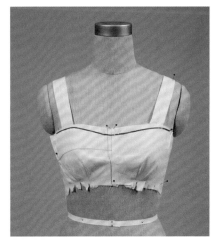

Step 1
- Mark and true the small drape, referring to the Checklist for Marking the Drape and Truing Fundamentals (page 74).
- Press the front and back bodice pieces flat.
- Scan the two pieces and enlarge to double the size.

- If the pattern piece does not fit on the scanner, tile it by making several scans of different areas, printing the pieces, and taping them together to create the full pattern.
- Note: It doesn't matter if your scan is rough, this will give you the correct shape and seaming. It can be fine-tuned when continuing the drape full scale.

Step 2
- Cut muslin pieces from the printed pattern, and pin the two bodice sections onto the dress form.
- Mark the top edge and add the strap (upscale by doubling measurement).
- Note any corrections, and mark with red pencil or red tape.
- Here, it appears the center front dart may be too deep, and need adjusting because there is some pucker in that area.

Scaling up the slip: the re-drape method

Step 1

- Press the pieces and check shape and size.
- Prepare muslin pieces for the front and back of the slip:
  - Calculate the dimensions for rectangular blocks panels of muslin by doubling the size of the smaller-scale pieces.
  - Mark grainlines.
  - Make any chalk marks that will be helpful when re-draping, such as the approximate position of darts.
- Begin draping the skirt front using the same techniques as for the half-scale drape.

Note: Because this is a mirror-image piece, only one side will be draped.

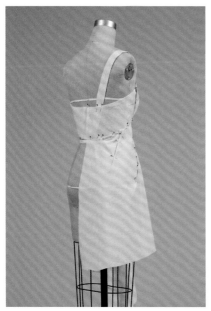

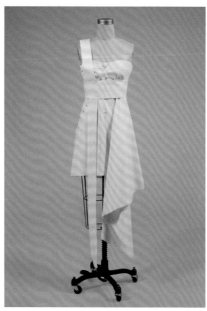

Step 2

- Drape the back skirt, pinning to the bodice.
- End the French dart at the hip past the side seam.

Step 3

- Drape the tabard, checking the proportions against the half-scale drape.

Step 4

- Before draping the cocoon wrap, experiment with some of the fabrics for the draped strips.
- Drape the cocoon using the same techniques as for the half-scale drape.

Step 5

- Finish the drape by adding the hanging strips and the feather and petal embellishments to the cocoon.
- Continue to add and adjust until you feel the design is complete.

Assessment

- See Assessment Protocols (page 59).
- Check the drape from different angles or in a mirror.
- Reflect on the drape to see if the feeling is conveyed: Will the wearer feel the soft earthiness of the Napa Valley almond blossoms falling in the rain?
- Does the concept contain an emotional punctuation?
- If you had a muse, visualize the dress in the situation you imagined.

- Note impressions about fabrication:
  - Is this fabric helping the concept to be expressed?
  - Are there other fabrics that might work better?
- Are embellishments and trims contributing to the emotional power or statement of the piece? Here, I feel they are adding strength to the look.

CHAPTER 5

Draping from an Illustration

OBJECTIVES

Observe and identify what elements of an illustration create the intended emotional portrait.

—

Cultivate the interpretive skills necessary in draping from design sketches.

—

Recognize what comprises a well-done flat sketch: right proportions and thoroughness of construction details.

Exercise: Draping from a Costume Design Illustration and Flat Sketch

Assemble a drape that matches the character portrayed by the illustration, and the proportions of the flat sketch.

Project: Draping from a Fashion Illustration

Deconstruct the attributes of a fashion illustration, translating the elements of an ensemble into the proportion and style that reflects the designer's intended mood and tone.

Draping from an Illustration

To drape from an illustration means to transform a two-dimensional image into a three-dimensional form that expresses both the look the designer intended and the mood and tone of the illustration. This chapter details formal, professional workroom methods of draping from an illustration or sketch. The challenge of hitting the right proportions as well as capturing the right attitude involves skill and practice.

In fashion and costume design, various types of drawings are done for different situations. "Design sketches" are often rough, working sketches that are done while a design concept is being developed. "Flats" are technical "blueprint" sketches for the workroom which include construction details, and "illustrations" are often done after the design is finished, and are used for editorial purposes such as advertising, branding or, in costume design, for presentation purposes.

The lines tend to blur; some designers are talented illustrators, and some don't sketch at all. There are many different ways for a designer to express their ideas; the point is to find the path that works best for you.

Ruben Toledo

Collaboration between illustrator and designer is fertile ground for heightened creativity. The famous partnership of Ruben and Isabel Toledo was a creative wellspring that produced award-winning avant garde fashion and art. Ruben's prolific illustrating and Isabel's draping and love of her craft resulted in elevated art forms for both of them.

> Our collaborations did not have a beginning or end. They vibrantly flowed out of us without rules or clearly defined borders. My watercolors became her dresses, which then became my sculptures and on and on... like a creative tennis game with a velocity and force all its own.
> *Ruben Toledo, 2020*

Fashion illustration by Ruben Toledo. The choice of pose indicates a strong and confident woman, the shapes and colors create a mood of whimsy and humor. (A turtle on a leash!) She is a woman in balance, the rounded curves of the hat, fan, bow, and turtle all flow and intersect with the many vertical lines, creating a vibrant, dynamic tension.

Design Sketches

An illustration or design sketch can be quite precise and detailed, or may be abstract, exaggerated, and free-form, hence requiring interpretative skill while draping. Ruben Toledo's work has such a wildness to it; a sense of artistic freedom, yet on closer examination, there is a lot of clarity of detail. Because Ruben is also an expert in construction, he has indicated the pleats on the off-shoulder section, and the lining of the skirt is clearly a side slit turn-back.

Christian Lacroix, like Toledo, has a beautiful, abstract sketching style, and again, is so knowledgeable about construction, one can easily see what he is intending. Each designer's style of drawing can be very revealing of their creative process. He explains his approach in Patrick Mauriès's book *Christian Lacroix on Fashion* (2008):

> *"Every dress that passes along the runway during a show is to some degree an evocation of the increasingly abstract graphic design that preceded it."*

At the other end of the spectrum, this design sketch (above right) by Karl Lagerfeld is extremely detailed, and the final dress is a very close match to its illustration. The proportions of cuffs and waistband, and the placing of the graphics, are all noted.

Karl Lagerfeld worked with the house of Chloé from 1964 until he began at Chanel in 1983. He was again with Chloé from 1992–7. His bold prints on Bohemian-style flowing dresses exemplified the joyous, modern spirit of Chloé, and elevated the brand to its still current, international success. This very specific style of illustration insures that the look of the design is executed as closely as possible to the designer's original vision.

Top: Design sketch by Karl Lagerfeld for the house of Chloé's Spring/Summer 1973 collection.

Bottom: The detailed sketch is brought to life on the runway with a very close likeness.

Bastide Rey for Lanvin

I visited Bastide Rey in 2016, during his time as head of the Lanvin atelier, and while there I caught sight of one of Alber Elbaz's sketches on the table. It was a very rough, but very beautiful, quickly drawn figure with a splash of black ink in the shape of a dress and a swatch of fabric stapled on. When I mentioned that there was a lot of room for interpretation there, Rey responded that he knew exactly what the designer wanted.

Of course, research would have been done. Rey knew what the collection was to be about, what style of ergonomics Elbaz preferred, and what kind of clothing he had been doing recently, and all this would have added up to Rey just "knowing what he wanted."

However, in addition to being a *modéliste*, Rey has his own individual, signature style of design. His talent, flair, and ability to give his clothes a unique look make him sought-after, and trusted to execute collections that not only exhibit the style of the brand for which he is working, but also reflect his own personal aesthetic.

This is the nature of draping; it encourages originality because a personal style always comes through. One must be able to read the subtleties, though—to recognize, in this case, which nuances are Rey's style emerging and which are those of the Lanvin brand.

Stéphane Rolland

These artistically rendered sketches by Stéphane Rolland display an attitude, but also incorporate enough detail to pinpoint design specifics. Compare and contrast these sketches with the photographs of the finished garments.

The finished design has become more interesting than the sketch. The addition of the ombré bodice adds flow to the color story as it moves from top to bottom. In the sketch there is quite a clear division between the white and the mocha, but in the runway version it blends beautifully. The sheerness of the skirt and the visibility of the undershorts break up the line a little, but make up for it by adding an interesting stylistic element.

Fashion Illustration

Illustration, as it preceded widespread photography, has been the fashion industry's standard method of communication for more than a century. Whether intended for the atelier team, buyers, or the general public as advertising, it is an art form that embodies the zeitgeist.

In the 1920s Erté was a major influence on fashion, and the pochoir prints of that period set the tone for haute couture in the first half of the twentieth century, with its Art Nouveau and Art Deco looks. The work of Antonio Lopez (known simply as "Antonio"), one of the great illustrators of the 1970 and '80s, was instrumental in defining the splashy, colorful look of that decade.

Illustrations of this ilk are most commonly done after the clothing is finished. The figures, usually elongated and slender, emphasize the lines of the clothing, and tend toward exaggeration, primarily expressing color mix, emotion, and silhouette. How detailed or how abstract, will determine the interpretive skills that are needed. As you try to match the mood, tone, and emotion in a three-dimensional drape, the key is to observe, and then identify what elements of the illustration create the intended emotional portrait.

The sketch is so dramatic—like a moment frozen in time. The challenge would be to finesse a drape that captures the dynamic mood of the design and also lands the transparent panels exactly as Rolland intended.

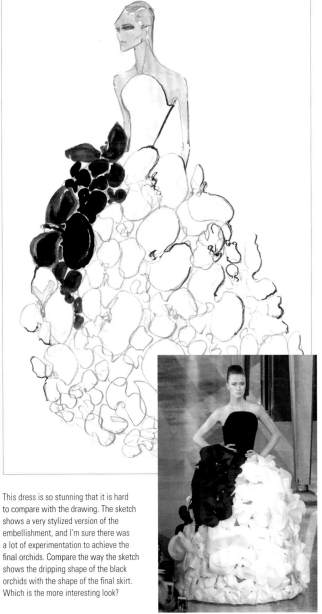

This dress is so stunning that it is hard to compare with the drawing. The sketch shows a very stylized version of the embellishment, and I'm sure there was a lot of experimentation to achieve the final orchids. Compare the way the sketch shows the dripping shape of the black orchids with the shape of the final skirt. Which is the more interesting look?

Technical Flat Sketches

The goal of a "flat" is a detailed sketch that clearly communicates the right proportions and construction details of a design. The challenge of drawing it correctly is again that of interpretation; and dependent on the sketch or illustration you are working with. While major changes will require consultation with the designer, the interpretation might include areas to tweak, simplify, or emphasize.

When mapping out a detailed flat sketch, foremost is to resolve the very important grainline configuration.

Some experimental draping with final design fabric can resolve that, as well as any decisions about underlining fabrics, which will greatly affect the look of a design. Seaming that is unclear can be tested on the half-scale form, and construction details such as topstitching can also be tested. All these decisions will affect the outcome of the design.

General Checklist for Draping from an Illustration

Preparation

Inspiration

- Aim for clarity, and focus on the intent of the artist or designer; what they are trying to communicate.
- Name the designs, and write verbal scripts of their "story."
- Identify which elements of the illustration evoke the story or intended emotional landscape.
- Use a muse to pinpoint the attitude or storyline.

Research

- Research the designer's past work.
- Research ways the chosen fabric has been used; historically and/or culturally.
- Use reference garments for measurements.

Fabrics/trims

- Use experimental draping to evaluate fabrics and finalize your choices. Note fabric widths.
- Consider possible nap or directional shading for seaming and yardage figures.
- Assemble, study, and measure any trims, treatments, or embellishments.

Flat sketches

- Map out the proportions so that they match the illustration, taking into consideration any exaggerated elements the illustrator has drawn.
- Indicate all the grainline decisions.
- Include swatches of self-fabrics and lining.
- Note support elements to identify: underlinings, fusibles, shoulder pads, crinolines, foundation, etc.
- Indicate all seaming and construction elements.
- Indicate any trims or embellisments.

Muslin preparation

- Match the type of muslin to use with the final design fabric.
- Make a muslin preparation diagram to help you cut the muslin economically.
- Tear, block, and press the muslin, and mark the appropriate grainlines.

Dress form preparation

- Select a dress form with the correct specifications, and pad it to size if necessary.
- Apply any support elements that are needed: shoulder pad, stuffed arm, crinoline, etc.
- Tape any areas that will help you to determine the proportions.
- Review the ergonomics for fit, size, ease, and stretch.

The drape

- Have the illustration and flat sketch nearby and in view.
- Drape in front of a mirror if possible.
- Take a moment to center and feel the energy you are trying to convey.

Assessment

- See Assessment Protocols (page 59).
- Compare and contrast the drape and the illustration. You may find it easier to do this by taking photographs of the drape, so that you can see both in two dimensions.
- Review The Ten Principles of Good Design (page 17) and The Ten Essentials of Couture (page 21), looking for any possible ways to improve the final look of the design.

Draping from a Costume Design Illustration and Flat Sketch

Pocono costume

The challenge in working with this sketch is in how to infuse the garments with this character's unique sense of disheveled earthiness. The proportions of the individual elements are key, they must be slightly oversized, but not sloppy. Because he is transcending specific time periods or historical and cultural milieus, care must be taken with the shapes and silhouettes to keep them timeless.

Preparation
Inspiration

• The illustration is very descriptive, but before draping the costume, read the script or libretto to gain further understanding of the role. This sketch is for the character of Pocono, the narrator of Peter Wing Healey's opera *The Spell of Tradition*. The director wanted the look to be a combination of Native American and Japanese peasant, but essentially, a traveler who has put together his clothing on the road.

Research

• Review images of historical clothing: *Noh* spirits, Japanese peasant clothing, and Native American robes and accessories.

Fabrics/trims

• Check the chosen kimono fabric (a loosely woven hemp) width. The kimono will be large and oversized, so if the fabric is not wide enough, where to seam it will be important to note. To arrive at the right support materials, various underlinings, buckrams, and fusibles were tested with the raffia fringe to give the the collar and *obi* the right weight.

Flat sketches

• Draw out flat sketches with construction and seaming details, adding swatches of the self and support fabrics.

Illustration of the character of Pocono by Jillian Ross, for Peter Wing Healey's opera *The Spell of Tradition* (2017). He is the narrator, a shaman with Native American and Japanese influences.

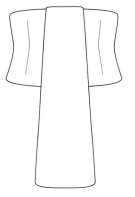

Muslin preparation

- Half garments will be draped as the pieces of the costume are symmetrical.
- Use the actor's measurements to draw the dimensions of the pieces for the muslin preparation diagram, calculated on half the total measurements, plus whatever fit or style ease is needed.
- The exception is the belt and front panel, as it will make it easier to get the correct proportion if seeing the whole pieces.
- The muslin will be a heavy cotton twill.
- Tear, block, and press the muslin pieces, and mark the grainlines.

Dress form preparation

Select and prepare an appropriate dress form:

- Evaluate the shapes and sizes of the forms available; choose one whose proportions are as close as possible to the size and shape of the actor who will wear the costume.
- Adjust the fit by wrapping with felt as necessary. Here, the actor was slightly larger in the waist than the form, so felt was wrapped until the correct measurement was reached.
- Note the yellow tape at the waist of the form. The waist was higher on the form, and the tape indicates the actor's real waistline. It was done in yellow so that it would not be confused with the black tape used for the style lines.
- Tape the important style lines with twill and pins, or sticky-tape. Here are marked:
  - The width of the *obi* waist wrap.

  - The collar piece, to delineate the space between the *obi* and the collar.
- Add any support elements that may be needed, such as the stuffed arm (see Checking proportions; drape to illustration, opposite).
- Review The Ten Essentials of Couture (page 21) to see what else might be needed, such as needles and thread for tailor tacking, or a steamer for shaping.

Fabric and trim preparation

- Before beginning the drape, several burn tests were done to test texture, color, and proportion. Being able to visualize the look of this treated fabric will help define the mood of the design while draping.

Bastide Rey: Draping to capture a mood

Draping is intuitive, so immersing yourself in the context of the collection will help to infuse it with the chosen tone. Collect your inspiration pieces—your taxidermied crow or full flowering peony, assemble tools and materials, set illustration and flat sketch clearly visible, and then take a moment to breathe and connect with the energy you want to convey.

> I could feel the dark and intense energy; it was the attitude of the collection we were making, and of course that mood influenced my work.

Bastide Rey, on his work in the design studio of Alexander McQueen

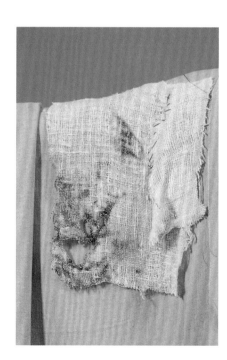

Burn tests on raw silk were done both with an open flame and with a microwave. Seen here is the test with flame.

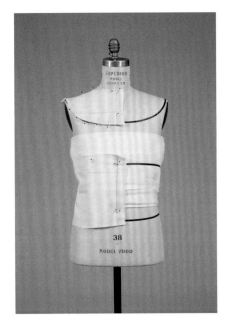

Step 1

- *Obi* drape: align the center front of the muslin with the center front of the form and smoothe the piece around to the back where the closure will be.
- Drape a shallow dart on the side seam.
- Begin the collar drape by aligning the center front with the center front of the form and smoothing the muslin across the chest and to the shoulder, clipping and trimming.
- Repeat for the back collar, and turn the shoulder seams front over back.
- Turn up the hem at the tape line.

Step 2

- Check and adjust the width of the *obi*, then turn under the upper and lower edges of the *obi* section.
- Begin the belt/center panel drape by pinning the center front to the center front of the form.

Note: This piece, although mirror image, is being draped full because the proportion is tricky to achieve and will be easier when seeing the whole piece.

- Turn under the edges of the center panel.

Step 3

- Drape the tie belt, devising an interesting knot treatment in the center front.
- Once the knot is done, adjust the length of the center front panel.
- Continue the collar drape by adding mock-ups of the embellishment on the collar lower edge and of the braid treatment at the neckline.
- Adding the embellishment to the lower edge of the collar will help you to work out the right point for the collar edge as it relates to the top edge of the *obi*.
- Check the drape in a mirror from at least 4 yards (3.7 m) away, to give you a different perspective.

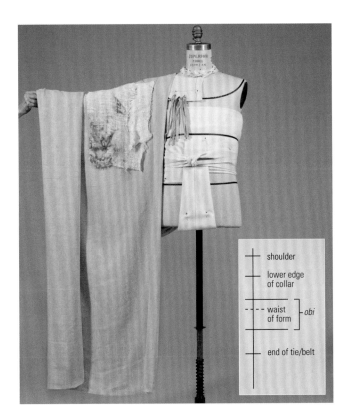

shoulder

lower edge of collar

waist of form — *obi*

end of tie/belt

Checking proportions: drape to illustration

- When draping, check the illustration and flat sketches constantly to make sure you are on track.
- Draw out or trace a proportion guide from the illustration (see inset) and then, holding it at eye level, stand at precisely the right distance from your drape to see if the proportions match.
- Take some photographs to study both drape and illustration in two-dimensional.
- What about closures? Would it have been easier to construct the *obi* and tie belt on a petersham ribbon with hooks to come off and on easily?

Here, an experimental drape is being done to check the burned and distressed fabric treatment, and to also set the proportions of the kimono.

The kimono draft

The study of the traditional Japanese kimono shows an ingenious garment cut without a single inch of wasted fabric. Edges are turned for support, and panels are carefully connected to maximize comfort and practicality as well as elegance and beauty. Because a basic kimono is essentially a very simple cut, it can be easily drafted using the checking measurements taken from the experimental drape.

Beginning with this basic pattern template, adjust the dimensions using the measurements taken above during the experimental draping to draft the new design.

- Body width: center back to sleeve seam
- Body length: center back to hem
- Sleeve width: sleeve seam to wrist
- Sleeve length: shoulder to end of sleeve
- Cut and sew all the pieces and assemble them on the form to assess.
- Here, the *hakama* (pant/trousers), hat, wig, and shoes have been added to help with visualizing the final outcome.
- Take time to adjust the final details and correct proportions.

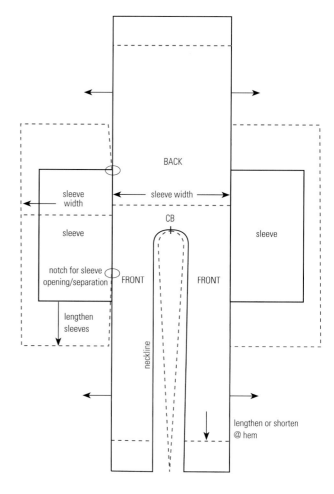

Assessment

- See Assessment Protocols (page 59).
- As this is a costume, be sure to consider the stage distance.
- The feeling of the piece is starting to emerge, the addition of the raffia trim helps to bring the drape into alignment with the illustration, enabling me to better visualize the final outcome. The black taped lines (in the images on the previous page) help to show the configuration of shapes and check that the proportions look right.
- Does the collar have enough support to hold the weight of the embellishment?
- Is the blue front panel too much of a focal point?

PROJECT:
Draping from a Fashion Illustration

Draping a new design from an illustration first calls for some context review: Who is it for? What is the price range? What is the intention of the illustrator or designer? Are you, like Bastide Rey, being given some freedom to make decisions on the look, or final silhouette of the design, or must you follow the illustration very literally? Best to know where you stand before you start.

Peignoir, bustier and tap pant set

A peignoir is a semi-sheer or transparent dressing gown, here worn over a corset style bustier and softly flared sleep short. A trousseau, or honeymoon set, will be worn by the bride after her getaway. This calls for it to be glamorous and sensual; made with heirloom quality workmanship, as trousseau pieces surely are; they are meant to be handed down to generations of daughters.

Preparation
Inspiration

- Study the illustration, the inspiration for this look is Hollywood glamour: romantic, feminine, the *femme fatale*. The lace has a sexiness, but in a delicate, flirtatious way.
- The muse is a young, beautiful actress going off with her handsome groom to the Amalfi Coast for a few weeks.

Research

- Research Hollywood's Golden Age which began in the 1930s with a sense of escapism and continued through the 1940s and early 1950s. Note favorite looks from glamour queens such as Jean Harlow, Rita Hayworth, and Marilyn Monroe.
- Study vintage lingerie from the 1930s through 1950s, noting the diaphanous, thin silks, the sensual ergonomics, often achieved with bias cuts, and period design elements such as revealing necklines and low backs.
- Pull reference pieces of lingerie from those eras. Measure necklines and distinctive proportions. A sleep short of that era would have a higher waist, and a fuller leg; the corset style tops would have waist emphasis and higher necklines than modern versions.

Illustration by Kathryn Hagen.

Fabric evaluation

Assess:
1. The visual quality of the drape
2: The tactile quality of the fabric (the "hand")
3: The mood and tone
4: Best construction details for the fabric.
5: Possible embellishments/ trims
6: Color
See page 28 for full list.

Fabrics/trims

Do some experimental draping with possible fabrics for the trousseau lingerie:

- Silk satin crepe: This has a luscious hand and a heavy drape; it would work beautifully in this design. It also references the satins used in the era of Hollywood glamour, but it may be too heavy for a trousseau piece when combined with lightweight lace.
- Silk charmeuse: This will be ideal for the bustier and tap pant, since it has a medium weight that will hold up well to the boning of the bustier.
- Silk chiffon: This is a traditional choice for a peignoir, but if it is too light and sheer, silk satin chiffon is a good substitute.
- Silk satin chiffon: This very attractive fabric is airy, lightweight, and sensual, and the satin sheen makes it semi-sheer. The hand is soft; it seems to drip like liquid and moves with grace. It will be used for the peignoir, which should capture the mood and tone of the set. This choice will also complement the delicacy of the lace.

Two types of French lace will be tested, both of which are lightweight enough to complement the silk satin chiffon.

For the bustier and tap pant yoke piece, fusible interlinings will be tested to provide the required support. The bustier may need something heavier to work with the boning.

Fabric widths: the silk satin chiffon is 45" (114.5 cm) wide. That will have to be taken into consideration when working out the seaming of the skirt of the peignoir that has a very generous hem sweep.

Colors: Those chosen by the illustrator will work perfectly. Black suggests night and mystery and signifies withdrawal, so it is perfect for a honeymoon getaway. The creamy gold of the underpieces has a rosy glow that will complement many skin tones, and the black lace relates nicely to the peignoir.

Flat sketches

An issue in question here is the cut of the skirt. We want to incorporate as much flare as possible and utilize the full width of the fabric at them. Upon checking the target specifications of the peignoir length, the skirt is slightly short. A solution is to cut the back bodice waistline down into a "V" which will allow a small, but valuable amount more for the skirt length.

Muslin preparation

- First assess which muslin will work best for the project. Draping in chiffon would align with the look and would be important if there were a lot of gathers. However, chiffon is tricky to drape with, and in this case, working with a muslin that has a light, crisp hand will be better for the draping, as it will help to more easily create the shape of the kimono-sleeve bodice and easier to see the balance of the peignoir skirt sections.
- Make a muslin preparation diagram to help you cut the muslin economically.
- Tear, block, and press the muslin, and mark the appropriate grainlines.

Dress form preparation

- Select a dress form with the correct specifications. In this case, the garments are to be made for a standard fit model size, so no changes will be made to the form.
- You will also need a pant form to drape the tap pants, and a stuffed arm for the peignoir.

The bustier drape

The bustier and tap pant will be draped first, so that the proportion of the peignoir neckline can be synchronized with that of the bustier, and the waistline with that of the tap pant. Check the proportions of the illustration constantly as you drape, the set of the straps, the depth of the neckline, width of the lace, proportion of cup size to midriff area.

Study the illustration for clues about what to emphasize. Are there areas of the illustration that are dramatized more than others? Be sensitive to the subtleties of the hand-drawn lines, interpreting the mood of the illustration into the contours of your drape.

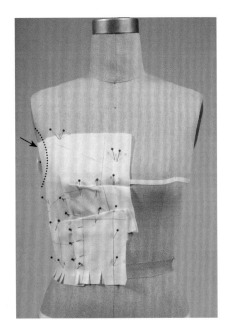

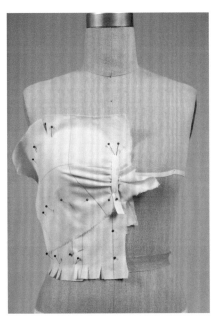

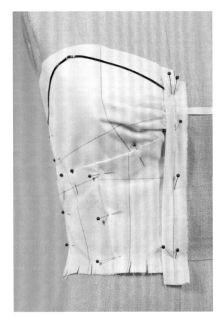

Step 1

- Pin the top center front section to the center front of the form for the lining of the bustier.
- Fold in a dart at the center front, letting the fabric hit very close to the form.
- Smooth the fabric over the top bust toward the side, draping very snugly toward the underarm area.
- Drape the center front lower panel, and the side front panel.
- Turn the seams front over side, and the lower panels over the top front.

Note: dress forms are harder than the body at this underarm point, so be sure to keep the drape close fitting here (see arrow).

Step 2

- Drape the outer top front by draping the piece over the darted front, but now pulling all of the ease toward the center front to create the gathers.
- Pin a length of elastic to the form to help you adjust and visualize the gathers.

Step 3

- Pin the lower front sections over the upper front.
- Pin the finishing band at the center front.
- Tape the top edge.

🖥 The tap pant drape

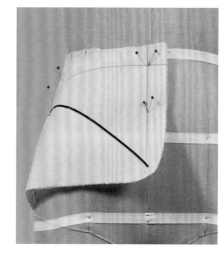

Step 1

- Align the center front of the muslin yoke piece to the center front of the form.
- Smooth across the hip and pin, clipping where necessary.
- Create yoke shape with styling tape.

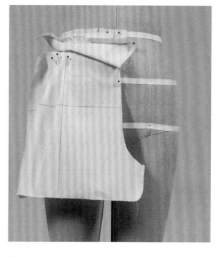

Step 2

- Set the front tap pant section to the center front of the form, keeping the lengthgrain perpendicular to the floor and the crossgrain horizontal.
- Fold in two tucks at the princessline, angled toward the side to keep the fabric away from the center front.
- Clip and trim at the crotch and pin toward the center front of the leg.

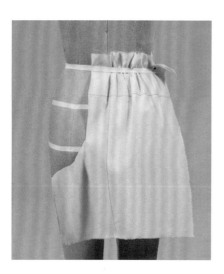

Step 3

- Set the back of the tap pant by aligning the center back of the muslin to the center back of the form.
- Tie elastic around the waist to help you adjust the gathers.
- Note: The back of the tap pant will have an elastic casing, so experiment with different widths of elastic now to confirm your width.
- Smooth toward the side.
- Trim away the center back above the crotchline, leaving enough fabric to meet the front at the crotch area.

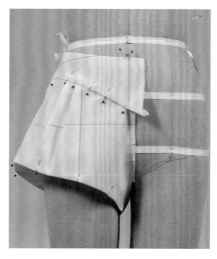

Step 4

- Join front and back at the sides, and balance the fullness, checking the sketch to make sure it matches the look. The muslin will be much stiffer than the final fabric, so check the drape of the silk charmeuse if you need to be sure of the amount.
- Turn the yoke over the front of the tap pant.
- Turn up the hem.
- Finish draping the back of the tap pant by turning up the hem and marking for elastic.
- Finish the front by turning up the hem.
- Add the waistband to the front.

Follow these steps to make the final design prototype for the tap pant and bustier:

- Mark and true the drape
  - Re-pin on the form to check for corrections
  - Transfer the drapes to pattern paper
- Prepare the fitting toile
  - Use the new paper pattern to cut a fitting sample
  - Conduct a fitting on the dress form or fit model
  - Apply any corrections to the pattern
- Cut and sew the final ensemble.

The peignoir drape

Before beginning the peignoir drape, review the illustration carefully to make sure you are clear about what the designer is trying to communicate, and what they want to emphasize. Define the intended mood, tone, and attitude with some phrases to keep you on track. Then try to isolate the elements of the illustration that illicit those feelings. Is it the luxurious and generous fullness of the skirt, the way the sleeve is a little long, or the back very close-fitting? Refer to your research images from the Golden Age of Hollywood glamour for insight on details or proportions.

As you drape, review The Ten Principles of Good Design (page 17) to make sure you have a good visual flow and an interesting silhouette.

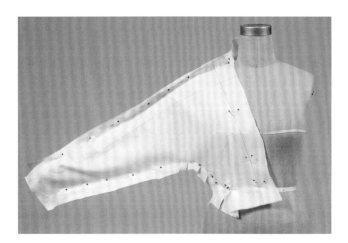

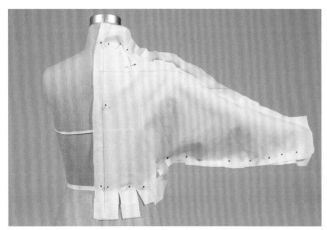

Step 1

- Drape the front bodice section of the peignoir.
- When draping the sleeve, consider the range of lift desired. This will dictate the amount of fabric under the arm.
- The sleeve should be slightly angled toward the front of the mannequin, mimicking the natural hang of the arm. This angle will cause the front section to have less fabric than the back.

Step 2

- Drape the back bodice section of the peignoir.
- If needed, remove the bodice to drape the skirt more freely.
- Turn the front seam allowances over the back at the top of the shoulder seam and at the underarm seam on the table, clipping as necessary.
- Test various angles until you are pleased with the balance.

Step 3

- Drape the front skirt by aligning the center front grainline with the center front of the form.
- Smooth the crossgrain across the high hip area, letting the crossgrain drop enough to give flare to the skirt.
- Trim and clip along the waistline for a smooth fit.
- Repeat for the back skirt.
- Pin the side seams together.

Step 4

- Reposition the bodice on the form.
- Pin the bodice to the skirt at the waist, turning the bodice seam to the inside.
- Level the hem and trim parallel to the floor.

Step 5

Check the back bodice:

- The center back should lie smoothly on the form from neck to waist.
- The sleeve should make a pleasing "break" (the fold at the armhole area) when the arm is down.

Step 6

Check the side view for balance. The front fold or break should be higher than the back, since it produces a more graceful look if the sleeve looks smaller at the front than at the back.

Note: You may want to re-position the bustier toile onto the form at this point to make sure the two necklines are well synchronized.

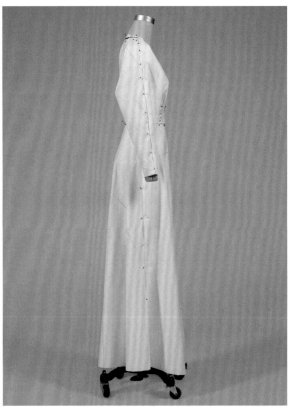

First Assessment

- Before marking the drape, take time to look at it in the mirror, assessing whether you have achieved the right degree of fullness and whether it is balanced from all angles.
- Check the drape against the sketch, holding the sketch at a distance to see it at the same proportion, and scan from top to hem, double-checking all the points, comparing drape to illustration.
- Assess the mood and feeling of the peignoir. Does it match the emotional tenor of the illustration?

- Identify which elements of the peignoir create the right emotional response, and determine whether those areas can be even more amplified or tweaked to heighten emotional effect.

Marking and truing:

- Use the utmost care to mark the drape, and thread-trace areas such as tucks or ease notches at the waist which need extra attention.
- Re-pin the pieces and reset onto the dress form to check for corrections.

Corrections

Review The Ten Essentials of Couture (page 21). Study the re-pin to see what areas could be enhanced with more care:

- Are there areas of stretch and/or ease?
- Will it need tear-away pattern pieces during construction?
- Is petersham ribbon needed at the waist of the peignoir or bustier?
- Does the bustier need any padding under the bust?

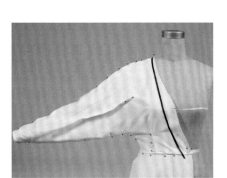

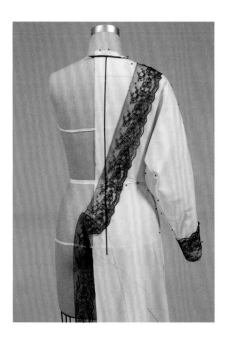

Step 1

- A correction has been made to the front bodice/armhole area of the peignoir.
- Because of the natural forward hang of the arm, this is an area where there should be less fabric in the front than the back.
- Check your drape and test to see if you can pin out a dart as shown. Having less fabric, especially with the arm down, will be a more flattering look if the bodice is a bit smaller in front than in the back.

See page 92 for instructions on making this correction.

Step 2

- The re-pinned peignoir muslin is now ready for the lace embellishment to be draped.
- There are two different laces, and they will be checked on the muslin to see which will work better.
- This one has a double "galloon," a scallop on both edges. Because of the length of the peignoir, there will be weight on the front edge, so it may not work to have a scallop edge such as this.

- The pattern will be corrected to enable the center back to be cut on the fold/mirror image, and then the lace will travel down the princess area seam in the back.

Step 5

Before finalizing the drape, review The Ten Principles of Good Design (page 17), and study whether there are any subtle things to be done to improve the flow or visual harmony of the piece.

- Where does the eye travel? Is it a good flow?
- Do the weight and intensity of the embellishment match the proportion of the peignoir?
- Think about finalizing details. Visualize a narrow rouleau type of tie belt, and then a wide sash with a bow to sense what will work best.

Step 3

- This lace has a straight edge on one side, which means that the scalloped edge can be zigzagged on to the fabric, leaving the straight edge for the neckline.
- This straight edge will work better than the scallop, because it can also have a binding or some other finish to give it stability.
- Don't forget to test the finishes.

Step 4

- Drape the lace on the back, and determine where it will end.
- It will have to make a sharp turn over the shoulder, or angle fairly straight down the back.
- Angling the lace down the back as shown will eliminate the problem of having a seam in the robe at the center back, which is how it stands at the moment.

Preparing a fitting toile

- Draft a paper pattern from the drape (or, if this is not for production, use the muslin itself as a pattern).
- Carefully mark all notches, and sewing indications.
- Cut and sew the toile:
  - Machine-baste (tack) the bodice front and back; and the skirt front and back.
  - Hand-baste, with a running stitch, the skirt to the bodice; the skirt hem; and the lace.

- After fitting the peignoir on the dress form and, if possible, on a live model (see procedure below), transfer any additional corrections to the pattern.
  - If the corrections are minor, proceed to the cut and sew of the final fabric peignoir.
  - If the corrections are extensive, it may be necessary to adjust the pattern and do a second fitting.

Conducting a Professional Fitting

- Check that the toile has been prepared properly:
  - All raw edges finished
  - Armholes and hems turned under and hand-basted
  - Closures prepared with zippers/snaps, etc., or ready to hand-baste
  - Underpressed enough to lie smoothly, but not creased or overpressed
- Have a "kit" ready for the fitting, ideally using a tool belt.
- Provide an adequate fitting room and mirrors.
- Do a "pre-fitting" on a form for obvious corrections.
- Choose a model with measurements as close as possible to the dress form used, and to the size specifications you are intending to hit.
  - Keep measurements close at hand so that during the fitting, if a sleeve length etc. is not right, you can compare your target specs to the models' measurements.
- Do any necessary fitting and pinning in the fitting room, until you and the model are comfortable with the fit. Pin with straight pins for fashion, and safety pins for costume and for knits. Baste where necessary for closures or delicate areas.

During presentation of the fitting sample:
- Assess the sample before beginning to pin corrections or adjustments. Start with the overall look, then scan down the body, discussing possible changes.
- When making adjustments, pin carefully where possible, opening seams where needed to adjust fit, cutting the fabric only when necessary.
  - Where additional fabric is needed, it may be possible to cut and patch carefully:
  - Have extra muslin on hand.
  - Have extra final design fabric on hand to patch or test for more fullness, etc.
  - Have extra lace or other embellishments on hand.
- For final hems, skirt and sleeves, compare the measurements of the model to your target measurements before adjusting.
- Finalize seam finishes and sewing details.
- If you are preparing for a photo shoot, show accessory options.

The final sample

After all corrections from the fitting have been transferred to the paper or muslin pattern, cut and sew using the highest-quality craftsmanship your resources will allow, and following as many of The Ten Essentials of Couture as possible (page 21).

Assessment

Compare and contrast the illustration and final trousseau lingerie set:

a. Review the look you were going for and the emotional tenor you wanted to express.

b. The silk satin chiffon and delicate black lace feel they are matching the level of glamour and femininity as seen in the artwork.

c. Visualize what other fabrics would work in this design. The heavier satin crepe would be a beautiful alternative, but its heavier weight would not have worked with this specific lightweight lace.

"Good Design"

a. The eye travels with the flow of the lace placements, and there are interesting focal points in both the back and the front waistline.

b. Review the historical or cultural references: Hollywood glamour. The low neck of the peignoir, the dramatic sweep of the hem, longer in back than front, and the lush, low armhole reference that period with a positive and familiar feeling.

c. The modern elements include the updated shape of the tap pant, the fit of the bustier, and the crisp lines of the lace as it meets the peignoir.

Final touches

If the trousseau lingerie set is being photographed for editorial, consider what additions will highlight the mood and tone. Perhaps a mule slipper with a kitten heel would add elegance to the posture, or a sparkle of jewelry at the nape of the neck would be an accent to try. Hairstyle and make-up are, of course, key and will help to set the right tone.

CHAPTER 6

Draping with the use of Two-Dimensional Surface Design

OBJECTIVES
Maximize the impact of a
two-dimensional surface design.

–

Understand the power of color.

–

Learn creative draping techniques that incorporate
two-dimensional surface design.

Exercise 1: Ombré, Airbrushing, and the use of
Novelty Dyeing Techniques
Develop a jacket design while exploring various dye techniques.

Exercise 2: Artisanally Crafted
Two-Dimensional Design
Solve a visual design problem by using two-dimensional
surface design techniques.

Project: Draping Using a Digital Print
Determine the correct scale and color story of a digital print,
to match original mood and tone of a design.

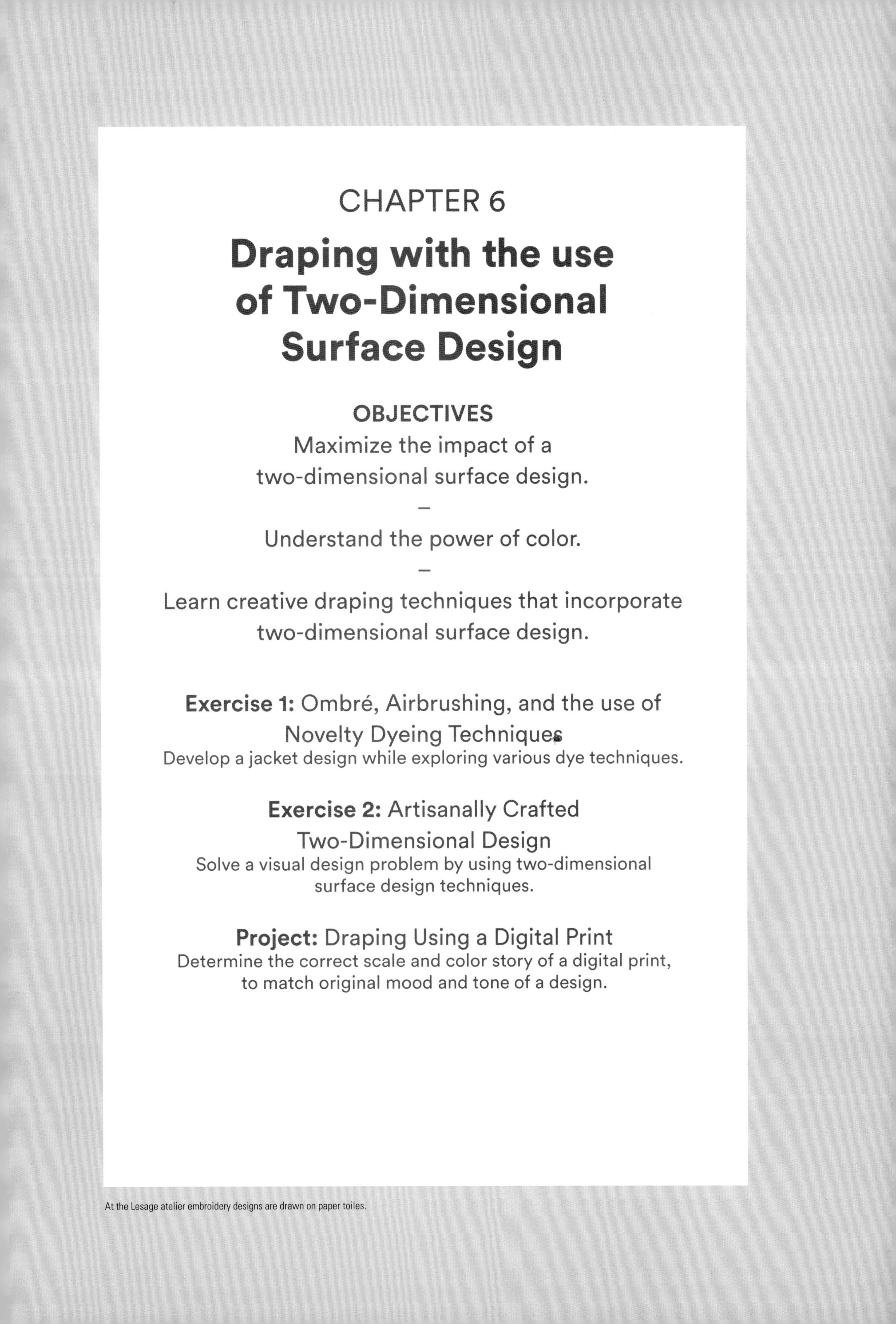

At the Lesage atelier embroidery designs are drawn on paper toiles.

Creative Draping with Two-Dimensional Surface Design

The power of color and symbol and the emotional resonance of print and pattern have been recognized and used throughout history. Surface design communicates a message or expresses inspiration; and can be done by handcrafted methods such as dying, hand-painting, and block printing, or by using screen, digital and sublimation-printing, all highly modern techniques.

The art of adding color and design to fabric is an ancient one. The Egyptians used resist dyeing for the fabrics of mummies. In Java, batik dates to the sixth century. It is believed that art was originally made to induce spiritual power, and symbols used on clothing to express sacred meanings or for rituals.

Egyptian symbols reflected their gods and goddesses, and the ankh (a symbol of life); Native Americans painted symbols on leather for ceremonial purposes. West African printed textiles signify specific roles—the hunter, the warrior, bride, groom, or expectant mother.

The variety of print and pattern techniques available enable designers today to create original fabrics. Integrated with creative draping, they provide a great tool for storytelling: setting a mood, an atmosphere, or creating a visual portrait of a character.

These Rodarte designs from their Fall/Winter 2014 collection conjure a space-age mood with their *Star Wars* digital prints in surprisingly oversized proportions. The familiarity of the images creates a prejudicial bias: everyone loves C-3PO and R2-D2.

Kenyan girl: With a rich history and tradition of patterned textiles, this fabric is also clearly decorative in its colorful exuberance.

Maximizing the Impact of a Two-Dimensional Surface Design

To enhance emotional impact, there must be an organic partnership between the two-dimensional surface design, the fabric, and its garment design.

Stay focused on the inspiration for your color, print, or pattern, determine the right fabric and the right match of application, and choose a garment design that matches the surface design, sketching different scales and placements.

The inspiration

Focus your inspiration. Have clarity on the concept and purpose: Is it symbolic, decorative, conveying a political message? Research the past; where it has been used before. Find the connective tissue between a symbol used in antiquity, and what it means now on a contemporary design.

The right fabric with the right match of surface design

The story of your surface design must harmonize with its fabric. Whether an earthy, handcrafted look such as stenciling or hand-painting, or a polished, modern one, such as sublimation printing, use your skill of visualization as the surface design is being developed, to "see" how it will look as a finished design.

Study the fabric for visual and tactile qualities, mood and tone, best color choices. If a surface design is strong and graphic, find a fabric with a strong lengthgrain energy. If it is a soft and lyrical graphic, a lighter fabric, perhaps draped on the bias, will define the tone and synchronize more with its surface design.

The principles of good design

Creative draping with two-dimensional surface design involves pinpointing not only the right fabric and application, but also developing the right design for it.

Depending on your skill of visualization, try some of the Mock-up Techniques outlined on page 151.

Scale and proportion play a large part, so continue to study different scales until you find compatibility with your design, or if you are firm on the sizing of your two-dimensional design, continue draping until the two harmonize.

Jeremy Scott's Spring/Summer 2016 ready-to-wear collection for Moschino made humorous yet stylish use of a graphic of police "caution" tape, a perfect match of fabric, surface application, and his design.

Understanding the Power of Color

Understanding the psychological and emotional power of color is fundamental to all design. Whether symbolic or decorative, color is an invaluable tool to help us tell our story, create a mood, suggest a tone. The spectrum of colors have long-standing historical, cultural, and socio-political connotations, so it is necessary to be aware of these when creating a chromatic narrative for costume or fashion.

During the Renaissance deep purple dye was obtained from a particular mollusk, and it was so costly that only royalty could afford to wear it. Hence the name "royal purple," and the enduring noble connotations. In more objective terms, it has been scientifically proven that the various wavelengths of the color spectrum affect us emotionally, psychologically, and energetically. Color has an impact on a deep level, and is sometimes felt only subconsciously.

Here follows a very basic description of the colors and their qualities. Experiment with color combinations and changes of hue and intensity, and try to be sensitive to how those differences subtly affect emotion and perception.

Primary Colors:
Blue = spiritual depth
Red = the physical
Yellow = the mind/ the intellect

Secondary Colors:
Purple = deeply relaxing to the nervous system
Orange = positive energy, enthusiasm
Green = balance, the calm of nature

The "Tints" have white added and soften the effects of the pure hues, create more ethereal moods.
Rose Pink = romantic love
Amethyst = considered the highest spiritual vibration

The "Shades" have black added and create more intense color effects.

Indigo (deepest of blue/blacks) = energizes the highly intuitive
Earth tones (oranges and yellows with black) = earthy, grounding
Black = has longstanding historical/cultural weight. Its intensity gives it a sense of power and authority, and of mystery.

Metallic gold = softening, magnetic energy
Silver metallic = dynamic, quickening energy.

Testing Color for Surface Design While Draping

Because surface design can act as the punctuation of a garment, it is important while draping to observe the effects of the colors being used.
- Try experimentally draping different colors of the same fabric. Study the mood they create. Some fabrics look better in intense, bright colors, and others in soft, muted tones.
- Try draping different color combinations; sometimes the effects of single colors are amplified when they are used in tandem with others.
- Experiment with color balance, perhaps using the half-scale form, to see whether a bright color works better on the top edge or on a hem.

Creative Draping Techniques to Use with Two-Dimensional Surface Design

With two-dimensional surface design, it is crucial to integrate this with the draping process so that the effects created on the surface of the fabric are synchronized with the drape of the garment.

There must be some freedom to improvise, or flexibility for change. While draping, that extra element can suddenly demand that a sleeve be a little fuller, or a fit more elongated; the two-dimensional graphic or surface treatment dictates the parameters of the design you are draping.

If the surface design is a familiar treatment—such as a stenciled border print that has been used in historical garments—it may be easy to work out the scale and placement. With a new and original concept, identify which mock-up technique will be most helpful for visualization while draping.

As designers, we have a specific vision we want to express, and our challenge is in communicating that vision to those who are helping us to realize it.

The mock-up is a way to communicate the vision of the surface design to our team, or to the artisans who will do the final work.

The more precise you are, the closer you will come to communicating your color story, proportion, scale, details, and placement, and the more assured you can be of getting the result you envision.

Mock-up Techniques

- Draw variations of the two-dimensional surface design on your original sketches or flats (see page 155).
- Draw the surface design on a paper mock-up of the garment (see below).
- Draw the surface design freehand on a fitting muslin (see page 179).
- Print out a photo of your fitting muslins, and draw on the copies to experiment with different ideas.
- Draw or computer-generate and print out a surface design, and pin it to the muslin drape. Try different scales and sizes by printing it larger and smaller, and work with the placement, since finalizing that will help you to determine the size.
- Experiment on the half-scale form by printing half-scale variations on fabric using digital or sublimation printing.

Creating a digital file may be most efficient, but it is sometimes better to follow a more hands-on approach by painting or drawing your surface design directly on to a muslin toile. The more precise you are, the closer you will come to communicating your color story, proportion, scale, details, and placement, and the more assured you can be of getting the result you envision.

The more specific the directions to the artisan, the closer the result will be to the look the designer intended. Here, at Lesage, the beading designs have been drawn by hand on a paper toile.

The two ombré tests for this Alpaca jacket create entirely different effects: The darker at the lower edge gives a sense of being grounded; the darker at the top, with a lighter hem, feels more protective and more powerful.

Ombré, Airbrushing, and the use of Novelty Dyeing Techniques

The galaxy jacket, part of the Dark Radiance collection, is a close-fitting bolero, or cropped jacket. It will have a generous collar with a high stand, and elongated sleeves that flare out over the hand, referencing the edgy glamorous club atmosphere that defines that group. It will be constructed using the block-to-drape method (see Chapter 3), with the addition of a two-dimensional surface design, and finished with an embellishment (see Chapter 7).

The dark-to-light ombré effect of this dress and the muted tones of the mauve create a mysterious, sultry mood. Ellie Saab, Fall/Winter 2014 Collection.

Galaxy jacket
Inspiration
• To create a jacket using dyeing techniques that reflect this photograph of our galaxy.

Research
• Study garments that have similar dyeing techniques, to pinpoint the effect you want.
• Examine bolero blocks, and choose one that incorporates the desired design elements.
• Use reference garments to show to the artisans doing the dyeing. The dress fabric shown in the photo to the right has been dip-dyed and airbrushed to achieve the mix of colors and variation in effect. The artisan is recommending a combination of airbrush and crystal dye process, which will give the piece a sharper definition than the ombré seen in the dress fabric to the right.

This dress fabric has the jewel-tone dye effect that works with the Dark Radiance inspiration.

• The classic ombré technique (as seen on page 151) is to dip the piece into the dye bath, rinse, then repeat, leaving the top part of the garment out of the dye. Each time you dip the garment, dye less of it, to achieve the gradated effect.

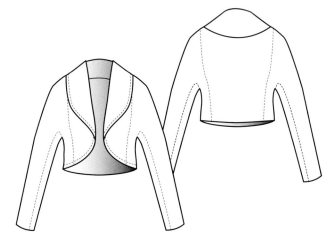

Flat sketches
- Use these to make decisions about grainline, seaming, and construction.

Fabrics/trims
- Use experimental draping to finalize the decisions about the fabric. Here, a raspberry-colored peau de soie was chosen and, after testing, was sandwashed to make it slightly softer and give it a more porous, suede-like texture.

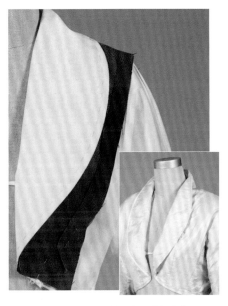

The fitting toile of the jacket with mock-up of the dyeing process to show to the artisan working on the project. Inset: The block chosen to use as a starting point for the bolero.

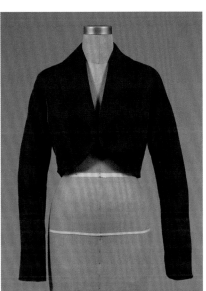

First the jacket was dyed to the deep garnet base color.

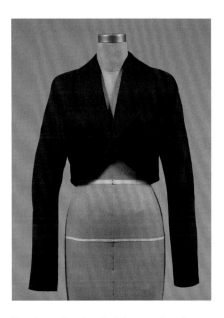

The artisan used a variety of techniques to arrive at the finished galaxy look.

Muslin preparation
- Create a muslin preparation diagram according to the chosen jacket block (sloper) (seen here).

Two-dimensional application on the drape
- The block-to-drape method will be used for this jacket. The first step is to review available jacket blocks to find one that is close enough to work with as a starting point.
- If you do not have such a block, find a jacket that is as close as possible to the finished look, and make a new block, using the draping method (see page 81–5).
- Create a fitting toile of the jacket incorporating the elements from the original inspiration:
  - Collar—generous volume with high stand
  - Long sleeves that slightly flare
  - High armhole, exaggerated shoulder height

- Dye techniques have been tested, first on muslin, then a test fabric, then on the on swatches of final design fabric.
- After dyeing, pin the strips to the jacket to help you visualize how it will look, and experiment with the position of the colors to determine where on the jacket you want lighter or darker areas.
- After the jacket was cut and sewn, it was sent to the artisans to carry out the dyeing process. First, the jacket was dyed to the deep garnet color base color.
- Next airbrush and hand-painting created the uneven, swirling effects. The collar was left untreated as it will receive an embellishment (see page 172).
- When returned, the shoulder pads were sewn in, the jacket lined and completed with the buttons and buttonholes.

Artisanally Crafted Two-Dimensional Design

In their earliest forms, two-dimensional surface design involved the handcraft techniques of painting directly on to fabric, stenciling, and block printing.

These traditional techniques can be used when a hand-done, rough-hewn look is wanted.

Brocade opera cloak
Preparation
Inspiration

- The designer's intent with this costume for the opera *The Spell of Tradition* was to follow the stylistic direction given by the director, for the costumes to pull references from many cultures and periods to create a "new language." The two-dimensional surface design will be a deliberately faux-looking simulation of a late eighteenth-century brocade.

Research

- Having determined that a handcrafted two-dimensional surface design is the right look for your project, study the effects of hand-painting, stenciling, and block printing.
- After studying the two examples shown here, hand-painted and hand stenciled, the block printing was chosen for use on the opera cloak.

Fabrics/trims

- Use experimental draping exercises to determine the fabric chosen, here a rayon bengaline.
- Carry out further tests to make sure it will work with your chosen surface treatment. After testing some of the paints to be used, it was discovered that the bengaline's lightly ribbed texture and slightly nonporous surface and weight made it perfect for block printing.

Above: Hand-painted roses by artist Robin de Vic. The hand-painted application (done on the wrong side of the fabric) gives the roses wonderfully varied texture and the choice of velvet adds extra depth.

Left: This stencil was hand-cut with an X-Acto blade on wax stencil paper, weighted on to the fabric, then carefully stenciled using textile paint and a flat brush.

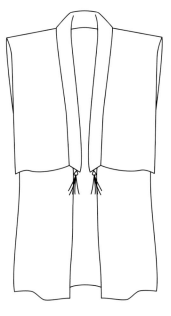

Flat sketches

- Use flat sketches to map out the right proportions and construction details.
- Here, the surface design has been indicated on this flat in two different proportions. The larger proportion (the right side of the cloak) will work best because it needs to be seen on a stage from a distance.

 Two-dimensional application on the drape

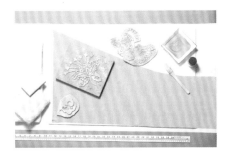

Step 1

Assemble the materials:

- A hand-cut block to use for the print (shown here, three sizes)
- Fabric for testing
- Paintbrush and gold metallic paint
- Sponge, water, and towel for cleaning

Step 2

- Using the brush, carefully paint the surface of the block. Testing the effects will determine how thickly to apply the paint.

Step 3

- Mark the fabric (see chalk-marked "X") for the placement of the block.
- Turn the block over on top of the fabric and press down gently.
- Lift the block quickly, taking care not to move or twist it.

Step 4

- Check the surface design to determine the appropriate paint density.

Step 5

- Clean the block after each print, with the sponge and water.
- Repeat the process.

Step 6

- Once the block print is done, analyze whether it must be amplified to be visible from the stage. If possible, take it to the stage and look at it under the lights.
- Determine whether any extra hand-painting or accent work is required. Here, assembled for testing, are:
  – Gold leaf for accents
  – Standard glitter
  – Black Swarovski crystals

> The most interesting way to create texture is to use a mix of techniques. It gives the costume an air of mystery if the viewer is not necessarily able to tell what is being used; is it crystals, paint, beading?
>
> *Dominique Lemieux*

When working with Dominique Lemieux on a Cirque du Soleil project, I was struck by how many different techniques were used in a single design. Dominique's skill is in mixing media to arrive at very new and unusual effects.

Shown here is the finished costume. The elements above have been added to the block printing on the front of the coat, adding depth and texture that will read well on the stage.

Assessment

- See Assessment Protocols (page 59).
- To assess the block printing effect on the costume, follow the assessment guide, then visualize the end results had you used other types of applications.

Be Prepared

For the best possible results, follow all the steps below when you are starting a new project.

Preparation
- Inspiration
- Research
- Fabric
- Flat sketches
- Muslin preparation
- Dress form preparation

Draping Using a Digital Print

The challenge with a digitally printed dress is in finding the perfect symbiotic match between the print and the fabric, and then the printed fabric with the dress design.

The goal is to enhance the mood and tone of the original inspiration. Using historical references, such as the film noir elements here, work powerfully towards achieving this goal.

Film Noir dress

Film noir is a specific style of Hollywood filmmaking originating in the 1940s. It evokes mystery and intrigue, shadows and dark alleyways, jaded detectives, and dangerous but beautiful women. This dress fits the mood of the Dark Radiance collection: glamorous, and exciting in its sense of mystery and the unknown.

Preparation

Inspiration

- An original flower print typical of the 1940s, which will translate well into a print for a film noir-themed dress.
- A vintage Lucite (acrylic) buckle is appropriate to the period and can be incorporated into the design.
- The muse is Lauren Bacall in *To Have and Have Not*, or Barbara Stanwyck in *Double Indemnity* (both 1944): stylish, slightly dangerous women.

Research

- Learn more about film noir: the actresses, sets, lighting, and props.
- Investigate 1940s' color stories in fabrics and prints.
- Rayon crepe was a signature fabric of the 1940s, giving the dresses of that era a lot of movement and creating a swingy, sexy look. Look for contemporary versions of that fabric.
- Search for other embellishments or trims specific to that period that could contribute to the look.
- Use reference garments for design inspiration, including attitude, types of necklines and sleeves.
- Take measurements: the sweep of skirt hems, shoulder width and height for 1940s-style shoulder pads.
- Review the ergonomics:
  - What is the look of the period? Should the garment be very fitted, oversized, or have a standard amount of ease?
  - Decide what it is about the balance and proportion of the film noir look that make it identifiable.

Fabrics/trims

- Do experimental draping to finalize the fabric.
- Be aware that some digital printing techniques require 80% synthetic content.
- Find a fabric with the slinky drape of the 1940s' rayon crepes.
- Design the print using the flower inspiration.
- Determine the scale and repeat of the print and work with the digital printing company to generate test samples of the print to choose from. Don't forget to supply the final design fabric for testing.

The style of this hand-painted original print is typical of the 1940s, as is the color story with the distinctive tomato red, jade green and black.

Flat sketches

- Use these to work on grainline decisions; use experimental draping with the final fabrics to determine whether to use a bias or lengthgrain cut on the skirt.

Fabric

- Include swatches of self-fabrics and lining on the flat sketch. Note the fabric widths.
- Identify the support elements: underlinings and fusibles; shoulder pads, crinolines, and foundation
- Seaming: using a half-scale drape if necessary. Decide whether it will be a wrap or have a side zip.
- Construction: Will the belt be real? Will it be a faux wrap?

Muslin preparation

- Decide on the weight of the muslin. This lightweight standard will not drape as softly as the final crepe, but will be soft enough to gather and plan the cascade. As usual when using muslin, it will be far easier to handle than the final fabric, especially when working the seam joins on tricky areas such as the bias sleeve.
- Tear, block, and press the muslin, and mark the grainlines.

Dress form preparation

- Select the correct dress form with the correct specifications, in this case a standard fit model size.
- Apply any support elements that are required: shoulder pad, stuffed arm.
- Carefully select the right shoulder pad for the dress form. Try to find or mold one with the 1940s' silhouette—slight S-curve, dipping in at the center of the shoulder. It is quite different from 1980s' shoulder pads.

The drape

- Have the illustration and flat sketch nearby and in view.
- Drape in front of a mirror if possible.

- Take a moment to center yourself, think of your muses, and feel the attitude that you are trying to convey.

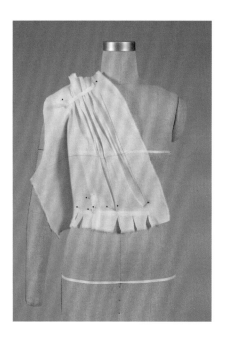
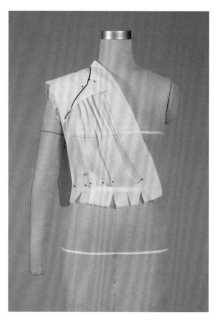

Step 1

- Start with the bodice front drape, determining the grainline.
- Here, the lengthgrain will follow the diagonal, since the finished edge there will need the strength of that grain. If the grainline were running vertically, the front edge would be on a bias grain and tend to stretch out.
- Pull in gathers to flow over the bust area.
- Clip at the waist to fit.
- Add a tuck at the princessline area.

Step 2

- Form the yoke of the dress. Tape the style line.
- Re-check your sketch to make sure you have the curve of the yoke right.

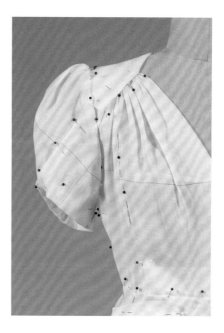

Step 3

- Begin the sleeve drape, starting at the cap with the center section, referring to the Sleeve Draping Order (page 84) if necessary.

Step 4

- Continue draping the sleeve by adding the front and back sections, working to create a balance with the center section.

Step 5

- The finished sleeve drape.
- A correction has been made to the front bodice, removing extra fullness as pinned. For the correction, see diagram on page 92.

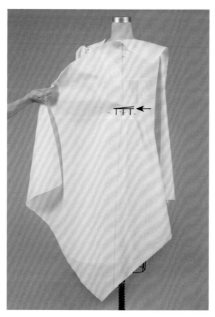

Step 6

- The underskirt will be draped on the bias, so begin the drape by aligning the bias grainline with the center front of the form.
- Pin down the center front and smooth across the hip allowing a flare to form on the side.
- Drape the back, also on the bias, beginning at center back, smoothing toward the side, allowing flare as in the front (not shown).
- Join side seams, pinning front over back (not shown).

Step 7

- Drape the overskirt with the flared cascade by pinning the bias of the piece down the center front, allowing extra fabric above the waist for the fabric to fall into the cascade after it is clipped and trimmed.
- Clip to waist along arrow as shown

Step 8

- Experiment with the fullness of the cascade.
- Trim the the curved outer edge of the cascade shape to balance with the skirt.

The print scaling tests

The flower print has been digitized and test swatches printed out in three different sizes to be checked on the muslin drape.

- The top print is the smallest, close to the original scale of the artwork.
- The second is too large.
- The lowest and medium sized scale shows the print pattern with the most clarity.
- The smallest scale will be used, because that scale looks the closest to the 1940s noir style.

Step 9

- Check the buckle placement against the cascade. It should look as though the buckle is creating the cascade by holding it together.
- Level the overskirt, finalize the flared cascade.
- Turn up hem of underskirt to match (not shown).

Step 10

- Finish the skirt drape by making the final adjustments to trimming the edge of the cascade.
- Mark the hem of the underskirt.

Marking and truing

- Carefully mark and true the muslin drape.
- Do the correction to the bodice that was pinned in Step 5 (see previous page).
- Use the new pattern to cut and sew a fitting toile.

The Fitting Toile

- The next step is to check the fitting toile on the dress form and continue testing the print.
- The fitting toile has been sewn in the final design fabric to check how it drapes and moves.
- The bodice correction that was done was successful and has worked well.
- The print is now being tested in the final design fabric for color tones and scale.
- As you check each print, use your skill of visualization to "see" what each would look like in the finished dress.
- The two prints on the right side of the form look the right period, and have interesting color stories, but don't quite fit the mood of the dangerous, bold, Film Noir muse.
- The print on the upper left of the form will be used for color, the one just below it, for size.

Digitizing pattern and print

After testing and choosing print scale and color tones, the print will be executed on the final design fabric. The choice will be to either print on running yardage, or digitize the pattern and print only the pieces needed, which is more economical for the ink costs. We will use this method, and calculated extra at seam allowances for adjustments or error.

- Digitize each pattern piece by scanning them in pieces and tiling them together individually, or taking it to a service that has a large scale scanner and can handle the larger skirt pieces.
- Make a marker (as in a cutting diagram) to engineer the print with economy of spacing on to the fabric.
- Digitally overlay the print on the pattern.
- Print the individual pieces.
- Cut and sew the dress.

Bodice and sleeve pieces engineer-printed onto the final design fabric.

Assessment

- See Assessment Protocols (page 59).
- The spirit of the Film Noir inspiration is there, the black and red are always glamorous and sexy, and combined with the jade green create a classic vintage 1940s' color story.
- Visualize the muse: Can you see Lauren Bacall solving a murder mystery in this dress?

CHAPTER 7

Draping with the use of Three-Dimensional Embellishment

OBJECTIVES

Enhance the emotional impact of a design with embellishments that reflect a designers' style.

-

Study the purpose and origins of embellishment.

-

Devise techniques to clearly explain concepts to other designers and artisans.

-

Identify and group the categories of embellishment.

-

Develop embellishments within a creative drape.

-

Exercise 1: Integration of Technology in Draping
Integrate electronic embellishments while draping.

Exercise 2: Embellishment Mock-Up Tests
Apply a variety of mock-up techniques to a draped dress. Testing scale, proportion, placement, and color of an embellishment.

Project: Embellishment Design Development
Follow Christelle Kocher's embellishment design process, exemplifying the importance of knowing your craft.

Alberto Ferretti dress mock-up for the engineered lace, flowers, and leaves.

Draping with the Use of Three-Dimensional Embellishment

There is an elegance to a simple, beautifully made garment. When a three-dimensional embellishment is added, the impact of the designed is enhanced, taking on a new personality as the visual and tactile textures create aesthetic depth and emotional resonance.

Embellishments, as with historical or cultural references, create prejudicial biases. Perhaps a heavily ruffled shirtfront reminds you of your grandmother, or a sprinkle of gemstones heightens a familiar sense of glamour. An interesting twist of fabric, a beaded flower, a pleated godet, can all create a compelling focal point and an emotional connection.

Creating embellishment can be a strong reflection of the designer's style and amplify the inspiration. It follows an intuitive path, and so, as with draping, it is very personal, a three-dimensional expression of a designer's unique aesthetic.

Working with embellishments often relies on hands-on craftsmanship, taking time, attention, and a singular vision to execute well. This chapter presents various tools for incorporating embellishments into the draping process to ensure they are well executed, and adding to the artistic statement of the design.

Three-Dimensional Embellishments

Possible forms of embellishment include:
- Quilting/appliqué, embroidery, and other forms of needlework
- Fabric treatments such as pleating, tucking, and multi-thread shirring
- Beading and sequin work
- The application of feathers, metal objects, and other ornaments

Lemarié feathers: peacock barbe, duck back, bird of paradise, pheasant.

Purpose and Origin of Embellishment

Three-dimensional embellishment has a profound effect on any design, often providing its emotional power. It can be seen on the earliest known clothing, and was added for a variety of reasons, such as:

- For spiritual or symbolic meaning
- For protective qualities, either physical or psychological
- As a show of wealth or stature, or as rank identification
- As a decorative art, pairing with artisanal traditions

Many cultures use ornamentation for spiritual or symbolic purposes. Native American tribal culture embraces the eagle as the highest species of birds, being connected to the heavens. Thus when adorning their clothing with its feathers, it symbolizes what is bravest, strongest, and holiest.

Wishram brides–to-be of high status wore the tusk-like dentalium shells, their removal signifying their readiness for marriage. In modern culture, many contemporary women still choose to wear pearls and white lace—symbols of purity, innocence, and hope—for their weddings.

Three-dimensional embellishment is used for its protective qualities, in both a physical and psychological sense. Often heavy beading, embroidery, coins or metal pieces were added over vulnerable areas such as the chest. This type of embellishment was surely a precursor to breastplates and armor, giving the wearer real physical protection from attack.

A Native American Wishram, adorned in an elaborate bridal headdress, beaded buckskin dress, neckpiece, and earrings of highly prized dentalium shells. Photograph by William Curtis in 1910.

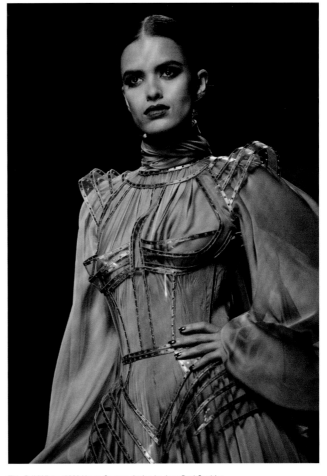

This Fall/Winter 2009 Haute Couture design by Jean Paul Gaultier incorporates a delicate metal embellishment in the style and shape of traditional armor. It provides a protective quality, albeit one that is more psychological than physical.

For centuries members of the military have been "decorated" with medals and ribbon flags to signify rank and accomplishment, each one indicative of a certain service or merit.

The traditional and often very ostentatious, bejeweled looks of royalty were clearly meant to set them apart from people of lower classes, and, especially in ceremonial situations, to indicate their wealth, position, and stature.

Embellished clothing may also exist simply for their aesthetic beauty. It is considered a decorative art—beautiful but also functional—rather than fine art, which stands on its own as a visual discipline.

Communicating with your artisans

There are long traditions of designers pairing with companies of artisans who create the embellishments for their designs. Karl Lagerfeld's work with the Lesage and Lemarié Ateliers is an example, as well as my own work with Park Pleating when creating my Jacaranda dresses with pleated insets and textured surfaces. Having a co-dependent relationship with one's artisans connects the designer to their community, expanding the circle of creativity. This is key to how work ventures into the avant-garde, which is the evolution of exciting new looks and techniques that emerge from a group of like-minded artists being inspired by and building on each other's ideas.

A key to the success of this symbiotic relationship is in communication. Experiment with a variety of mock-up techniques to find which way works best. The closer one comes to communicating what they want, the more satisfying the results will be.

While it is important to know as much as possible about the craft being used on your design, it is also important to give creative freedom to the artisan who is doing the work for you. Because they are the experts in their field, they often have a good design sense and excellent suggestions. A good pairing of designer and artisan inspire creative results.

The richly bejeweled dress of King Henry VIII was meant to impress and intimidate visiting royalty and peasants alike.

An embellishment developed by Karl Lagerfeld in conjunction with the house of Lemarié for its cruise 2016/17 collection shown on the streets of Havana, Cuba. This is a perfect example of the pairing of designer and artisan to create excellence in the decorative arts.

Categories of Embellishment

Historical examples of embellishment fall into defined categories, while with contemporary design, the purposes are more interwoven. Something created for pure artistic and decorative effect may also carry a deeper symbolic meaning, or have a subtle protective quality to it. A couture beaded and embroidered dress may be commissioned as a decorative art piece, but when worn, clearly indicates the wearer is of a certain economic stature.

Whichever combination of categories, an embellishment is a strong reflection of the individual style of its designer.

Needlework: Quilting, appliqué, and embroidery

Quilting, or the technique of putting two fabrics together with a layer of padding in between, has been dated to ancient Egypt. During the twelfth century the Crusaders wore quilted garments under their armor for comfort, warmth, and protection. Early American settlers popularized quilt-making for warmth and, later as a decorative art, often using the technique of appliqué: topstitching one piece of fabric onto a base fabric. It reached a notable peak in the unique and beautiful American Amish quilts of the 1850s, which are highly treasured today.

The purposes of quilting are many. Quilted fabrics are a visual reflection of the community that crafted them, they offer protective warmth, and are decorative art as well.

It is interesting to note the difference in the following two designer's quilting styles. Valentina Marie Kiisel, has a lyrical, traditional style using floral motifs and a soft, but vibrant spring color story. Natalie Chanin (next page) uses earthy, mineral tones for her modern abstract shapes.

An appliquéd quilt by Valentina Marie Kiisel, *c.*2001.

Treatments and Embellishments

A treatment is using the self fabric in a three-dimensional way, and embellishments are three-dimensional additions to the fabric.
- Quilting/appliqué, embroidery, and other forms of needlework
- Beading and sequinwork
- Fabric treatments such as pleating, tucking, and multi-thread shirring
- The application of feathers, metal objects, and other ornaments

The art of appliqué—stitching layers of fabric on top of others—developed in the eighteenth century and is seen in this detail from the modern quilt in the top image.

Today quilting is slow fashion at its best, combining excellence of craftsmanship with using small scraps of spare fabric or, as Natalie Chanin did, founding a business on using recycled T-shirts to a practical and beautiful end.

The art of embroidery, that of adding a sewn thread motif to the finished surface of a piece of fabric, is thought to have originated in China. New techniques were pioneered by the Phrygians, and then passed on to the Romans and Greeks. The first Roman embroideries were panels of contrast cloth which trimmed the borders of the clothing (which sounds a lot like appliqué). When all clothing was still hand-stitched, embroidery involving highly complex techniques was applied to nearly all articles of clothing. Embroidery in its various forms was practiced for centuries by virtually all classes in a predominance of cultures.

This dress by Alabama Chanin, an example of reverse appliqué, shows a rough-hewn hand-sewn look that is intriguing in its layered, detailed effects.

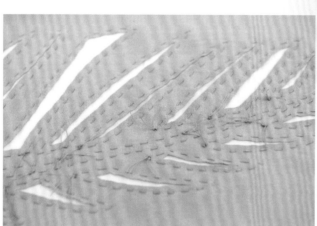

Fabric treatments: Pleating, tucking, and specialty stitching

Pleating, or specialty stitching techniques such as tucking or multi-stitch shirring, adds a three-dimensional textural embellishment. Artisans and specialty stitching companies continue to develop new and inspiring fabric treatments for designers to incorporate into their work.

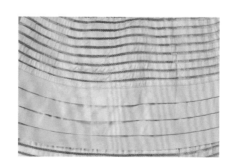

Far right: Apricot sunburst pleated godet by Park Pleating, for Jacaranda, by Karolyn Kiisel, 2006.

Right: Vintage cotton dress with multi-tucking and faggotting.

Beading and sequin work

The history of bead making dates to 3100 BCE with the Egyptians making beads by firing clay, lime, soda, and silica sand. Seed beads were being used on religious items in 1200, and in 1770, Charles Germain de Saint-Aubin's book, *Designer to the King*, documented complex, precisely detailed embroidery techniques as well as the social values, working conditions, and aesthetics of his time.

The embellishment work of Chinese fashion designer Guo Pei is astounding in its complexity, and attention to detail. Beading and sequins are an integral part of the powerful textures and shapes she crafts. Her rise to success has been supported by the hundreds of experienced artisans who work on the embroidery for her designs—designs that are available only to her private clients.

Guo Pei's embellishments are examples of the finest quality decorative art of that culture, yet also hold symbolism. The dragon she often uses in her work is an ancient symbol of power, strength, and good luck in Chinese culture.

Guo Pei, Legend of a Dragon Collection, 2012.

Three-dimensional applications: Feathers and flowers

Adding dimensional elements to a fabric, such as feathers, flowers, metal coins, or safety pins, creates a compelling visual and emotional intensity. They may elicit a prejudicial bias, or become an iconic symbol as the camellia has become to Chanel.

Lemarié for Christelle Kocher

In the 1880s the Lemarié studio had the reputation of being the finest of the many feather workshops in Paris. The feathers—taken from birds of paradise, herons, swans, peacocks, ostriches, and more—were cleaned, tinted, trimmed, and curled to adorn the high fashions of the moment. Later flowers were added, dahlias, peonies, orchids, and roses made of organza, tulle, leather, and velvet.

In the 1960s Coco Chanel turned to the house for her iconic camellia, and Lemarié's reputation as the best in the craft was confirmed. In 1996 the studio was acquired by the fashion house Chanel, and it is used by many contemporary designers.

Today their thriving workshop has brought Lemarié into the twenty-first century. It is renowned for its innovative and beautiful use of feathers and flowers, and also a vast array of interesting materials, including plastics, newspaper, crystals, and semiprecious gemstones.

Kocher is a contemporary French designer exploring the sensibility of mixing the "high" with the "low," the traditional with the modern. In her work, this means pairing luxury fabrics and embellishments with street fashion. This bold and somewhat irreverent concept has been developing for some time in the work of designers who have pulled athleticwear or streetwear into the realm of high fashion through the use of top-level craftsmanship.

Kocher's work is inspirational because she has been able to ground herself in what she knows best. Her feel for Parisian streetwear and her work environment at Lemarié, where there are voluminous archives of samples to study and a huge selection of feathers and gemstones to choose from, have nourished her individuality, and ability to create groundbreaking, unique collections that are rich, colorful, and very beautiful.

Creative Draping and Developing Embellishments

An embellishment must be integrated holistically into the garment, an organic and complementary balance between embellishment, fabric, and design of the garment. Ideally, they are developed simultaneously, so they will harmonize; physically with the shapes and construction style, and subjectively, with the inspiration of the design.

The twofold process of developing an embellishment during creative draping involves firstly development work to determine what will express the inspiration best, while creating the most interesting and complementary effect. Secondly, a plan for how to communicate your concept to the artisans, choosing a mock-up technique that can best represent your ideas. The key is lots of testing and experimenting, and communicating your comcepts well. When developing a three-dimensional embellishment, review the Designer's Aims and Aspirations (see page 10) to ensure that you are maximizing the effect of the ornamentation.

Find your focus: Review the theme or mood or your inspiration boards.
- Does the embellishment add to that, and expand and articulate the tone?
- Have clarity on the purpose: Is there a symbolic meaning? Does it have protective qualities such as quilting for warmth? Is there a subtle political message, or is it clearly for decorative beauty?

Incorporate research: Collect cultural and historical images similar to your embellishment

Recognize the principles of good design:
Study and analyze:
- to what degree this element will become a focal point
- how it will affect any construction issues, such as the seaming and proportions
- if it will affect the integrity of the fabric's surface or hand?

Establish your ergonomics: Have a sense of:
- The relationship between the scale of the garment and the intended proportion or scale of the embellishment.

Acknowledge the ethics of slow fashion: Consult your conscience, and use fair-trade labor and sustainable materials wherever possible.

Apply quality of craftsmanship: Know your craft:
- Learn as much as you can about the techniques of the craft that will be used on your design.
- Give the artisans as much information as possible about the result you want.
- Pursue artisanal excellence by welcoming feedback from the artisans who will be working on it, and allowing them some creative freedom.

The famous Chanel camellias have been made by Lemarié in a great variety of colors and materials.

Integration of Technology in Draping

The mood and tone, ergonomic attitude, and the jewel-toned, crystal-dyed color scheme of the galaxy jacket (page 152) were all inspired by the NASA starry-sky and cosmic swirl images of the Dark Radiance theme.

After seeing the jacket dyed, I wanted to take it one step further by adding "stars," thus accentuating that feeling of the mystery and beauty of outer space.

Galaxy jacket
Preparation
Inspiration
- Inspiration for the stars on my jacket came from studying embellishments that used crystals, looking at the NASA photos again, and imagining how I wanted the jacket to look in a darkened room.
- I found inspiration in a moment I recall from a live performance by Miwa Matreyek. The piece integrates her own projected animation and her own shadow in interaction. The show just sparkled with energy and playfulness, had a beautiful, soft lyricism, and a whimsical sense of wonder.
- To capture the essence of the art piece, the design must have that sense of depth and mystery. The electronically lit "stars" will need a companion embellishment to artfully conceal the lights themselves, a "platform"/control panel, and the wiring. Some draping and experimenting with different fabric treatments will be necessary to craft something that will synchronize with the electronic elements.

Research
- Images with electronic lights on clothing, noting what elements you feel work best.
- Fabric treatments that have been used to conceal lights and wiring.

Fabrics/trims
- Test fabrics for the embellishment: They must be light for the space-like mood, but opaque enough to hide the electronics.
- A combination of straight-grain and bias-cut chiffons and organzas were experimented on (see next page). A sheer version of the jacket's jewel tones, will provide a cover for the electronics with its three-dimensional depth, and also a soft, sensual, element to the collars.

Documentation image provided by artist Miwa Matreyek, from her live performance, *Myth and Infrastructure: Dreaming of Lucid Living*, 2010. Animation, performance and design: Miwa Matreyek.

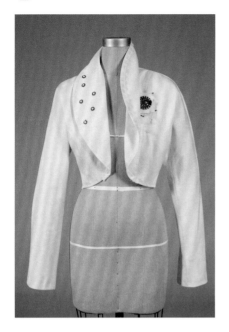
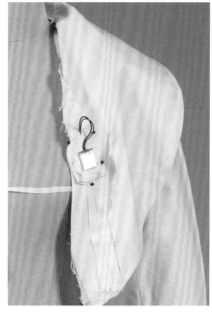
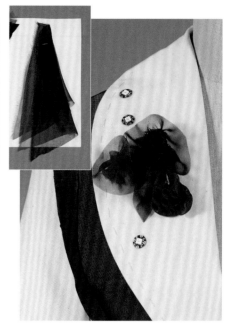

Step 1

- Work with the muslin fitting sample of the galaxy jacket (see page 153).
- Craft a pocket from muslin to hold the lighting platform.
- The on/off switch and battery must be on the inside of the jacket, because the outside will be heavily embellished, so determine the position on the inside of the lapel.
- There will need to be an opening through which to pass the wire to the inside of the jacket; this can be the princess seam. Mark it for the opening.
- Lights are positioned and their placement will be marked on the pattern.

Step 2

- Drape a pocket to hold the battery, and be sure to mark the position.
- After truing and marking the muslin, mark the position of the battery, platform, and lights on the pattern.

Step 3

- The positioning of the lights, battery pack, and platform will now be double-checked.
- Seen here, jewel-tone fabrics being tested for embellishment.

Step 4

- Shown here, the jacket has been sewn in the final design fabric, and dyed (see Chapter 6).
- Stitch down the electronic platform.
- Stitch the lights with the wire conductive thread.

Step 5

- The lapel embellishment must now be applied to cover the electronics.
- Create the embellishment on the lapels improvisationlly, using the rosette and chiffon strips that were tested as inspiration.
- Hand-sew the strips of jewel-tone bias chiffon to hide the wires and enable the lights to sparkle through the sheer layers.

Assessment

- See Assessment Protocols (page 59).
- Check the technological aspects in a darkened room, since they don't show up well in a lit photograph, and try it on a model if possible. Does the embellishment provide enough of an emotional punctuation?
- The embellishment feels luscious and interesting, and serves the purpose of camouflaging the lights and wires?
- Review the vision of the inspirational MIWA image. Does it capture the mood you wanted to express?
- Visualize the muse to see if it still fits the situation you imagined.

Embellishment Mock-Up Tests

With this complex embellishment project, the right choice of mock-up techniques is important because there will be two artisans working on the three embellishments: the engineered lace, the embroidered leaves, and the three-dimensional flowers.

As a designer, the closer you can get to giving your craftspeople a clear road map of proportion, scale, color story, details, placement, and so on, the more certain you can be of getting the result you envision.

Alberta Ferretti flower dress

The beauty of this dress lies in the graceful balance of the fitted lace bodice, the full, flowing skirt, and the delicate embellishment. All three must harmonize for this complex combination to work.

Preparation
Inspiration
- The quotation: "Fashion is strength, fragility, and poetry" by Alber Albaz is my inspiration. It resonates with my Ikebana inspiration board.
- This poetic dress by Albert Ferretti with its strong, but fragile, delicate embellishment is worn by a woman as if she is emerging from a forest having used flowers and vines to wrap and adorn herself. The ornamentation creates a protective quality, albeit psychological rather than physical.

Research
- Research historical uses of this type of floral reference by other designers.
- Reference garments: Look at skirts with large chiffon hem sweeps to calculate how much yardage will be needed to drape the skirt.

Mock-up Techniques

- Make a variety of physical samples of the three-dimensional idea. Experiment with pins, glue, or any rough techniques to come up with unique ways of working with the fabric or other materials. They can be refined later by experienced artisans (see page 179).
- Draw variations of the three-dimensional treatment on your original sketches.
- Draw the three-dimensional design on a paper mock-up of the garment (see page 151).
- Draw the embellishment freehand on a fitting muslin (as done with this project, see page 179).
- Print out a photograph of your fitting muslins, and draw on the copies to experiment with different ideas.
- Photograph your sample or sketch of a three-dimensional design, then print it out and pin it to the muslin drape. Try copying it various scales, and use those to work with the placement, since finalizing that will also help you to determine the size (see page 179).
- Experiment on the half-scale form by printing half-scale variations on to fabric using digital or sublimation printing.

Fabrics/trims
- Experimental draping: Check different weights of chiffon or georgette to finalize decisions about the skirt.
- Assemble various materials and trims that are options for the embellishment.

Flat sketches
- Include sketches of three types of embellishment: the lace texture, the leaf embroidery, and the three-dimensional flowers.

Muslin preparation
- Create a muslin preparation diagram.
- Tear, block, and press the muslin, and mark the appropriate grainlines.

Dress form preparation
- Prepare the dress form by applying style-line tapes to match the sketch. Study the photograph carefully as you apply the tapes, and visualize the negative space to help you create the shapes.
- Adjust the dress form for runway model proportion:
  - Lower the waistline by ½" (1.3 cm) to allow for longer center back neck to waist.
  - Add padding at the dress form waist to smooth the line for the new waist.
  - Make the waist tape yellow so that it will not confuse you while you are draping.

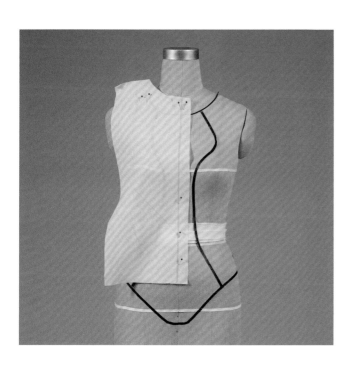

Taping for General Guidelines

It can be a useful technique to tape the style-lines onto the dress form before beginning the drape. However, remember that draping involves intuitive, subtle decisions as you create your final shape. Do not let yourself be controlled by these tape lines, just use them as general guidelines to get you started, and feel free to move them as you go along if the drape calls for it.

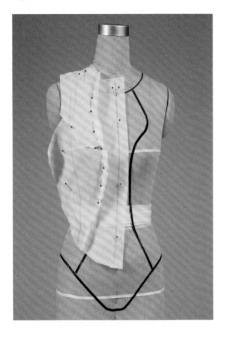

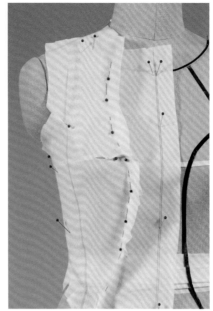

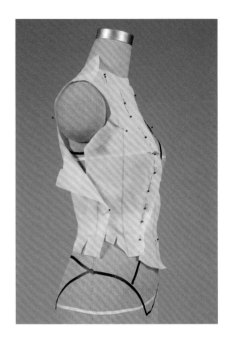

The bodice drape

Step 1

- Align the center front bias lines on the muslin to the center front of the dress form, and pin.
- Pin the side front with bias lines running vertically, then pin a small tuck (approximately ½"/1.3 cm) for ease at the bust and armhole, as shown.
- Wrap the muslin toward the back as far as it will go laying smoothly.

- Paying attention to ergonomics is key here. The bodice is bias cut, so it can be somewhat fitted, but there must still be some slight ease in the fit, for comfort and for the fabric to flow.
- These tucks will not be sewn, but will become ease in the seams. This means that it will involve more work to mark the drape, note the ease on the pattern, and sew it correctly. However, the effect will make it worth the extra labor: The bodice will fit better, hug at the armhole, and allow for shape at the bust.

Step 2

- Drape the center back, with the bias lines running vertically.
- Seen here, the muslin section cannot wrap far enough. Try angling the muslin in different ways, and if it still doesn't work, the section will have to be pieced.

Beautiful Pinning is an Art

Take the time to pin accurately and smoothly. Keep your pins parallel when first pinning wrong sides together, then perpendicular to the seams when turning front over back. You want your tools to recede so that you can focus on the shape you are creating.

Patching Muslin while Draping

When working with bias pieces, it can be difficult to plan the exact dimensions. You must follow the curves of the body and make decisions as you go.

When in the middle of a drape, and the fabric runs short, don't waste time, or interrupt your flow to stop and re-cut the piece. Simply patch on a small piece of muslin by cross-stitching the pieces together and keep draping.

*It is critical that the grainline of the piece added matches that of the main piece.

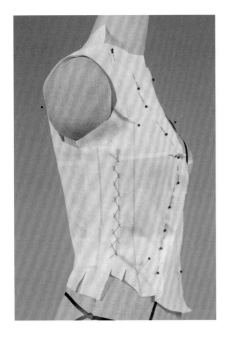

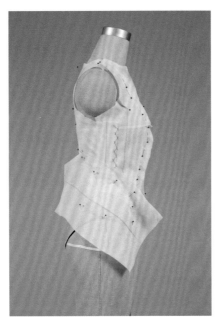

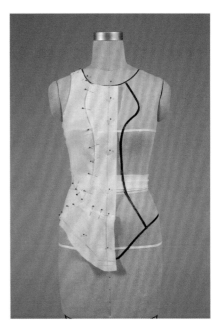

Step 3

- Bring the back piece around to the front to connect with the front side piece.
- Smooth the pieces on top of each other, and pin.
- Piece the two fabrics together with a cross stitch and continue.

Step 4

- Drape the lower side piece by wrapping toward the front. Note how the piece fits ergonomically; the bias line nicely follows the hipbone.
- Here, I have had to shift the back tape down a bit to accommodate the shape I want. Check in again with the ergonomics before finalizing the set of the piece (see page 176, Step 1).

   Note: When working with style lines that have been pre-taped on the form, remember that it is more important to pay attention to the shape you are forming, and drape outside the lines if necessary.

Step 5

- Tape the lower center front section.
- Finish draping the bodice by reviewing all the style lines.
- Turn all seams to the inside, front over back.

Step 6

- Clip and turn the armhole and neckline.

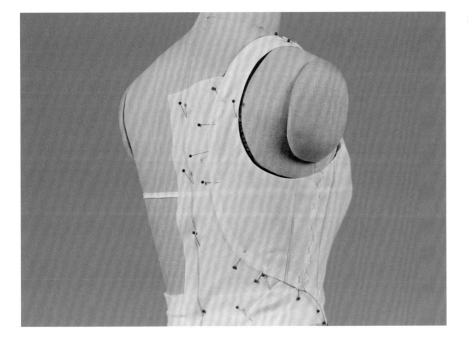

The skirt drape

Step 1

- Begin the skirt drape by aligning the bias of the muslin with the center front of the form.
- Clip the top edge of the skirt to match the bodice as you pin the skirt to the bodice along the lower front edge.
- Continue pinning the skirt around toward the side seam area.

Step 2

- Begin draping the back skirt by aligning the bias lines with the center back of the bodice.
- Smooth toward the front and join the side seams, which will fall toward the front about 5" (12.5 cm).

Step 3

- Finish the skirt by turning front over back at the side seams, trimming where necessary.
- The top edge seam allowance of the skirt is now folded under and pinned to the bodice (see below photo).

Embellishment mock-ups on muslin drape

- Do a drawing of the flower embellishment; rough sketch will be fine.
- Copy it in a few different proportions, seen here: small, medium, and large scales.
- Pin the paper copies onto the dress, following the position of the Ferretti photograph.
- Color some of them in if it helps you to visualize the finished flowers.
- Take a step back to view the dress from a distance, or in a mirror, and determine which of the three different scales of the embellishments will work best.
- The medium-sized scale of floral embellishment has been chosen.

Fitting sample with embellishment mock-ups

- Work with the craft house or artisan who will make the final embellishment by showing them the mock-ups and explaining the look that you want.
- Optional: Make a three-dimensional flower to bring the mock-up closer to the desired embellishment, and pin to the bodice to help with visualization.
- Ask them to create several choices of sample flowers for you to choose from.
- There may be two more additional "send out" processes to complete the dress:
  - A lace firm who will craft the engineered lace pattern for the bodice.
  - An embroidery house that will do the leaf embroideries.
- Here, the mock-up technique of hand-painting directly on the muslin has been used to show exactly the proportion and style of lace and leaves wanted.
- Shown here, the final dress with three dimensional flowers and hand-painted mock-up embellishment, ready to show to the artisans who will do the work.

- Mark and true the drape. Make a paper pattern, or use the muslin draped pieces as a pattern.
- Cut the bodice in a lighter-weight muslin and cut the skirt in chiffon to check the drape in a fabric the same weight as the final design fabric.
- Make additional paper copies of the chosen size and pin to the bodice for placement plan.

Assessment

- See Assessment Protocols (page 59).
- View the dress from a distance, holding up the photograph to compare the two. Check proportions and level of embellishment, making sure it is the right mood and tone, but not overpowering the light fabrics of the dress.
- Does it convey "strength, fragility, and poetry"?

Hand-painted leaves and lace, three-dimensional flowers by Claire Fraser

Embellishment Development

Bringing an embellished design to life takes not only the skill of visualization to "see" the finished piece, but also a knowledge of the craft that will physically realize it. Christelle Kocher's years of experience as design director of Maison Lemarié has given her an intimate knowledge of this medium, enabling her to exquisitely realize her design seen at the end of this chapter.

Christelle Kocher's Lemarié Embellished design

Christelle Kocher used an inspiration from the Nari Ward artwork, *We the People* to create the skillfully designed camisole on page 187. The success of this compelling and beautiful piece is inextricably linked to the complex and unusual bead and feather embellishment. The result is striking and perfectly realized because she is so well versed in her craft, and knowledgeable of the capabilities and techniques used at Lemarié. In addition, working so often with the Lemarié team means that she was able to trust their decisions with the details of executing the work, offering them some creative freedom in the practice of their craft.

The following is the process that Christelle Kocher used from inception to completion of a runway look for her Spring/Summer 2017 collection.

Lemarié showroom sample.

Preparation
Inspiration:

- Kocher's inspiration was the mood created by the colored shoelaces in this artwork: the pattern of their placement, their bright perkiness, the suggestion of movement as they hang from the wall, and their everyday-object sensibility.
- One of the core tenets of her design work is in portraying the tension of opposites, combining the "high" and "low." Here, the low is the practical nature of the shoelaces, the high, the couture quality feather and flower work of the Lemarié studio.

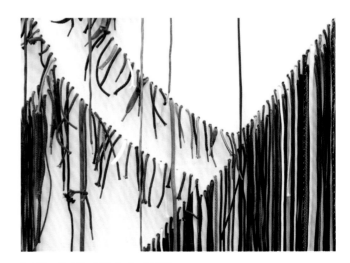

Detail from Nari Ward's *We the People* (2011).

Research:

- Prepare to work with embellishment by researching how that type of ornamentation is most commonly done. It is important to have a thorough understanding of the processes so that you can improve the quality of craftsmanship where possible, or even create in the work subtle nuances that you otherwise would not have noticed. Visit the workshops, discuss the craft with the artisans, and have an appreciation of the artistry it takes to accomplish what you are looking for.
- Find reference samples to set the tone for your design, as well as define proportions, color stories, and details that you can adapt to match your own ideas.

Lemarié showroom samples. Ms. Kocher might review such samples to find techniques or stylistic embellishments which would be helpful as reference examples in communicating her new ideas, or perhaps just as inspiration.

Mini exercise

Note: Follow Christelle Kocher's process as a guide to create your own embellished design:

- Find an inspiration.
- Select the fabric for the design.
- Assemble a variety of materials to use for the embellishment.
- Determine how the embellishment will be done, and use the highest-quality craftsmanship available to you.
- Drape the new design, and follow the steps to the finished toile, incorporating the embellishment at the appropriate stage.

The Lemarié studio is a treasure chest of tools and materials. A veritable wall of metal dies—many very old and some fairly new—are stored here, ready to make every imaginable style of flower petal come to life.

A selection of dies with wooden handles.

A second selection of dies.

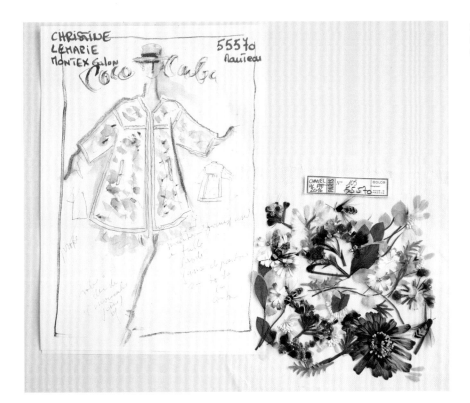

Studying the work of other designers brings inspiration and also more knowledge about the details of the craft. Here is a sample that has been used by Karl Lagerfeld.

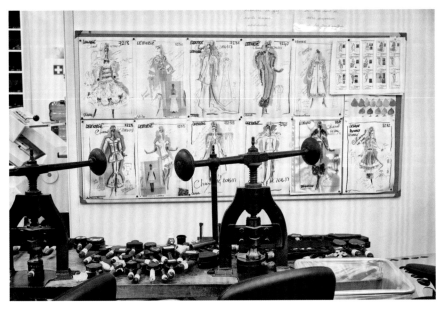

The die presses with sketches by Karl Lagerfeld seen behind the table.

The dies are inserted into the press manually and the die-cutting machine cuts each flower individually.

Every flower in the Lemarié studio is individually handcrafted, petal by petal.

Here, a signature Chanel camellia is being crafted out of sequin petals.

First, the petals are individually hand sewn before being molded into their curved shapes.

The wood-handled, metal shaping ball is being heated over the flame of a spirit lamp.

The petal is now pressed onto a pillow with the heated metal shaping ball to achieve just the right level of curl.

The various tools used to shape the flower petals: shaping balls, crochet hooks, knives, and a rayette.

The finished Chanel sequin camellia.

Beginning work on Koché's sample: first the feathers are clipped.

The tips of the feathers are dipped in a glue.

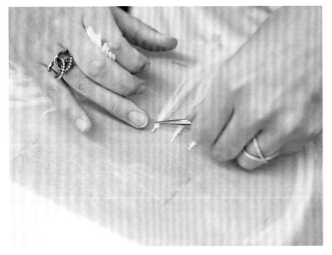

The small individual clusters of feathers are hand-sewn onto the base of silk mousseline (chiffon).

The feathers are carefully hand sewn.

The small embellishment sample has been done with tambour-style embroidery, and is now ready to present to Christelle Kocher.

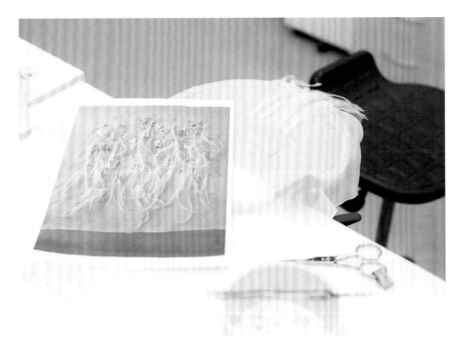

Step 1

- The camisole has been draped on the dress form, marked, trued, cut, and sewn into a fitting sample/toile.
- After studying the proportion and sizing needed for the design, Lemarié is contracted to do the beaded and feathered embellishment.

Step 2

- The finished Lemarié embellishment sample is now checked for general look, color, proportion, density.
- The spacing and density are working; the bright, perky colors echo the feeling of the Nari Ward inspiration piece.
- The workmanship is perfect.

Step 3

- Pin the finished sample on to the drape or fitting muslin to test it for positioning on the garment. Note the length and where the beading will stop.
- Check the color balance, the size of the beads and feathers, the proportions, and the density, volume and fullness.
- Note any changes to communicate to the artisans.
- Before finalizing the sample, review the original inspiration again to make sure the embellishment is on track.
- At this point, notes are given to Lemarié for any corrections to the sample. The position of the embellishment will be marked on the camisole pattern, and transferred to the camisole fabric by thread tracing. Then the cut fabric camisole pieces or a block of fabric large enough to cut the camisole pieces is then returned to Lemarié for the production process.

The finished camisole is seen here on the runway for Christelle Kocher's spring/summer 2017 collection. In sync with Christelle's philosophy of mixing couture elements with street style, the show was held under the brand new canopy of the Forum des Halles shopping center, on a busy concourse that also serves as an exit from the underground mall and Châtelet-Les Halles station.

Assessment

- See Assessment Protocols (page 59).
- Seeing the design on a runway is truly getting the long-range perspective. The piece has impact and has succeeded in the goal of incorporating Lemarié's luxury component with the street style attitude. The relaxed cut of the trouser contrasts well with the close-fitting, embellished camisole.
- Fabrication: The fabric is working well. It is soft and has some flow and drape to it, helping to give the feathers the same sense of movement as the look of the Nari Ward shoelaces had.
- Embellishments: The beads and feathers make an impact; their size and proportion show well from the distance seen here.
- Take some photographs to study and compare the runway piece to the drape.

  – The bust area is fitting well.
  – The soft "V" of the top edge works well to echo the shape of the hemline and the general soft, curvy, feminine energy of the camisole.
  – The straps seem slightly close together; placed a bit further apart along the top edge of the camisole would result in a more ergonomically harmonic look.
  – The length may be slightly more flattering if a few inches shorter or longer, rather than finishing at the fullest point of the hip.
- The trouser and camisole fabrics coordinate in texture and with hand. The matching tonal quality of the fabrics and embellishment is soft and sensual.
- Journal some notes.
- Sketch any other ideas that are generated from this look.

CHAPTER 8

Draping for Costume Design

OBJECTIVES

Incorporate the aspirations, tools, and techniques of creative draping, to design and drape a costume.

—

Understand the sequential stages of costume design.

Exercise 1: Half-Scale Design Development
Formulate quick drapes to test composition, color balance, and visual tone. Sketch the drapes to stimulate ideas for final costume design.

Exercise 2: Experimental Draping
Deduce final fabric choices using experimental draping techniques to finalize the right combination for a theater costume.

Exercise 3: Improvisational Draping
Resolve issues within the design process, using improvisational draping.

Project 1: The Minuet Dancer Costume
Apply a combination of draping methods to develop a costume design for a specific character. Drape and construct the costume, assessing the effect of the design within the overall tone of the production.

Project 2: The Beaumarchais Costume
Apply a combination of draping methods to develop a design for a specific character, with a focus on executing a dramatic look, with an exaggerated emotional or psychological effect.

Draping the *kataginu* over the finished brocade *obi* for the character of Beaumarchais.

Draping for Costume Design

Costume designers imagine, develop, and create the costumes for a production or performance. The skill is in creating character and storytelling, capturing the imagination of the audience by setting a tone, evoking an atmosphere, then weaving a spell with texture and color.

Costume design is a collaborative effort, working not just with actors and performers, but also directors, writers, production designers, choreographers, visual effects teams, and hair and makeup artists, all contributing to the creative style or tone of a production.

Draping for costume design necessitates a wider approach than working on a single garment. It may involve a large cast of characters or a single character with a variety of costumes made of separate pieces, accessories, and props that all affect the final look. These elements must come together, in a complete picture for the costume design to be brought to life.

As the designer assists in the storytelling with their interpretation of a characters' style, it is important to express an original voice. A costume designer who can develop their own unique style, offers something recognizable and memorable that makes them sought after.

Building a Costume

In the field of costume design, the term "building" is often used, referring to the traditional way a costume is developed in live theater. The actor may first be given basic pieces to rehearse in; for example, they may need to accustom themselves to wearing a corset, a large skirt, or a long kimono. Once the base costume is established, additional pieces and accessories are added, building the costume as the actor builds his or her character.

When costumes are being "built" instead of rented or purchased, all of the methods introduced thus far can be utilized in your design and development.

Costume designer Dominique Lemieux was part of the original creative team of Cirque du Soleil. She began sketching her whimsical, unusual costumes in the early days of the company, helping to define its style with her focus on strong, quirky characters. Note the interesting textures in the illustration, which became one of her signature design strengths. Cirque du Soleil performer from Allegría, 2019. Illustration by Dominique Lemieux.

Using all of the techniques of creative draping

- Experimental draping
  - Evaluating fabrics for design development
  - Providing research and/or presentation boards for the director or art directors
  - Helping to visualize costumes as pairs or a group by assessing selections of fabrics on dress forms
- Improvisational draping
  - For design development and detail studies
- The block-to-drape method
  - Using blocks (slopers) as a shortcut
- Draping with a half-scale form
  - Exploring tricky construction and seaming
  - Checking period silhouettes
  - Working with color balance and focal points
  - Viewing costumes as a group
- Draping from an illustration
  - Recreating specific proportions of an illustration
  - Capturing the mood and tone of the illustration.
- Draping with use of two-dimensional surface designs
  - The importance of testing for scale and proportion
- Draping with the use of three-dimensional embellishments
  - Using their emotional and symbolic meanings to build depth to a character's costume.

Aims and aspirations for costume design

The Designer's Aims and Aspirations (see page 10) have specific points when applied to costume design.

Find your focus

Inspiration is having a full understanding of the script, the characters, and what the costume should communicate.

Incorporate research and reference garments

- To understand the cultural and historical context of the production.
- To understand your own context, economically, and creatively.
- To stimulate original ideas, and help get the team on board with your concepts.

Recognize the principles of good design

- The heightened importance of the emotional/psychological impact of color in costume.

Establish your ergonomics

- Review the type of fit the director may want, and make sure to convey that to the actors.

Acknowledge the ethics of slow fashion

- Consult your conscience when it comes to fabric and labor choices. Be vigilant.

Apply quality of craftsmanship

- Know your craft.
- Know where you stand; keep a close grasp of your resources—from overall budget to the skills of your stitchers.

Costumes of Quality

The quality of costumes will be dependent upon the budget. A very important skill for a costume designer is in knowing how to present a realistic budget, being able to accurately figure fabric costs, assess the size of the crew necessary, and any additional costs for outside help with specialty services. A carefully calculated budget may enable you to take the extra steps needed to high quality of craftsmanship.

The Stages of Costume Design

In this chapter, we follow the stages of costume design, following the design-through-production process of two characters from *The Spell of Tradition: Two Noh Operas on the Life and Afterlife of Benjamin Franklin*, an opera by Peter Wing Healey, produced in Los Angeles in 2017. The costumes, the Minuet Dancer and Beaumarchais, both appear in a dream sequence. The Minuet Dancer is a whimsical, chorus-like member of the ensemble, who flows between the other actors with balletic moves. Beaumarchais, an historical character, was an early supporter of American independence, and also a musician, diplomat, and highly regarded member of French society in the court of Louis XV.

All costume design projects will benefit from following a systematic approach to the process. Being thorough and resisting the temptation to take shortcuts will ensure you are designing the best possible costumes.

The Stages of Costume Design

1. Inspiration overview
   • Collecting research images and reference garments

2. Synchronizing a vision with the director
   • Getting to know your characters
   • Preparing boards: fabrics, colors, concepts

3. Design development
   • Draping on the half-scale form
   • Experimental draping with fabrics
   • Improvisational draping

4. Final illustrations and working flats
   • Creating the final illustration
   • Flats/technical sketches from the construction crew.

5. Building the costumes
   • Meeting with the actors; taking measurements
   • Draping, constructing, and fitting the muslin toiles
   • Preparing for the final fabric fitting on all pieces
   • Accessories and props

Inspiration overview

Initial inspiration for the costume design will come from the script or libretto. This, in addition to notes from the director, will provides a basic roadmap for the project. Notes given by *The Spell* director were:

• Mix and match period references to create a "new visual language"
   – Find the balance of fantasy and reality (determine the stance between a historically correct period vs. no period)
• Tone: high degree of exaggeration (both in Noh and late eighteenth-century styles)
• Mood: one of awe and wonder
• Production value description: "Brittle, spare, slightly fake."

Before meeting with the director to synchronize visions, let your imagination percolate and your personal inspiration come into focus. Journal some notes on what colors, mood, and tone you would like to see in the production. Create mood boards for the characters; include various elements of the costumes.

Mood board: research of late eighteenth-century wrist and jabot (necktie) treatments, as well as a general color palette for the dream sequence.

Creating authenticity in period costumes

Christine Edzard, creative director of Sands Studios, which incorporates the Rotherhithe Picture Research Library, maintains that the only way to achieve an authentic look and make a costume that "feels" the period is to duplicate the technology used in that era. Her philosophy is to study the period references in great detail and copy, not adapt, the techniques.

Her costumes for *Little Dorrit* are famous for their authentic look, and were made by period methodologies.

Presenting your research images

Well-chosen research images are crucial for:
- Clarifying the cultural and historical context of the production.
- Providing visuals to bounce your ideas against while you are in design development.
- Communicating concepts to others on your team.

The *Spell of Tradition* inspiration images: a mix of late eighteenth-century and Japanese Noh style

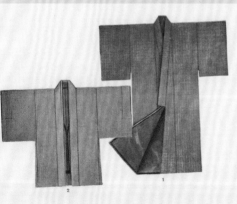

Clockwise from top left: Incroyables and Merveilleuses, 1794; late eighteenth-century women; Marquis de Lafayette, 1791; Kanze Noh Theatre "Okina" Performance at Time Warner Center on July 13, 2016 in New York City; formal *kamishimo*, worn by Japanese samurai, 1878; and traditional Japanese kimonos.

Reference garments

Reference garments help to hone your sense of ergonomics for a production, and also coordinate your vision with the director and others on the team.

Collecting kimonos of various proportions helped focus the scale and volume I wanted to see on stage for *The Spell*.

193

Synchronizing the vision with the director

Before meeting with the director, study the script, do scene breakdowns, note fast changes, duplicate needs.

- Meet with the art director to discuss general tenor of the production:
  - Coordinating color concept between sets/costumes
  - Discuss lighting style and affects on costumes

- Develop "character boards," identifying:
  - Attitude/personality traits of characters
  - Volume, shape and silhouette, wigs, accessories, props
  - Scale of exaggeration or focal points, accents
  - Foreshadowing: costume elements that hint at future story elements

Planning fabrics and construction style:
  - Create color, texture, and detail boards to help ground your inspirations.
  - Construction plan: consider budget, resources, tailoring needs, specialty stitching needs, dying, etc and create a sequential flow with color tones and textures to illustrate the storyline. For example, in *The Spell*:
- Act I: in a forest, the train crash, colors and textures earthy, grounded, dark
- Act II: the dream sequence, apparitions, fabrics light, ethereal organza overpieces, sheers, pastels

Design development

As you begin designing the individual characters, draw on the techniques presented in earlier chapters to stimulate creativity. Hands-on practices such as experimentally draping with fabrics, working on the half-scale form, and draping improvisationally can all be helpful. Take photos and do rough concept sketches while you work. Also, review the work of other designers, absorbing the qualities of their work you aspire to.

> Don't be afraid to be influenced by those you admire.
>
> *Anthony Powell, costume designer. Interview with the author, 2017*

These costume designs for *Camelot* by Tony Duquette in 1961, were done by draping on the half-scale form, the method itself an engaging way of presenting the ideas as well as his intended mood and tone.

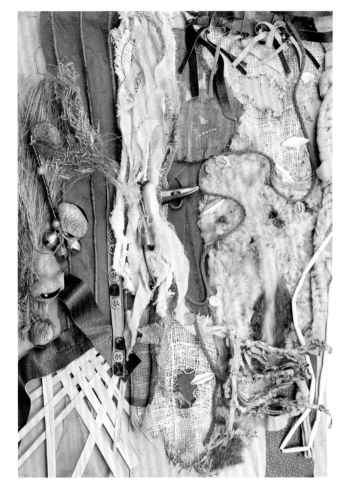

The mood board for Pocono, the narrator, whose costume combines the looks of Native American shaman and Japanese peasant.

EXERCISE 1:
Half-Scale Design Development

Working on the half-scale form saves time. An ensemble can be draped quickly, fabric combinations tested, color balance checked, and silhouettes easily compared on the smaller scale.

Minuet Dancer

A successful mix of late eighteenth-century and Japanese Noh styles is challenging. The fabrics for this costume were chosen at the experimental draping stage, and here the design and composition are being worked out. The Option 2 combination seems to work best, and after working with the drape of the *obi*, a balanced proportion has been reached.

Ornamentation for Communication

Ornamentation, whether a two-dimensional application or three-dimensional embellishment, will be included in both the Minuet Dancer and the Beaumarchais costumes, as it is important to the late eighteenth-century aesthetic. Also the director, Peter Wing Healey, believes that ornamentation communicates on many levels. In theater, it serves to draw the audience in, opening up the energy in a design and creating an emotional connection between actor and audience.

Base pieces: bustier, pant (trouser), and kimono combination.

Option 1, adding a pink lantern-shaped skirt and tulle underskirt.

Option 2, with white pleated skirt and pink bubble skirt.

Back view with *obi* flourish.

Left: Working on the half-scale form is a design development tool, so while working on the compositions, some rough sketches were done to start experimenting with how the final Minuet Dancer costume might look, and what embellishments might be used.

EXERCISE 2:
Experimental Draping

At this stage in the design development, experimental draping was done to finalize fabrics and trims. The sequential flow of color tones (set up on page 194) will help to amplify the story arc. Carefully consider your color choices for the actors individually and as part of the ensemble, noting which actors appear on stage together. It may be helpful to list the emotional qualities of the colors to see how they correspond with the personalities of the characters. For example:

- Sybilla: Earth tones—rusts, browns, greens— because she is close to nature, of the earth; green is balance; she is intuitive, a nature witch.
- Minuet Dancer: Pink and white: ingénue colors; pink is love and affection, the white, youth and innocence. She dances freely in between the characters, connecting them, lyricizing the moments.
- Beaumarchais: Blue, silver, cream, perfect for his dream sequence. The blue connects with dream/ spirit and the silver is brightness of mind, pointing to him as the intellectual of the group.

For the experimental draping of the Minuet Dancer costume
- The goal was to find the right composition of pinks and whites.
- The "pant" was mocked up in the two colors first, and then the bubble skirt over them.
- The bustier and kimono fabrics were pinned on from the back.

For the experimental draping of the Beaumarchais costume
- The pant fabric was pinned at the waist with a deep inverted pleat to imitate the look of the *hakama* pattern.
- The brocade *obi* was then pinned at the waist.
- The faux brocade was tested for the "lapels."

Top: Holding up a white board to cover half the drape made it easier to visualize the combinations. The two pinks (skirt and bustier) blend well, and the pant fades toward a pale skin tone, giving the dancer a little more height.

Right: Various laces were pinned on to see which shades of ivory best complemented the gray of the hemp/silk pant and the silver of the *obi*.

Inset (right): Promotional photos were needed for the opera, so an experimental drape was done of the Ghost of Benjamin Franklin. Draped on a model, using an existing kimono and *obi*, a *kataginu* mock-up was created, and various fabrics and laces collaged together.

196

Experimental draping for the "Ghost" drapes

In Act I, the opera singers are traveling from New York to Philadelphia by train. The train crashes and all are killed. They reappear as ghosts. Since there is no time for a costume change, fabric will be draped over their costumes to indicate their now otherworldly status. Here, various fabrics are being experimentally draped to test for the degree of sheerness over the costumes. Test as may fabrics as necessary to find one that looks right. If it is a stage costume, it would be helpful to test on the stage with the lighting, which may change the look.

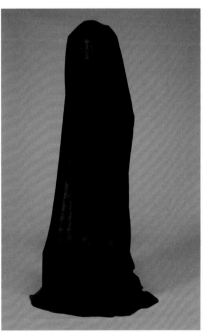

The silk marquisette is fairly sheer and has an airy look, but may not be ghostly enough.

Here, the chiffon was pinned over the hat with gathers to add volume. This creates a very different look, with lots of vertical lines developing. This could be interesting, since the scene takes place in a forest and the set has trees that would echo these lines, enabling the figures to harmonize with the background.

This polyester georgette is light and thin, but opaque. It is too dark to use.

EXERCISE 3:
Improvisational Draping

A very useful purpose of improvisational draping is working out details of a garment that are difficult to sketch and simply need be done on the form. Here, it is being used to develop designs for the back of the Beaumarchais kimono.

Beaumarchais kimono

A traditional Japanese *obi* usually has a large bow or closure in the back, but rather than be so literal, I wanted something more unusual, which might add a reference to the late eighteenth-century look.

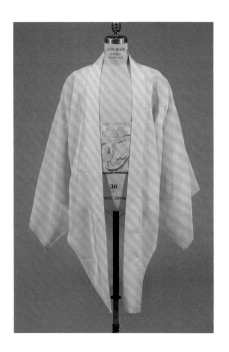

Step 1

- Starting with the basic kimono, the project is to come up with a back costume that references the late eighteenth-century look.

- The first step is to pull the fabric up in the back to reference the period's lower in front/higher at the back angle. Note the side view and the new angle formed by pulling up the back.

- Drape the fabric into a cascade at the center back, which also is a reference to the historical period we are aiming for.

Step 2

- Here the back has been pulled up into the cascade.

- An *obi* has been created from muslin.

- It seems quite large, which could work, but it also looks a bit too feminine, with the small bow finish.

Step 3

- A second *obi* choice with a vertical bow flourish works better, because its clean, simple lines contrast well with the busy cascade and sleeve drape.

Note: When preparing to build the *obi*, study authentic Japanese *obi* to see how they are traditionally cut and sewn. For authenticity, incorporate some of these methods if the budget allows.

Design Development: Sybilla Forest Spirit

Step 1
Sybilla, color and texture direction.

Step 2
Experimentally draping fabrics on the form.

Stages of costume design: final design illustrations

At this stage of the Costume design process, the inspiration boards have been reviewed with the director, the character boards are done, fabrics and colors selected. Draping on the half-scale form, as well as experimental and improvisational draping exercises, has helped with design development. Next the final illustrations will be done, then handed off to the construction team to draw out the flat sketches and begin the plans to build the costumes.

Step 3
Design sketch.

Step 4
Flat sketch with petticoat detail.

Step 5
Draping the petticoats.

Step 6
Sybilla: Final costume.

PROJECT 1:
The Minuet Dancer Costume

The costume has a mix of elements which create the Japanese Noh Theater influence, and the late eighteenth-century looks. As it is a dream sequence, the layers have varying degrees of sheerness, which will make it challenging to execute well. It needs to have the richness of a 1776 court ensemble, and yet the exaggerated simplicity of the Noh.

Final illustrations and flat sketch blueprints

Once the design development exercises have been done, the information gained from the experimental, improvisational, and half-scale draping exercises can be used to sketch multiple designs for the costumes. Before choosing the final design, review The Ten Principles of Good Design (page 17) and relate them to costume design:

The finished illustration:

Before completing your final illustration, check with the director or actors about any updates in quick changes, or movement restrictions that may have developed in rehearsal. Remember that these illustrations should be scaled to the actors proportions, so have photos of them on hand.

Minuet Dancer illustration by Barbra Araujo for *The Spell of Tradition*.

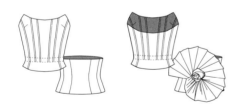

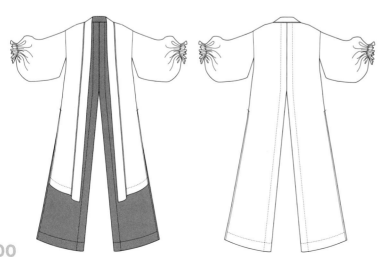

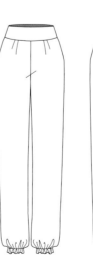

Preparation
- Meet with the actors and take measurements.
- Dress forms: customize to fit actors' sizes and postures.
- Prepare muslin and support materials.

Drape the base costume and/or rehearsal pieces
- Cut and sew the muslin fitting toiles.
- Mark and true the drape, use the muslin drape as a pattern, or transfer to paper.

Drape consecutive/overpieces (on top of the existing ones)
- Cut and sew the muslin fitting toiles.

- Mark and true the drape, use the muslin drape as a pattern, or transfer to paper.

Fitting the muslin toiles
- Notes from actors regarding mobility and fast changes.
- Do corrections to pattern.

Final design fabric fitting
- Cut and sew final design fabric garments

Assessment
Self-assess the costume first on the dress form, and review The Ten Principles of Good Design (page 17).

Preparation

Meet with the actors and take measurements:
- Note idiosyncrasies and/or posture issues.
- Discuss movements, range of lift, fast changes.
- Try on reference garments to familiarize the actor with the costume scale and ergonomic concept.
- Determine what rehearsal pieces will be needed.

Muslin preparation:
- Choose the muslin that is most similar to the final design fabric.
- Map out the muslin preparation diagrams.
- Tear, block, and press the muslin, and mark the grainlines.

Dress form preparation:
- Select the dress form closest in size to the actor, pad up where necessary.
- Add stuffed arm and a head form if possible to help with proportional issues.

Drape the base costume and/ or rehearsal pieces

The base pieces are: bustier, dance pant (trousers), and an *obi*. After the fit of these are perfected, and the dance pant tested for mobility, I will add a (purchased or rented) kimono for her to work with. Different lengths and volumes will be tested, observing them in motion; also giving the dancer an opportunity to rehearse in them. Accessories or props, especially ones that will be tricky to work with, may be necessary to supply for rehearsal. Shoes are also important to give the actor the correct posture and silhouette.

Above: The fan for the Minuet Dancer was created early in the process so that the actor could work with it during rehearsals.

Below: The final design ballet shoes will be important for the performer to rehearse in as she has many complex dance steps to execute.

201

Corset: is worn as an undergarment for support, and also to shape the silhouette. The classic version is boned and snug fitting, often with lacing.

Bustier: a term often used interchangeably with a corset, because it is also snug-fitting, and uses boning for support. It is, however, considered more as a decorative outergarment. First popularized in the mid-twentieth century as lingerie, it then became fashionable as outerwear, often made with silks and brocades and the addition of various embellishments.

Foundations: are the basis for other garments, often for heavy, voluminous garments such as eveningwear. They are intended to be worn as an underlayer to which other fabrics can be stitched. Most commonly made of a medium-weight cotton or linen, they are also sometimes made of a fine silk mesh, especially for bridal.

Silk mesh foundation: Note boning on seams and petersham ribbon at waist.

Draping the bustier

The bustier will be made using the block-to-drape method. The pattern will be adjusted to the measurements of the actor, and new style lines draped for the upper and lower edges.

Shown here: a muslin of a foundation block that will work well for this design. Although the pattern has a center front seam, this one has been cut on the fold, giving it a flatter front that will go well with the Japanese Noh influence.

First, calculate how much to add or subtract from the pattern pieces to fit the actor. Create a chart adapted from the one below to record the measurements of the block pattern pieces, the corresponding measurements of the actor, then noting the pattern dimensions to be changed.

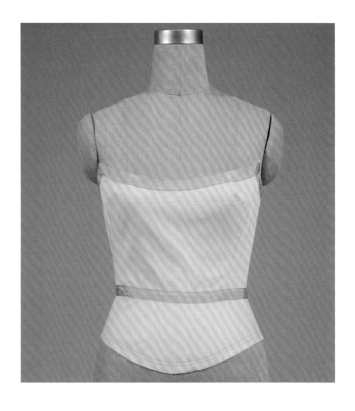

Pattern measurement conversion chart

	Measurements		Adjustments			
	Pattern	Body	–	–	Notes	Target Measurement
Bust						
Underbust						
Rib cage						
Bust apex to waist						
Waist						

For our Minuet Dancer, we need to add only a small amount of extra fabric beyond the pattern edges, as the actor is quite close to the measurements of the block.

Estimate how much muslin will be needed for the bustier drape by doing a layout of the pattern block. Leave extra in between the pieces to allow for what you may need to add. It will be draped as a half muslin as it is mirror image.

Prepare the muslin, and mark the lengthgrains on the muslin to correspond with the grainlines on the pattern pieces. One crossgrain per piece will suffice.
- Align the pattern pieces onto the prepared muslin, matching length and crossgrains.
- Trace the block on to the muslin.
- Refer to the actor's measurements and mark any adjustments to the size
- Note here the extra muslin being added to the side seams from the underbust area to the high hip to allow for the larger measurements of the actor in those areas.

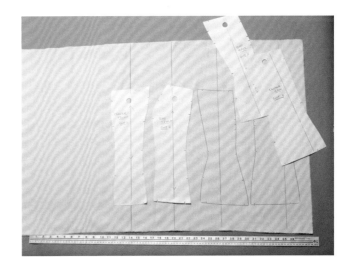

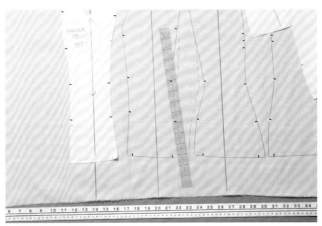

Drape the bustier, and continue by marking and truing the drape. Re-pin to check your work, then enter any corrections onto the pattern and prepare a toile for fitting on the actor. It will be helpful to add the boning and closure before the fitting to help with accuracy. At the fitting, secure a ribbon around the waist to confirm the distance between bust point and waist.

Shown here is the bustier in the base fabric, ready for fitting and rehearsal.

Note the long darts that have been added in the front section. Because the bustier was cut without a center front seam, and because the actor was quite narrow in the rib cage, it needed a closer fit in the front. Adding darts wherever necessary for a better fit is fine when the underlayer will not be seen. In this case, it will be covered with a stretch paillette covered fabric, which will smooth nicely over the boning and fitting seams.

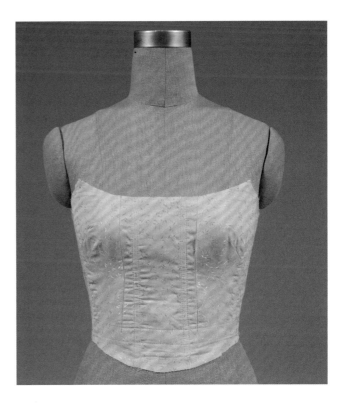

Draping the Dance Pant

The look of this pant is light and ethereal. It needs to be slim-fitting; there is a lot going on in the costume and it needs to recede. It will be lightweight silk mesh, cut on the bias, which will give a close fit and also provide plenty of movement.

The bias grainlines are marked with a double line, but here, on this lightweight muslin or mesh, it may be easier to thread trace the grainlines.

Draping from a flat sketch

It's important to continually check the flat sketch during the draping process, but allow yourself some artistic license so that you can move seams or adjust proportions as needed.

Flats sketches to drape from may be far less detailed than a flats for technical design, such as those done for overseas production. There, all seaming and construction details must be spelled out exactly, with design details such a plackets and pockets drawn accurately to scale.

Calico Preparation for Dance Pant

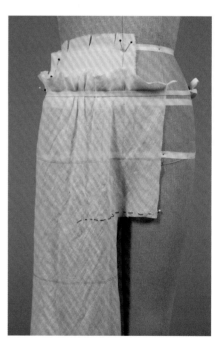

50" (127 cm)

45" (114.5 cm)

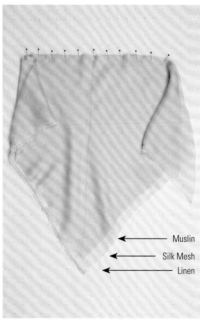

← Muslin
← Silk Mesh
← Linen

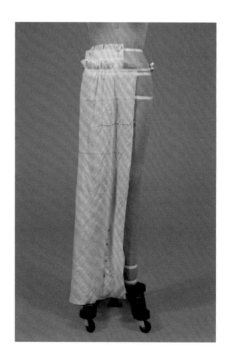

Step 1

- The muslin for draping should be as close as possible to the final design fabric. Because it will be cut on the bias, it will stretch and hang a certain amount.
- Shown here: testing a muslin option to see how much it will drop when draping.
- Calculate mathematically how to adjust the pattern after the drape.

Step 2

- Drape the yoke, starting by aligning the center front of the yoke piece with the center front of the form.
- Drape the pant front by setting the bias grainlines vertically and wrapping toward the center back.
- Use elastic to hold the piece in place, and adjust the gathers. Pin the inseam, beginning at knee level. Estimate the ankle width and pin the inseam down to the ankle.

Step 3

- Slash horizontally, estimating the crotch depth.
- This fabric has been thread-traced using a measurement from the actor.
- Pin the inseam up to the crotch.

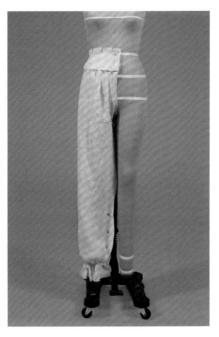
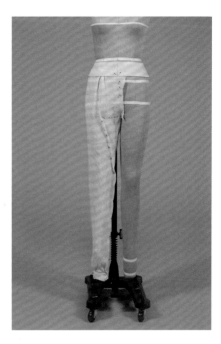

Step 4

- Repeat for the back, trimming the excess fabric from the center back.
- Pin the inseam up to the crotch.

Step 5

- Tie elastic around the ankle to check the length and width.
- Turn the yoke side seams front over back, lower edge to inside.

Step 6

- Mark and true the yoke and pant and re-cut (cut yoke as full piece)
  - Refer to the Checklist for Marking the Drape and Truing Fundamentals (page 74).
- Re-pin the trued pant onto the form to check
- Corrections: The gathers are moved away from the center front, and the pant leg is narrowed slightly.

Step 7

- Cutting the pant leg in one piece means that all corrections must come from the inseam, rather than having a side seam to adjust as well.
- Here, a long diagonal dart has been pinned to take in the pant leg.
- For this correction on using this dart to reduce the size of the pant, see page 92.

Step 8

- Complete the above correction on the dance pant pattern.
- Correct for the difference between the muslin and the final design fabric. (See Step 1, opposite, testing for stretch.)
  - Calculate how much length to remove in the pant legs.
  - Slash and close the pattern half the amount above the knee and half below.
- Cut and sew the pant, and prepare the toile for a fitting or rehearsal.

Engineering the pleated skirt

Preparing a pleated skirt requires working closely with your artisans. Eddie Moya at Park Pleating studied my sketches, showed samples, then recommended a "graduated accordion style" pleat. I provided a rough skirt length and asked them to produce a sample section to check on the actor during the muslin fitting for length, and for the proportion of the pleats.

A variety of pleating samples done by Park Pleating helped to visualize the right type of pleating for the skirt.

Draping the *obi*

The *obi* is a traditional Japanese belt that usually fastens in the back. Here, the flat surface of the *obi* will give a reference to the Japanese Noh tradition. Because the *obi* drape is improvisational, just estimate how much fabric you think you would like to see on the back of her kimono, and start there. Although you don't know the final shape yet, try visualize the right volume of fabric to be seen here.

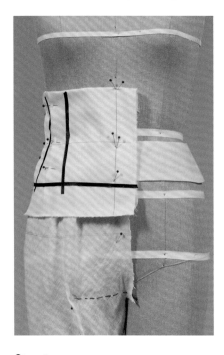

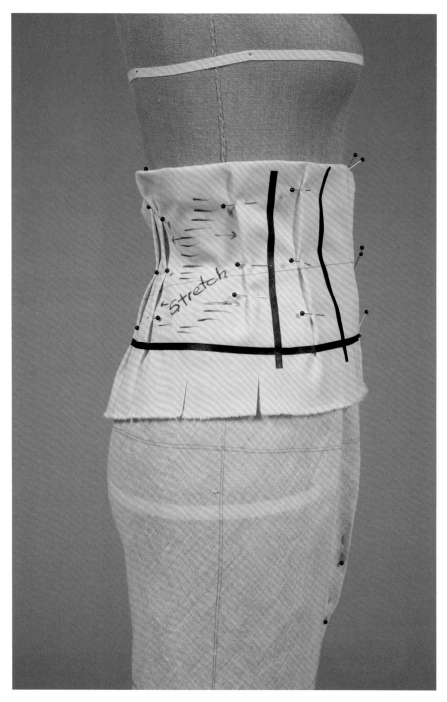

Step 1

- Align the center front of the muslin with the center front of the form.
- Smooth all the way to the center back.
- Create a dart at the front and back princesslines.

Step 2

- Tape an area on the side for stretch. Since this is a dance costume, it will look like a flat *obi*, but have shape and stretch.
- Tape the lower edge and the top edge (not shown).
- Turn under the top and lower edges.

Step 3

- Mark and true up the muslin, then transfer to a pattern
- Cut, sew, and prepare the *obi* for the fitting.

"With fit and movement, there is a huge difference between the needs of a Martha Graham dancer where the focus is on the body, and an opera singer who needs room to breathe."

Peter Wing Healey, founder, artistic director, and president of the Mesopotamian Opera, Los Angeles, California

Draping/drafting the kimono

The Minuet Dancer kimono will be created in the same way as Pocono's kimono (see diagram on page 136.) The final design fabric will be experimentally draped on the dress form to arrive at a volume, notes will be taken from the half-scale form drape, (see page 195) and a new technical sketch done, then a pattern will be created from that information. A muslin toile will be cut from that pattern and prepared for a fitting.

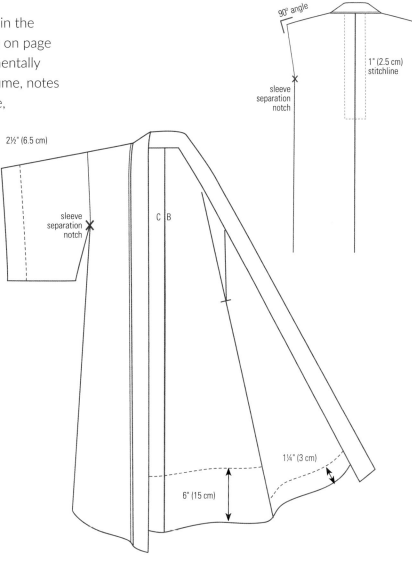

2½" (6.5 cm)

sleeve separation notch

90° angle

1" (2.5 cm) stitchline

sleeve separation notch

C B

1¼" (3 cm)

6" (15 cm)

Costume Fitting Guidelines (see also Conducting a Professional Fitting page 144)

- Review the original notes from the director, the characters' "story," and your own goals for the costume so that you are clear on points you are looking for.
- Hold the original costume inspiration in your mind and keep the illustration close at hand.
- Take photographs and have a note taker assist you (or use your phone).
- Include all accessories and props in your analysis, reviewing proportion and functionality before the fitting with the actors.
- Have extra hat and shoe size choices if possible.
- First fit all pieces of the ensemble on the forms to save valuable time with the performer. Review the proportions, checking them against the illustration and flat sketches.
- Make any obvious corrections at this point.

- Fit each garment onto the actor, pinning corrections as you go, until together as an ensemble.
- Give the actor time to get comfortable in their costume, and make sure there is an adequate mirror for them to see what they look like.
- View the costume from different angles, and at a distance; observe how it moves.
- Check with the actor about any special movements, fast changes, or concerns about mobility.
- Mark all corrections carefully before removing any pins; transfer the corrections to the patterns.

Fitting the muslin toiles

Fitting the muslin toiles gives the pattern drafter a chance to see how the pattern is working and check closures and seaming, and gives the designer a first look at how all the pieces are working together.

- The bustier in the base fabric and the muslin dance pant are tried on the Minuet Dancer actor.
- Here, the pant is being tested for freedom of movement.

- The pant is too long.
- A very quick way to shorten a pant is not to shorten it at the hem, but to take a tuck somewhere else on the pant.
- Here, a 1½" (3.8 cm) tuck is pinned, which will be taken off the length of the pant later.

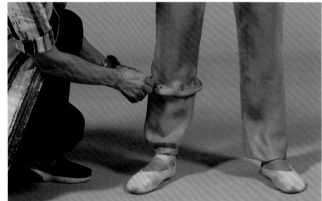

- The pleats are well proportioned, but the skirt will be made 2" (5 cm) shorter.
- The kimono is checked for movement.
- The *obi* is checked for proportion.
- The pleating artisans have supplied a panel of trial pleating which has been stitched onto a length of grosgrain ribbon for easy fitting.

Assessment from the fitting:
- The pant will be shortened.
- The *obi* will be narrowed and balanced, because it looks heavy on the left side.
- The sleeves will be lengthened.
- The kimono and neckband need 6" (15 cm) more length.
- The skirt will be shortened.
- The *obi* flourish will be reduced in size.

The remaining pieces of the costume—the final pleated skirt, embellished overskirt, and wrist flounce pieces—can now be draped over the rehearsal/base costume, and prepared for the final fitting (not shown).

Final Design Fabric Fitting

Review the original notes from the director, the character's "story"; and your own goals for the costume.

Foremost in assessing a costume is whether it is helping to create the character. Be aware of what elements of the costume are crucial to that. Hold the original costume inspiration in your mind, and keep the illustration close at hand.

Assessment

- See Assessment Protocols (page 59).
- The Minuet Dancer fits the director's desired "brittle, almost fake" quality, delicate and slightly stiff, yet she conjures a world of complexity with the layers of sheerness, variety of textures, trims, and embellishments.
- The costume feels light, whimsical, and ethereal, perfect for the dream sequence. A chorus-like sprite, she connects the others through her dance, her soft pinks magnetic and drawing affection. The details of the costume support the feminine, harmonious look.
- Ergonomic Quality: Discuss with the actor whether the costume is comfortable and works to move in.

- Look at the costume individually and also analyze how it fits with the rest of the ensemble.
- Are the historical (late eighteenth century), or cultural (Japanese Noh Theater) references clear?
- Review the The Ten Essentials of Couture (page 21). Try tweaking the wristlets or position of the *obi*, the lengths of the two skirt sections, and observe how slight differences can change the tenor of the look
- Take photographs of the actor to compare to the illustration. They will be easier to analyze when both are in a two-dimensional format.

PROJECT 2:
The Beaumarchais Costume

Beaumarchais is an erudite intellectual in the Act II Dream Sequence. The costume will be a mix of styles: the proper late eighteenth-century gentleman with Japanese *Noh* theater style, referenced by the typical oversized, exaggerated look of that tradition. Break down the ensemble into the individual garments and accessories. Follow with flat sketches, to use as blueprints for the costume build.

Preparation
- Meet with the actor and take measurements.
- Discuss movements, range of lift, fast changes.
- Try on reference garments to familiarize the actor.
- Determine what rehearsal pieces will be needed.
- Gather any needed base pieces.

Muslin preparation:
- Choose the muslin that is most similar to the final design fabric.
- Map out the muslin preparation diagrams.
- Tear, block, and press the muslin, and mark the grainlines.

Dress form preparation:
- Select forms closest to the measurements of the actor.
- Pad up to match specs, marking with twill tape any areas needing special attention.

Beaumarchais illustration by Barbra Araujo for
The Spell of Tradition.

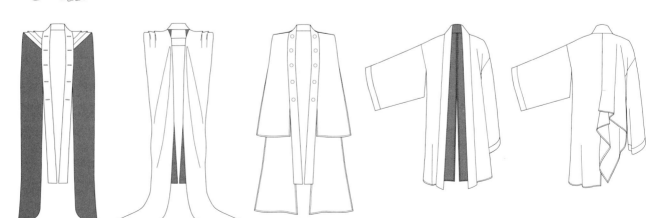

Draping the base/rehearsal pieces

The base pieces for Beaumarchais consist of a T-shirt (purchased), a *hakama* pant (trouser), and a kimono.

Drape/draft the rehearsal kimono

Give the actor an opportunity to work with a possibly unfamiliar and voluminous garment type by making a muslin rehearsasl kimono. The hand of the muslin should reflect your final fabric. This will also give the costume designer a chance to see the kimono in action on the actor and determine final volume and length. Study the kimono draft on page 136, draft a pattern, then cut and sew the muslin kimono.

Draping the *hakama* pant

Originating with the samurai, the *hakama* is a traditional wide leg Japanese pant. Research shows when fullness of the fabric needed to be out of the way—perhaps when men were riding or hunting—the fabric was pulled in at the lower leg. Interestingly, the wrapping then changes the silhouette of the traditional wide leg *hakama* to one that echoes the look of a late eighteenth-century pant.

Using the block-to-drape method, drape a *hakama* pant, adjusting it to the measurements of the actor, and adding an improvisational drape for the leg wrap. See Resources (page 248) for patterns or simply start with a large rectangle, following the draping steps.

 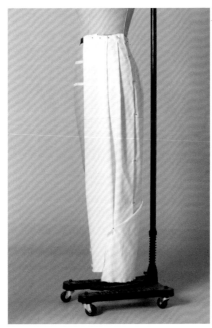

Step 1
- Trace the *hakama* block onto the prepared muslin, adjusting dimensions per size of the actor, or start with a simple rectangle, estimating fabric needed for drape.

Step 2
- Begin at the center front and drape the pleats of the *hakama*.

Step 3
- Pull the fabric around to the center back.
- Drape one inverted pleat at the center back.
- Adjust the balance at the waist from the side (as shown).

Step 4
- Mark and true the drape.
  - Refer to the Checklist for Marking the Drape and Truing Fundamentals (page 74).
- Use the muslin draped pant section as a pattern, or transfer it to a paper pattern.

Step 5
- Cut one pant leg only. (Before cutting the second leg, the pant will be tried on the actor.)
- Sew the pleats.
- Topstitch a length of grosgrain ribbon to the top of the pant to hold the pleats in place.

Step 1
- Fasten the ribbon around the actor's waist.
- Mark the waistline fastening point as reference for future closure.
- Check the length and hem up if necessary.

Step 2
- Draping improvisationally, work with the ankle tie piece to pull in the lower leg.
- Pin in some tucks to reduce volume if necessary for it to lay smoothly.
- Determine where it will need to be sewn to the pant, and where you want the ties to finish.

Step 3
- Check the kimono for width, length, and sleeve length.
- Check the center back neck opening, and adjust it if it is too wide or too narrow.

Improvisational Draping on a Live Actor or Model

In some cases, it is helpful to drape on a live person so one can observe the ergonomics of the design; how a certain element fits and moves, and needs to be synchronized with musculature. When this is necessary:
- Prepare the muslin in such a way that the work will go as quickly and smoothly as possible. Here, the pant section has been sewn onto a length of grosgrain so it easily ties at the waist.
- Supply whatever undergarments or shoes that might be needed (here, a T-shirt and leggings).
- Prepare a few different proportions of muslin ties to experiment with the leg wrap, and practice. beforehand on the dress form so that you have some ideas of how it might work.

Multiple Fittings with Actors

- It is always helpful to have multiple fittings with the actors, but not always possible.
- Take accurate measurements. The more precise you can be, the closer you can come to a good fit.
- Visualize the actor's body shape in the costume during the draping process.
- Be efficient, fast, and thorough during the fittings to maximize your time and theirs.

Assessment and corrections
- The pant fits well, but the lower leg wrap should be tighter.
- The pleats inside the wrap will be stitched down, to remove bulk.

- The three-quarter length of the kimono works well. The width will increase by 4" (10 cm) on each side, and the sleeve will be 5" (12.5 cm) longer.
- The proportion will be tested with the overpieces before the final design fabric is cut.

Building the overpieces

Now that the base rehearsal pieces are in work, refer to them to help you visualize the right proportions when building the kimono with lapels, the *kataginu*, *obi*, and necktie/jabot and wrist accessories.

Draping the *obi*

The *obi* is a traditional Japanese belt worn over a kimono, usually a straight rectangular piece with a back closure, sometimes in the form of a bow, or other shape.For the back flourish of this *obi*, refer to Improvisational Draping, Exercise 2 (page 62) and use the *obi* flourish draped there.

Draping the kimono

Working with the rehearsal kimono, determine final length and sleeve length after observing the kimono in rehearsal. Refer here again to Improvisational Draping, Exercise 2 (page 62) and see the kimono back drape, which gives the historical reference to the late eighteenth-century court style.

- Adjust the back cascade until it reaches a good balance, then pin to the center back seam.
- Carefully tailor tack the cascade on to the back of the kimono.

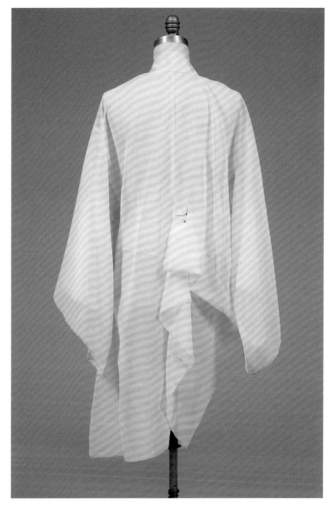

Truing the kimono pattern for the back cascade

Step 1

- Make sure the positions of the cascade tailor tacks are precise and accurate.
- Release the tailor tacks carefully at the center back cascade.

Step 2

- As they are released, make sure the tailor tacks are intact and clear.

Step 3

- Note the angle of the tacks to mark on the pattern, then use arrows for direction.
- Use carbon paper and a tracing wheel to mark the exact location.

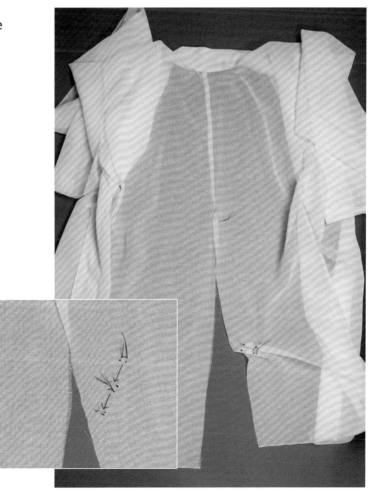

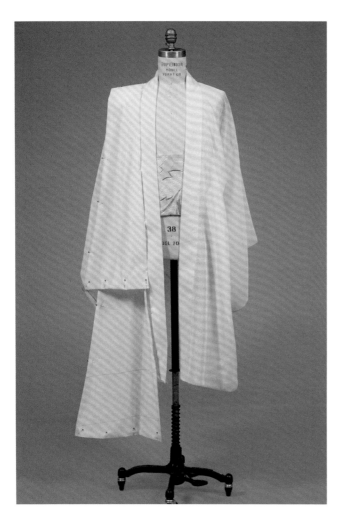

Draping the lapels

This element references the late eighteenth-century look and will be comprised of two different lengths of lapels.

Drape the under layer first, then use styling tape on both of them to study the proportions. Finish the neckline with a kimono band (a lengthgrain, rectangular piece.)

Creating your own fabrics

In costume design, surface design and three-dimensional embellishment techniques provide a rich opportunity to create your own fabrics. If a vintage fabric must be duplicated, the look of a late eighteenth-century frock coat produced, or a particularly detailed stage direction followed, there are numerous ways to achieve a desired result.

When we first started, there was a lot of hand-painting and embellishing; hand dyeing, airbrushing and specialty stitching. Later, when the company became larger, [the pieces] had to be mass-produced, so different production techniques had to be used. Printing and silkscreening replaced the hand-painting.

Dominique Lemieux, costume designer, on her work with Cirque du Soleil

Adding a two-dimensional or three-dimensional texture to the lapels

While draping the lapels, have a length of the final design fabric close at hand (as is always recommended). Practicing the skill of visualization, determine whether its print could be enhanced, punctuating the look of a late eighteenth-century brocade.

Experiment during draping with samples of hand-painting, block print, or screen print on top of the final fabric.

Before finalizing the embellishment to the print, refer back to your construction plan (see page 194) to align the project with your budget and resources.

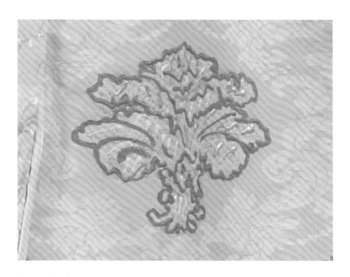

Lapel fabric being tested with handpainting in periwinkle and silver to enhance the baroque look of the pattern.

Draping the *kataginu*

The *kataginu* is a samurai piece that is both protective and dramatic. When draping it, make sure the pleats are even and precise, as the samurai's would be.

The muslin should be stiff enough to stand out dramatically. If necessary, fuse it, or add an underlining of buckrum or heavy organdy.

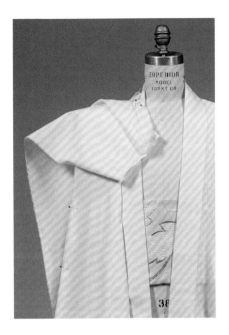

Step 1
- Set the shoulder pad for height.
- Start with the lengthgrain going over the shoulder.
- Start the tucks: they will be angled outward and tucked downward.
- Check the back length and balance.

Step 2
- Adjust the three tucks so that they are even.
- Angle the piece so that the shoulder stands out, as seen in the sketch.

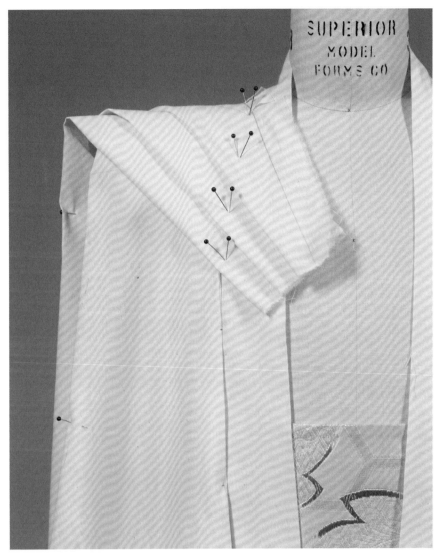

Step 3
- Drape a new band in the front to hold the *kataginu* in place.
- Check the button sizing; these will look as if they are holding it in place, so need to be substantial.

Step 4
- Mark and true all draped pieces.
- Cut and sew the muslin toiles and prepare for the fitting.

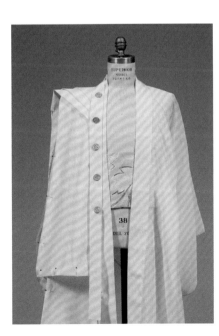

Prepare for the final fitting:

Before cutting and sewing the garments for
Beaumarchais in the final design fabrics, review
The Ten Essentials of Couture (page 21). There are
many complex sewing procedures to be done with
this costume. Details such as the back cascade of
the kimono need to be very carefully marked and
sewn exactly as draped. The fabrics are varying
weights and need individual attention and testing
for underlinings and support structures. The *kataginu*
needs the appropriate amount of lift. Make a plan
before you begin and be vigilant with your team to
make sure the details are properly constructed. After
the pieces are sewn, add accessories, and any other
elements, such as cuff pieces, necktie and jabot. See
Costume Fitting Guidelines (page 207).

Opposite: Study the two costumes together; they have the
same level of complexity and embellishment, which ties them
together. The pastel colors and sheer fabrics help to place
them within the Act II Dream Sequence. Visualize how they
will work with the rest of the cast. The costumes of all the
actors on the stage must be cohesive in the same way that a
fashion collection creates a visual collage..

Assessment

- See Assessment Protocols (page 59).
- Upon reviewing the original mood board and the
  illustration, the costume feels successful in helping
  the character to express dreamlike whimsy, while
  holding richly layered meaning and seriousness of
  intent. The age and handsome, intellectual look of
  the performer fits the costume well.
- The oversized shapes and proportions create an
  exaggerated physical and emotional impact. The
  kataginu is a dramatic finishing touch.
- The final fitting for a costume is to "crisp the lines,"
  according to Dominique Lemieux, Cirque du Soleil.
  The layered complexity needs all the details to
  coordinate perfectly; a "crisper" feel.
- The overall costume looks like it could use refining
  and more definition. The floral pattern could have
  lines integrating it with the background so it reads
  as a texture.
- The lace could be a bolder pattern so that it is
  more obviously a lace from the stage distance.
  Perhaps if the jabot had a trim on the edges it
  would have more definition.

- The Noh Theater mixed with the late eighteenth-
  century court elements:
  - The faux Baroque print on the lapels gives a
    flavor of the period, as well as the generous wrist
    lace and jabot.
  - The *obi*, *hakama* pant, and Japanese shoes add
    the Noh touches.
  - The shoulders of the *kataginu* look like they could
    be more exaggerated. A stronger support fabric
    may accomplish that.
  - The *obi* pattern is great, and shows up well.
  - The pant/lower wrap has a good ergonomic
    quality; it looks and moves well.
- Regarding grainlines working together: The main
  elements of the costume are strongly lengthgrain,
  and the kimono bands and pleats of the *hakama*
  reinforce those strong vertical lines, which in
  turn reinforce the strong masculine energy of
  the character.
- The flow of the gathered wristbands and the
  bias-cut flounced jabot add a contrasting softness
  to his costume.

CHAPTER 9

Draping the Heirloom Design

OBJECTIVES

Define a modern heirloom design.

–

Understand the qualities of authenticity.

–

Evaluate examples of upcycling clothing and textiles
to create heirloom designs.

Exercise: Heirloom Design Development
Apply improvisational draping techniques on the half-scale form
to determine the best use of an heirloom fabric with
a three-dimensional embellishment.

Project: Draping the Modern Heirloom Design
Construct a modern heirloom dress, incorporating
the use of two-dimensional surface design and
three-dimensional embellishments.

Embroidered embellishment by Maison Lesage for Karolyn Kiisel, 2019.

Draping the Heirloom Design

Heirloom-quality clothing is, in essence, clothing of elevated stature, intended to be kept for generations. Draping an heirloom design is similar to all draping projects, yet must incorporate more. It must integrate the Aims and Aspirations studied throughout this book.

The inspiration must start with a spark of desire to enlighten or uplift with clothing, so The Ten Principles of Good Design (page 17) must become second nature and The Ten Essentials of Couture (page 21), common practice. The goal is to raise the quality of the design: concept, drape, construction, and embellishment, to the highest level of artisanal excellence possible.

The heirloom design must have a sense of authenticity, meaning that it is inherently the right design in the right fabric for its intended use, the style of construction fits it, and the colors imbue a chosen psychological or emotional state of mind. The addition of trims or embellishments are decorative, but also add a symbolic note or a strengthening of the concept.

The following chapter explores creating the modern heirloom garment of today. It follows the process of creating a contemporary, original design, drawing on the various draping approaches covered in previous chapters to stimulate creative inspiration and originality and bringing the design to fruition with excellence in craftsmanship, and depth of meaning,

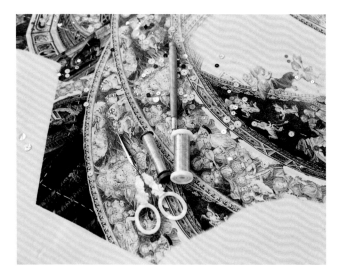

Preparing to start the embroidery: The thread-trace on the printed fabric indicates the edge of the tabard pattern.

The Qualities of an Heirloom Garment

Family heirlooms are handed down through generations. Our modern, contemporary heirloom garments are treasured for:
- A sense of authenticity
- Designs derived from timeless cuts of Eastern or Western culture
- Exhibiting artisanal excellence
- Incorporating the inherited; using antique textiles, needlework, or jewelry
- Offering an element of spirituality, symbolism, or radiating healing qualities
- Holding cultural or ancestral gravitas
- Manifesting superior decorative craftsmanship

Modern Heirloom Garments

Contemporary couture can be heirloom quality, as can traditional clothing from ancient times, when a precious piece of hand-woven cloth was sewn with pride in workmanship, and incorporated elements such as inherited precious stones, jewelry, or perhaps a surface design with symbolic meaning or spiritual significance.

"Modern" clothing may mean that it is simple, comfortable, and seasonless, or that it is made of the most current fabrics or construction methods. Or, it may mean the designer is forward-thinking, and following Slow Fashion ethics, striving to coax the best possible work out of the artisans while paying fair trade labor pricing, and using low carbon footprint textiles.

We tend to think of heirloom objects or garments as ones we have inherited, but the time has come to change that view. As designers, our ultimate aspiration should be to make the modern, heirloom-quality clothing of today, designing clothes that exist on their own merit, beyond trends that are sustainable and durable enough to last for generations

It means discovering and following our own unique creative paths, so that we create a legacy of beauty, originality, and authenticity; valued additions to a modern heirloom collection.

Lesage

The Saints Descend to Earth dress crafted in this chapter, is an original, modern, heirloom design created by myself and Hubert Barrère of Maison Lesage. Working with such a prestigious atelier ensures the artisanal excellence of the embellishment.

Maison Lesage, Paris's oldest embroidery atelier, was founded as Michonet in 1858. Its exquisite embroidery designs were highly sought-after among the fashion elite, including the father of haute couture, Charles Frederick Worth. In 1924 it was bought by Albert and Marie-Louise Lesage, and this family—embroiderers for generations—succeeded in continuing the legacy of the historic atelier. One of Lesage's techniques, Lunéville embroidery—which dates back to 1810, from the town of Lunéville, France—requires many years of training to reach Lesage's signature high level of expertise.

The artistic and skillful work of the Lesage family brought them much success. They became known for

Lesage for Saints Descend to Earth: beginning the embroidered overlay,

technical innovations, such as the vermicelle carré-style beading created for Madeleine Vionnet, and for designing avant-garde motifs, such as those of Elsa Schiaparelli, with whom they worked from the early 1930s. Francois Lesage, the son of Albert and Marie-Louise provided stunningly beautiful embroideries for all the great designers of Paris, including Yves Saint Laurent, who worked with them exclusively for over 40 years.

By the late 1970s, haute couture had reached a low point, and fashion houses worldwide were becoming more reliant on their ready-to-wear lines to survive. The many embroidery ateliers in Paris began to suffer, becoming an endangered species. In 2002 Chanel's chief designer, Karl Lagerfeld, wisely purchased Maison Lesage to ensure the precious and historic studio would remain.

Today the Lesage archives constitute the biggest collection of couture embroidery in the world, containing some 75,000 samples. Each year the company adds new and exciting designs to its rich heritage, contributing to the collections of such major design houses as Dior, Louis Vuitton, Valentino, Yves Saint Laurent, and, of course, Chanel.

The unique heritage of Maison Lesage is due to its visionary leadership, and their very skilled artisans. They hold a legacy of excellence in design and craftsmanship that will continue to co-create modern heirloom designs for the designers of the future.

Authenticity

Clothing that is "authentic" is the real thing, not an imitation. It is the chef's apron that is the right design, in the right fabric, constructed with the appropriate level of workmanship. It is the sturdy motorcycle jacket truly meant to be worn for speeding along a desert highway, not worn by a celebrity to a Hollywood party; the leather hunting jacket a man has worn in the Montana woods for decades before handing it down to his son, nicely softened and broken in; the perfectly cut, stylish 1950s' red brocade dress that Mother wore to her epic Christmas parties.

> We want the real thing; the authentic stuff, an honest object. The quintessential white cotton shirt, the perfect lace nightgown found in Florence, the well-cut jeans; fabrics and colors which fit the function and offer integrity. Objects with aura.
>
> *Li Edelkoort, fashion forecaster, View on Color, 20/20, 2005*

Authenticity: Classic, French white cotton nightgown, *c.*1940, still in use.

Li Edelkoort's description of "objects with aura" is an interesting notion. To recognize clothing with an aura, we have to slow down, feel the fabric and have an informed sense of what we are looking at. A designer producing modern heirloom clothing should consider what would make clothing radiate an aura that a consumer would notice.

Timeless cuts

Many traditional ethnic shapes have persisted in fashion for centuries because they work. The caftan (or kaftan) is a perfect example. It is an ancient form, and also a contemporary resort-wear staple. It is simple enough to be hand-stitched, provides a blank canvas for embellishment, is comfortable, and, as do most garments cut from simple rectangles, falls with an elegant and regal drape. Because of their timeless cuts, the sarong, dashiki, kimono, and toga have been beloved and worn for centuries.

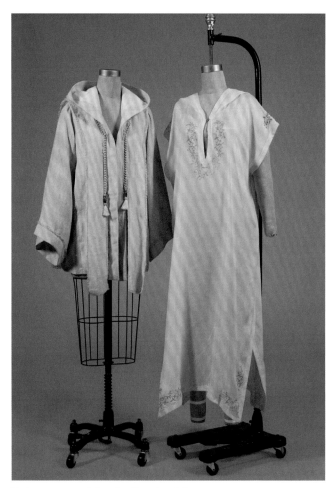

Timeless cuts are practical, comfortable, and regal. Hemp silk burnoose, and cotton caftan: Tara West Meditation-wear by Karolyn Kiisel.

Artisanal excellence

In ancient times, clothing that was handmade carefully with pride in workmanship was valued and treasured. Modern sewing and construction methods have become increasingly complex, and are also highly prized for their quality. Whatever the techniques used, heirloom clothing exhibits excellence in craft.

An element of spirituality or symbolism

A history of heirloom garments will show that many were worn by royalty or spiritual leaders. These were the people and institutions that could afford the best fabrics and the highest-quality workmanship.

The early fifteenth-century Ming emperor Yung Lo once had a vision of a black hat or crown that signified his spiritual position, and it is still worn today by the Karmapas of Tibet in the famed Black Crown ceremony. Italian designer Ludovica Amati designed clothing while spending time in the Peruvian rainforest with the Shipibo tribe, and used on her clothing an ancient print that is intended for healing purposes. There are many New Age designers who consider their work to have balancing or healing qualities, using colors that refine energies, align chakras, or gemstones that heighten awareness.

The embroidered appliqué seen here was done for a contemporary, ecclesiastical chasuble created for an Episcopal church in Lake Arrowhead, California. It was designed by Clifford+Challey, who specialize in unique embroideries that draw on environmental elements, personal interests, architectural details, etc of their clients. The colors and motifs here symbolize various elements of nature found in the area, such as the pine, dogwood, and lupines. The purple violet color signifies the Lenten season, a time for reflection and repentance.

Chasuble by Clifford+Chally for St. Richard's of Chichester, 2009.

Inherited clothing or textiles

In Russia, aristocratic, medieval clothing often had precious gemstones sewn onto them, following a cultural style of embellishment, as well creating a valuable heirloom for sons or daughters. Many people inherit their grandmother's linens, hand-embroidered or interestingly appliquéd. Using inherited textiles or clothing to re-purpose, adding gemstones or jewelry pieces to our designs, is creating new, modern heirloom garments.

Flowered embroideries were appliquéd to the cut fabric sections of this black faille coatdress before it was sewn. Removed from an antique silk jacket that was too ripped and frayed to be worn, the still intact embroidered sections were cut from the jacket, preserved carefully with fusible interlining, and sewn by hand on to the new coat.

Repurposing embellishments in this way is a worthy effort, and reinforces the values of slow fashion. Using inherited fabrics or clothing, adding gemstones or pieces or jewelry to our designs, is creating new, modern heirloom garments.

Above: Embroidered floral motifs from an antique Chinese jacket have been appliquéd onto this black faille coatdress by Karolyn Kiisel, 2011.

Above inset: To determine the placement before sewing, copies of the embroidery were printed out and placed on the muslin fitting toile until the final position was determined.

Superior decorative craftsmanship

The complex and exquisitely embellished embroideries of the Maisons Lesage and Lemarié are examples of extraordinary craftsmanship that elevates the work into the realm of art. The great breadth and richness of styles and techniques in the French tradition is due to them incorporating a mix of these modalities from around the world: those of Europe and also of Persia, India, China and the Middle East.

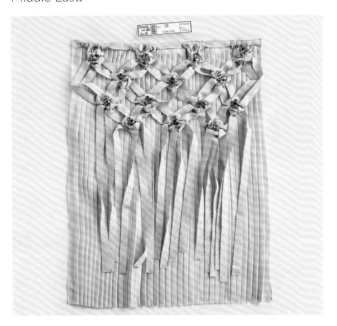

Cultural ancestral gravitas

Some of the heirloom clothing of indigenous tribes and ancient cultures has been passed on through generations. The Native Americans created countless examples of beautifully embellished clothing over centuries. When their culture was decimated over a short period of 100 years, the heirloom garments that were saved, assumed a cultural, ancestral gravitas, because they are significant visual records of a moment in time that is lost forever.

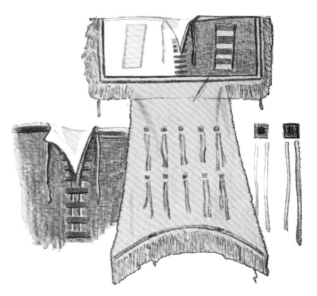

Left: Artisanal excellence exhibited in this Maison Lemarié embellishment for Chanel.
Above: North American native dress, illustrated by Max Karl Tilke c. 1850.

Hiroki Nakamura, visvim WMV

Hiroki Nakamura is a designer who is truly creating the modern, heirloom clothing of today. The worth of his clothing is evident in its depth, thoughtfulness, and high craft.

Mr. Nakamura uses repurposed textiles, but more importantly, updates them and makes them his own. He takes inspiration from heirloom garments (vintage Americana, Japanese EDO period garments, French workwear, Native American, and Finnish Sami culture clothing) and strives to create that blend their old-world charm and quality while adapting them to modern life.

He works directly with textile mills to analyze vintage fabrics and determine how to recreate them. Hiroki often works with artisans and craftsmen who keep alive practices and traditions that would otherwise go unnoticed outside of their worlds or perhaps go dormant without their care and knowledge.

Hiroki Nakamura hand-details garments made of his original Dry Denim® fabric in Tokyo in 2017. Using denim milled for visvim in Japan, he employs a complex and difficult to control technique which generates the authentic character and "dry" feel of vintage denims; those worn hard "under the strong west coast sun and washed over and over again with powerful American washing machines." The varied textures, colors, and finishing processes all work to give each of his visvim designs their transcendent and unique quality.

> We draw inspiration from the archives of human history, revisiting old knowledge and applying it to the world today. It is not our goal to simply reproduce what was done in the past. Our intention is to collaborate with the past and update things for our contemporary lifestyles by applying current industrial knowledge, to make something new that can withstand the test of time. At visvim we aspire to create "living traditions.
>
> *Hiroki Nakamura*

EXERCISE:
Heirloom Design Development

Advanced exercise: Find a piece of vintage fabric and follow the steps outlined here to create your own modern heirloom design. Experimentally draping with the fabric first will help to generate design ideas. Draping a muslin first on a half-scale form, as done here, helps use it to its best effect and with economy of cut.

Shibori and shells

Antique Shibori dyed cotton will be combined with delicate, ecru shells for this design, which is inspired by the Earth's Heritage board, and the concept of listening to nature. Creating clothing with "aura", taking the time to feel the rawness of the frayed fabric edges, and the smooth, delicate texture of the shells to figure out what type of design will best exhibit the interesting qualities of these two elements.

Heirloom clothing embraces slow fashion, slowing the pace of fashion as it is thoughtfully made, with the intention to grace the wearer with its gravitas, depth, and longevity. Therefore, a timeless silhouette, such as a tunic, will be best, and taking the time to hand-string the shells will be worthwhile.

Preparation
Inspiration
• This vintage fabric was purchased from a traveler long ago and its origin is unknown. The deep indigo and cream colors and its faded, fringed qualities make it unique. The shells were collected during beach walks in oceanside by the family home, and include some brought to me by a friend from New Zealand. The shells are delicate in appearance, but stronger than they look.
• I want to convey the feeling of warm sand under bare feet, a breeze flowing through the loosely fitted shibori, and senses filled with the ocean's salty, damp air. It should be worn with a sense of comfort, and of gratitude for the beauty of the materials.

Research
• This dyeing techniques dates to mid-eighth century Japan. It uses resist, sometimes wax, more often tying or clamping the fabric together to form patterns. It has been widely adopted by many cultures with a variety of interesting effects.

Fabric trims
• Start with experimental draping, and fabric evaluation to gain depth of understanding of this valuable fabric.
• Without cutting the fabric, drape it to get a feel for it's weight and hand.
• Study the volume to evaluate what designs will work for the amount of fabric available.
• Note variations in color, fading, or areas that must be avoided.
• This fabric was woven in long, narrow strips, which were then sewn together by hand. It is damaged in several places.

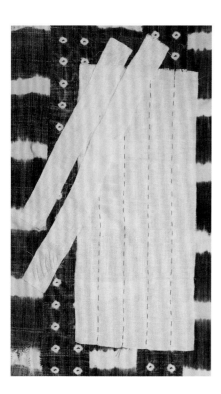

Here red stitching indicates the width of the hand-sewn strips, and shorter pieces indicate those with damages.

Design development:

To work out the design of the tunic top, duplicate the proportion of the fabric in muslin and drape it on the half-scale form:

- The muslin has been smudged with blue pastel chalk to indicate the two different shibori patterns—one with dots, one with stripes—to help keep track of the placement.
- Drape the tunic top on the half-scale form.
- The pieces seemed to fit together very naturally. There were just enough strips to create the body of the tunic, a sleeve, a belt, and a neckpiece. There was even enough fabric for a pocket and flap.

Create a flat sketch from the half-scale drape to work out exact placement of button, closures, etc.

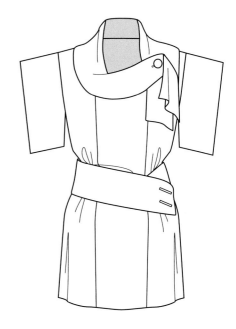

▮ The drape

Step 1

- Cut or unpick the strips of the final design fabric as per the stitched lines on the half-scale drape, to begin the full-scale drape.
- See pages 112, 117, 123 for the various methods of upscaling a half-scale drape. Because we have limited fabric to work with, simply re-draping full scale, using the numbered pieces on the half-scale drape as a guide will suffice.
- First, cut out a hole in the middle of the main panel for the neckline, then a half strip attached to each side and the side seams joined.
- Experiment with the belt to see which pattern looks best at the waist.

Step 2

- Fold the sleeve in half, with the fold at the top of the shoulder.
- Here it was pinned about halfway down the armhole, since it seemed to drape better if left separate from that point down.

Step 3

- Drape the collar with the opening on the left shoulder, overlapping the underneath part that draped from the center back to the left shoulder.
- Stitch the pocket and flap on to the belt, which fastens with a button.
- Add the shells:
  - If they need strengthening, paint them with a gel medium.
  - Make holes carefully using a fine drill bit.
  - Sew on the shells individually using a waxed cotton cord.

Assessment

- See Assessment Protocols (page 59).
- The tunic top feels like a timeless silhouette and cut, and yet has the practicality of the removable scarf collar piece and belt.
- The vision of the original inspiration or mood board has been realized; the design feels comfortable and modern, and reflects the Earth's Heritage sensibility.
- The shells with their soft, creamy color, and lovely sound are contributing to the emotional statement of the design.
- Take some photographs to study.
- Journal some notes.

Draping the Modern Heirloom Design

Advanced Exercise

Choose an inspiration from a historical period where ornamentation has some personal meaning, or was was used symbolically. Translate that expression into a contemporary design. Following the steps here as a guideline, create your own modern heirloom design.

Saints Descend to Earth Lesage embellished dress

The story of the inspiration for the Saints Descend to Earth dress starts with my visit to the richly historic and exquisitely detailed medieval cathedral in Siena, Italy. Inside, the frescoes of St. John the Baptist were protected by finely detailed, filigreed wrought-iron gates. Viewing the frescoes through the gates seemed like seeing something precious and mysterious through stained glass or a kaleidoscope. The saints in the frescoes felt both protected and protective.

Before beginning work on a project that you intend to be an heirloom piece, review the Ten Principles of Good Design (page 17). Aim for a design that is timeless; beyond trends. Think about the timeless templates discussed in Chapter 3 The Block-to-Drape Method. Integrate The Ten Essentials of Couture (page 21) to ensure that your work will achieve excellence in craftsmanship. Take all the proper steps in the muslin, preparation, the draping process, and in executing a thorough fitting with a muslin toile; it will all accrue toward a worthy result.

> The image of the iron-filigree gate protecting the frescoes feels like a symbol of the rich baroque preciousness of our historic embroideries being protected by the modern structure of Lesage.
>
> *Hubert Barrère, Creative Director, Lesage*

Opposite: The frescoes of St. John the Baptist, viewed through the iron filigreed protective gates.

Right: An image I used to study the color palette and line quality of the frescoes.

Below: The archive room at Lesage towers with floor to ceiling drawers; a treasure chest of embroidery samples dating as far back as the 1850s.

Preparation

Inspiration

A subsequent visit to the iconic Maison Lesage in Paris, and seeing their exquisitely detailed, beaded, and sequined embroideries, reminded me of what I had just seen at the Siena Cathedral. When I showed my photographs of the gated frescoes to the creative director of Lesage, Hubert Barrère, the inspiration for the dress was complete.

Hubert showed me more of the beautiful embroidery samples from the extensive Lesage archives, which he felt were the perfect mix of modern and baroque. Our concept for the design: digitally print the dress or coat with the image from Siena Cathedral, and then embellish that print with a Lesage embroidery. Finally, a three-dimensional printed piece will be layered on top to signify the wrought-iron gates.

Research

My research included:

- Studying images and photographs of the Siena Cathedral frescoes to determine which part of the image would work best as a print.
- Studying dress and coat shapes that exhibited a timeless quality.
- Studying the historic samples of Lesage.
- Educating myself in the techniques to be used so that I could communicate as well as possible with the Lesage team on the embellishment design.

Design development

The style of the dress or coat will be contemporary but classic, as it is intended to be an heirloom. It must have enough open space to enable the print and embellishment to be shown well.

A preliminary group of sketches were done to show to Hubert. The design is discussed as we continue to look at samples of embroideries and trims to crystallize ideas for the embellishment.

Fabric

After experimentally draping a variety of fabrics, the choices I felt would handle both the digital printing and embellishment best were a wool/silk blend and a four-ply silk crepe. Both are substantial with a heavy drape, yet are also pliable and luxurious feeling.

They will both be tested during the digital printing process to determine which choice will work best.

Above left: Sketches that have timeless template elements: bomber jacket, classic blouse, and trenchcoat.

Above right: Looking at embellishment samples with the lily and rosette filigree gate patterns.

Bottom: The design is finalized; the dress will be full-length, and more fitted than the sketch so it will be suitable for eveningwear. The sheer front panel will be omitted.

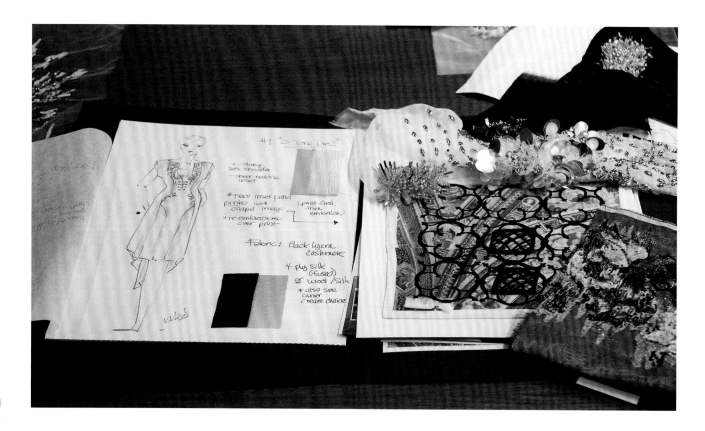

Flat sketches

After the fabric choice is made, the construction details can be confirmed, and a flat sketch done. The dress and tabard will be constructed separately, which will make it easier to send out for the embellishment. Stylistically, the tabard follows the fashion forward look of an overdress. Although the fabric drapes beautifully on the bias, the length grains will be set vertically, which will strengthen the stability of the dress and emphasize the vertical lines of the tabard.

Muslin preparation

It is always important to choose a muslin that behaves in a similar way to the final design fabric. Here I have chosen a cotton twill, which has a slightly heavier hand than the standard twill. I will wash it before draping, to bring it a little closer to the drape of the silk choices.

- Create a muslin preparation diagram.
- Tear, block, and press the muslin, and mark the appropriate grainlines.
- Dress form preparation: Set the stuffed arm on the form to aid in the off-shoulder drape.

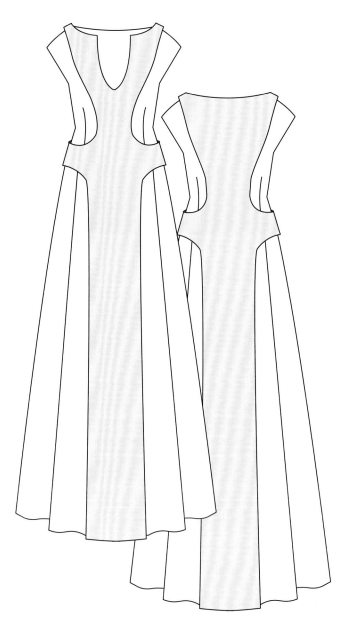

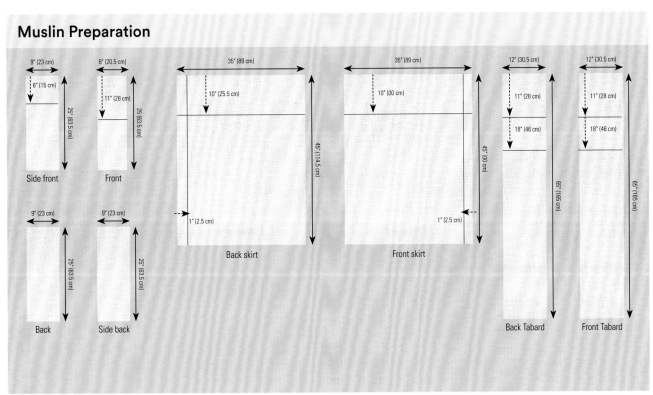

Muslin Preparation

Side front — 9" (23 cm), 6" (15 cm), 25" (63.5 cm)

Front — 8" (20.5 cm), 11" (28 cm), 25" (63.5 cm)

Back skirt — 35" (89 cm), 10" (25.5 cm), 45" (114.5 cm), 1" (2.5 cm)

Front skirt — 35" (89 cm), 10" (00 cm), 45" (00 cm), 1" (2.5 cm)

Back Tabard — 12" (30.5 cm), 11" (28 cm), 18" (46 cm), 65" (165 cm)

Front Tabard — 12" (30.5 cm), 11" (28 cm), 18" (46 cm), 65" (165 cm)

Back — 9" (23 cm), 25" (63.5 cm)

Side back — 9" (23 cm), 25" (63.5 cm)

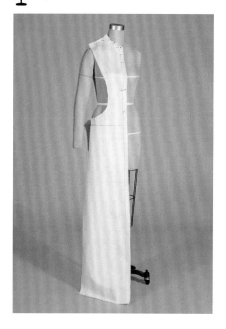 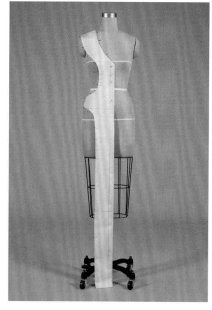 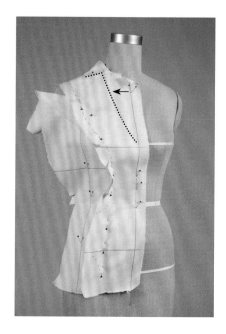

Step 1

- To design the tabard shape, align the center front grainline with the center front of the form, then trim and clip the neckline and shoulder area.
- Roughly tape or mark the upper tabard shape before cutting away the side front area, leaving a minimum of 1" (2.5 cm) seam allowance. Tape or mark the shape below the hipline, review from a distance, then trim away.
- Repeat for the back.

Step 2

- Remove from the form, then mark and true the tabard, so it can be used for the dress drape.
  Note: The shape can be fine-tuned later after the initial drape.
- Prepare the trued tabard muslin piece:
  - Machine baste along the seam allowances all edges.
  - Clip the curves (for a smoother turn), then press under at the stitch lines.
  - Hand-baste seam allowances to the inside.

Step 3

- With the center front bodice piece, the block-to-drape method will be used because the dress must be the same shape as the tabard.
- Trace the top part (high hipline to shoulder) of the trued front tabard shape on to a new piece of muslin to start the dress drape.

Note arrow: dotted line is the tabard pattern neckline marked onto muslin

- Pin, aligning center front grainline with center front of form, and set the shoulder as for the tabard
- Set the side front section with the center grainline dropping vertically.
- Clip the armhole and begin pinning the princessline seam. Check the ergonomics of the sketch: It should be fitted at the waist but have more room at the armhole.
- Trim the side seam area at the waist to help the section lie smoothly.

For the unusual fit of the sleeve drape with the low armhole, a reference garment is used. This Chloé sleeve, from the Spring/Summer 2018 collection, has the look that is needed here. Using this image as a reference will help target the desired sleeve shape.

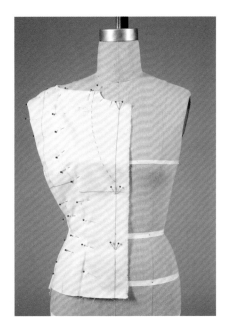

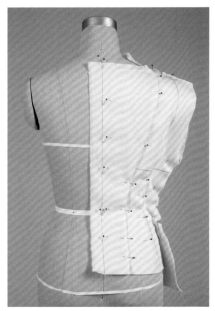

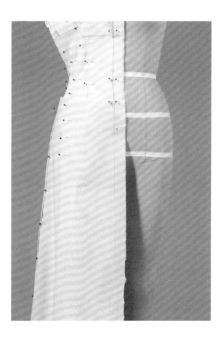

Step 4

- Pin the center front section over the side front section.
- Finalize the shoulder and armhole area.
- Pin a dart in the center of the side front panel if the waistline needs to be pulled in a little more tightly.

Step 5

- Repeat the block-to-drape step from the front by tracing the back tabard pattern on to the back muslin piece.
- Begin the back drape by pinning the center back and across the shoulders.
- Repeat as front Steps 3, 4, and join the side seams.

Step 6

- Drape the front skirt, folding a deep pleat at approximately the princessline area.
- Repeat for the back.
- Fold the side seam front over back.

Step 7

- Place the trued and prepared tabard muslin piece over the dress, aligning center front and backs.
- Check the tabard proportion and shape over the pinned dress.
- Assessment and adjustments:
  The tabard flares out slightly over the bust and would benefit from some shaping. This will be done during the construction process, but when marking, note the area approximately 2" (5 cm) above and below the bust apex. This should be eased in about ⅜" (1 cm) so that it will hug the bust area and give the tabard more shape. This construction detail could also be used on the top edge of it as it moves from the front toward the side so that it shapes over the high hip area.

Note: Leave the center front pinned all the way up to the neck seam of the form for as long as possible while draping. It will help to stabilize the bodice while working on the armhole and back pieces.

Marking and Truing

- Use the utmost care in marking the drape, making sure to mark areas of ease (as explained above) at the bust and high hip, and marking where the tabard matches the dress.
- True the pattern, then add seam allowances and re-pin onto the form
- Make additional corrections as necessary.
- Cut and sew the muslin fitting toile.

Correcting the fitting toile

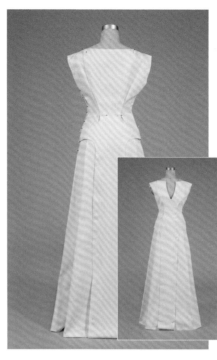

Step 1

- Place the dress fitting muslin on the form to be checked.
- Assess the overall look.
- Assess fit, depth of neckline, and armhole shape.
- Refer to the Chloé sleeve on page 232 to see if that same graceful shape has been achieved.

Step 2

- Pin the tabard over the dress, matching at the side seams and positioning it over the fitting muslin.
- Make sure that there is a smooth connection where the tabard pieces meet at the side seams.

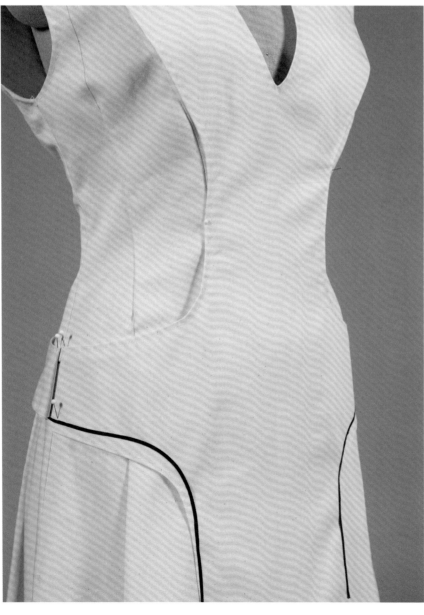

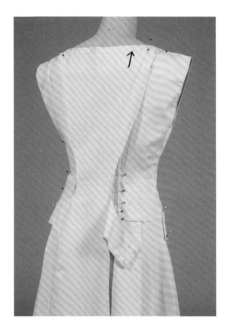

Step 3

- Assess the tabard shape and correct with tape if necessary.
- Here, the front tabard needs new line at the hip. Carving it a little further inward will result in a slightly more flattering line.

Step 4

- Take in the back at the princess panel seam for a slightly closer fit.
- Adjust the back tabard to match. Shown here, the back shoulder of the tabard being lifted and matched to the dress neckline. The pattern will be corrected to reflect that.

Digital Printing Steps

Print option A: hand-painted design.

Print option B: evolution technique print. Note: slightly blurry, embellishment to add definition.

Print option C: wasatch technique print. Note: like blurred effect, but colors a bit dark and monotone.

Print alternate 1: evolution technique print. Note: scale too large.

Print alternate 2: sublimation technique print. Note: print too dark.

Step 1:

- The next step is obtaining the necessary copyright permissions so that there is a digital file to work with. The print purchased is of the entire cathedral ceiling, but will give lots of choices for how to work with it for the printing of the dress tabard.
- Analyze it carefully, enlarging a few areas to study what areas of it will work best for the tabard shape.

Step 2

- A number of printing technologies are available. Send panels of the two fabric choices, the silk/wool and four-ply silk crepe, out for testing so that you can analyze which results work best on the two fabrics.
- Print option C, hand-painted sample: This quite different approach could work for a lighter, more painterly style.
- Print option B, evolution technique: Results in a slightly blurry effect. If the embellishment added the definition, it could be an interesting look
- Print option C, the wasatch technique: less color definition, a monotone look.
- Print alternate 1 shows checking color saturation on a larger scale of the evolution technique.

- Print alternate 2 is a sublimation technique and has been chosen as the technique to work with although it is noted that the colors here are slightly dark, and will need adjusting.

The ones on the four-ply silk crepe seem sharper, so that will be the fabric choice. The four-ply silk crepe must be treated with a coating to absorb the digital print, then after the printing will be washed. I have learned from experience that washing silk often results in interesting textures, so I felt confident this fabric would work well for this project.

Step 3

- Test on chosen fabric for scale and color tones until you are satisfied with the results.
- Continue testing the sublimation print, and submit "Color Reference chips" for the digital artists to use as a guide.
- Here, two different test prints were done for color tones.
- Test prints for fusing before printing.

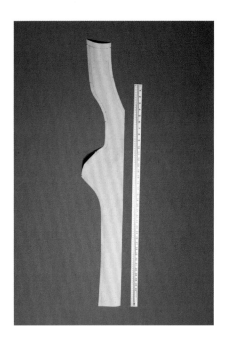

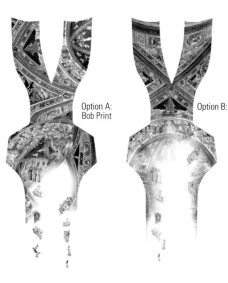

Option A:
Bob Print

Option B:

Step 4

- Prepare to print the fabric for the tabard piece.
- First the tabard pattern must be digitized so that the print can be engineered to fit exactly on the pattern.
- Place a ruler by the pattern to ensure the scale is correct.
- Scan the pattern.

Step 5

- Next, a digital file of a print design must be created for the tabard pattern piece from the copyright print. This is a time-consuming and important job because it must be engineered to fit perfectly on to the digitized pattern piece. Also, the general spirit of the print should be reflected in its positioning. Try several versions, both symmetrical and asymmetrical, before choosing the one that is right for the design.

Two options to choose from have been created for the tabard design, one symmetrical, and one asymmetrical.

The asymmetrical design has been chosen. Now, generous seam allowances will be added to the print design to allow for any inaccuracies in the printing of the fabric.

Saints Descend to Earth

As discussed in the Introduction regarding the Inspiration boards, it's good to use descriptive words to help define your work. At this point I decided to name the project Saints Descend to Earth. I love the way the print fades out as it moves down the tabard toward the ground. The saints are singled out; they drop lightly and slowly as feathers toward the Earth, as we hope they will do.

Step 6

- To test how the print will look on the tabard, a paper test of the chosen version is printed out on paper to check on the fitting muslin.
- Position the paper print on the fitting muslin.
- Pin gently at the shoulders and side seams to hold it in place.
- Note any adjustments that need to be made to the print design.

Step 7

- To reproduce the look of the filigree wrought-iron gates in the cathedral, two different graphics were pulled from the gate photo and have been printed on clear acetate to work with scale and position.
- One is a circular rosette pattern (shown here) and the other a pointed one, lily.

Note two different scales to check.

- Seen here is the lily pattern.
- Shown at neckline: segments of the wrought-iron gate to experiment with.

The chosen graphic and scale will be sent to Lesage for use in constructing the three-dimensional part of the embellishment.

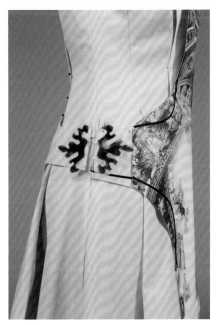

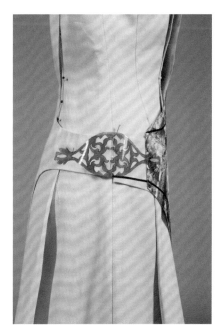

Step 8

- I thought another interesting element to the embellished dress would be to add custom-molded metal closures for the tabard—at either the neckline or hip-band closures.

- After considering the several options, I decided that because the dress was already fairly complex, it would be best to keep the three-dimensional treatment on the front only as the representation of the wrought-iron gates. Perhaps a metal closure would seem too literal.

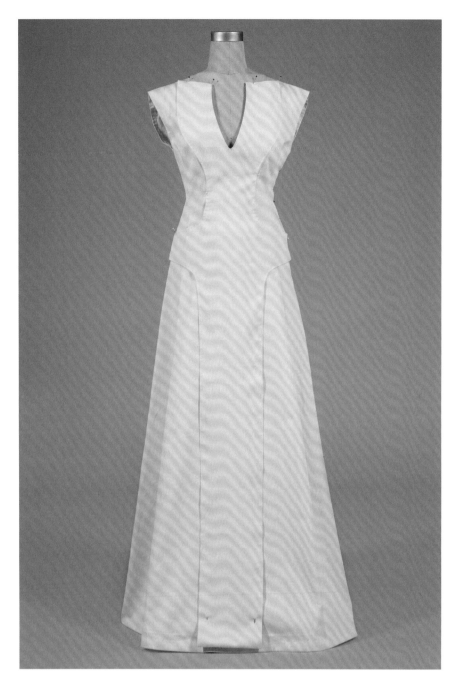

Step 9

- Cut panels of the fabric to send out for printing. Fuse the fabric pieces first for stability. The embellishment will add a considerable amount of weight, so the fabric will need some support.
- Mark the lines of the pattern on the fabric panels with a thread trace.
- Leave large seam allowances (at least 2"/5 cm) all the way around to allow for any printing imperfections that might necessitate shifting the piece on the fabric.

Step 10

- Save the printing firm's test pieces to send to Maison Lesage for doing an embellishment sample (proposition).
- Hubert will have a sample of the embellishment done so that we can then confer on any issues or additional ideas.
- Decisions and adjustments are then made:
  - Density of embellishment
  - Balance of sequins and beads
  - Color choices

Step 11

- Check the proposition on the fitting muslin.
- Send any necessary corrections or feedback to the supplier before they begin the work:
  - The direction given is that the embellishment should be heaviest at the shoulder and become gradually lighter towards the lower edge of the tabard.
  - The embellishment on the lower part should have a sense of "connecting" the saints falling. At the moment, with just the print, they look a little lonely, and could use a light touch of threads or beads to fill in.
  - The overlay should be open enough that the print and embellishment can be seen through the openings.
  - The filigree overlay should be most intense at the shoulders and disappear around the hip area.

Step 12

- The printed tabard piece is now sent to Maison Lesage for completion.

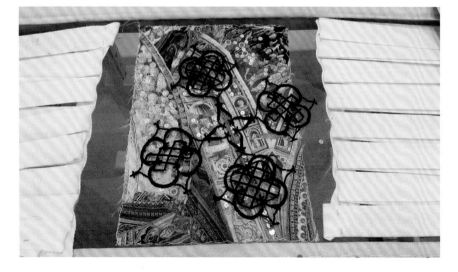

The sample proposition submitted by Lesage is pinned to the drape and studied for proportion, color, and intensity of embellishment, and spacing of the three-dimensional overlay.

Hubert Barrère and the primary artisan discuss Saints Descend to Earth details. The Lunéville technique (with hook) will be used, which is a specific type of tambour embroidery.

The embroidery and embellishment at Maison Lesage

The environment at the Lesage embroidery studio is one of precision; quiet formality. The craftspeople are highly skilled and well-trained, their surroundings are impeccable, and the feeling of pride in their work is palpable.

Now that the tabard panel is at Lesage, there are many steps to complete the project. One of the first is for Hubert and the primary embellishment designer to confer on the techniques and materials.

I will offer input into these decisions, but since they are the artisans who will be doing the work, I want to give them as much creative freedom as possible within the guidelines of the design.

First the sequin and beading pattern will be applied, following the look of the sample. When that is finished, the wrought-iron filigree overlay will be done.

Clockwise, from top left: The array of materials to be used is assembled at the embroidery table; gold metallic thread of the highest quality is used for the sequin work; gold mottled sequins, and smooth apple-green sequins.

The embroidery work begins on the print. The thread-trace line (note white stitchline on print) is the sew line of the pattern, so the beads and sequins will stop precisely at that line.

Following the lines of the print for the embroidered embellishment.

The level of detail in following the visuals of the print adds much depth and richness to the artistic statement.

The wrought-iron filigree overlay process

A scaled print-out of the rosette and lily pattern to be used. This design will be printed on a very light paper of the tabard pattern in preparation for the picking and chalking process.

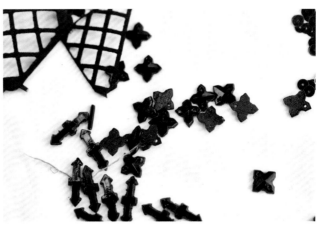

Materials for the overlay: black jet glass beads in fleur-de-lis shapes, and black three-dimensional printed cage pieces.

Picking and chalk-marking for the overlay process

The chalk and felts used in the marking process.

Tools used for the chalking-marking process.

The time-consuming picking work begins. Shown here, the work being done by a small electric machine. In the studio there is an interesting old hand-operated machine from a different era which must have been far more time-consuming to use.

The picking perforates tiny holes in the delicate paper, which in the next step will enable the chalk markings to pass through. The picking process took about 12 hours to complete for the front tabard piece.

With the weight holding it in place, the perforations in the paper enable the chalk to fall through and mark the netting under it.

The rosette and lily overlay pattern starts to emerge as the chalking progresses.

A fixative is applied over the chalked pattern.

The full pattern in the marked netting.

Here the paper is under the netting to show the pattern outlines.

The Lunéville technique of embroidery works the beaded embellishment from both sides of the fabric at the same time.

The Saints Descend to Earth tabard embellishment is completed within a week, and sent back to Los Angeles for the final construction of the dress and its tabard.

- The embroidered and embellished tabard arrives from Lesage. There was a hushed silence among my team when the embellished tabard was unwrapped at my studio.
- It is a very exciting moment to see the beautiful work.
- Note the hand-stitched shape of the tabard.

Cutting and sewing the dress

- The dress is ready to be cut and sewn.
- Wash the four-ply silk crepe for the dress pieces to remove the coating. The crepe weave will twist and shrink during washing, so it must be re-blocked into shape on a needle table.
- Fuse areas of the dress, as for the tabard, where needed for weight and support.

Hand embroidery, meticulous and exquisitely crafted, is awe-inspiring, but it is not about all the hours of sewing, or the technical expertise. It strikes a deeper chord, touches the soul in a way we cannot explain. Above all, ours is a profession of love and perfectionism, a demanding love. Every day we honor our imperious muse with our own hands. Like all tired lovers, we often rebel against the tyrannies of our mistress; it's a wonderful love story!

Hubert Barrère, Creative Director, Lesage

The workmanship is extraordinary, the artisans have created a beautiful piece of art.

Couture details

- Before finishing outer edges with silk piping, ease the tabard in the areas marked with pins, as was done in the drape to give shape over the bust and high hip.
- Sew the piping very carefully, watching for any embellishments in the sew line, which will have to be moved.

- Here, a layer of hymo and a soft lambswool have been stitched inside the tabard to give loft and support. It will also serve to soften any dimensional bumps on the inside lining of the dress.
- The seam allowance of the piping has been clipped and cross-stitched to the hymo, to help it to roll inward.

Assessment

- See Assessment Protocols (page 59).
- The original inspiration is represented well in the embellishment.
- The four-ply silk crepe has the desired luxuriousness, yet also the weight and stability to support the embellishment.
- Ergonomic quality: the fit has just enough ease to look form-fitting and sensual, yet also comfortable. The shape of the belt in the back is in just the right place.
- Construction quality: the couture details in the construction add to the overall success of the design.

Incorporating qualities of the modern, heirloom design:
- Authenticity = the "real thing." The dress is a good design for both the fabric and the embellishment. It was developed thoughtfully, its embellishments carefully considered and expertly done, and was constructed with the highest possible quality.

- Timeless cuts: The tabard design dates back to the Middle Ages, yet the concept of an overdress is appearing in contemporary collections. Thus, with the mix of old and new, it can be considered a timeless cut.
- Superior decorative craftsmanship: The artisanal excellence of Lesage under its skilled staff and director is of extremely high quality, and without reserve, can be called a work of art.
- An element of spirituality or symbolism: As Hubert articulated, the symbolic significance of the dress is that just as the wrought-iron gates of the Siena Cathedral protect the ancient frescoes, so Lesage's modern structure protects the ancient preciousness of its legacy.
- The spiritual side of the image of Saints Descend to Earth is a quiet wish for just that grace which we all need in our busy, modern lives, a way for our clothing to help make our world a better place.

Glossary

Avant-garde Ahead of the rest, the most advanced in any field, usually with experimental or unorthodox techniques

Baby hem A very delicate, narrow hem, twice turned and usually finished with a ⅛" to ¼" stitch.

Baste (tack) A loose stitch meant only to hold seams or hems in place before a final stitch is made.

Bias line The grainline that is at a 45-degree angle to the length- or crossgrains, resulting in a drape where the threads can open, give, and stretch.

Bolero A waist-length jacket.

Buckram A very stiff support textile, often used in millinery.

Bustier A corset-like garment that is intended to be worn as outerwear, usually with boning on the seams as support.

CAD (computer-aided design) An automatic pattern-making system that has pattern-making and grading software.

Cascade A circular cut piece that when falling vertically, creates a flowing diagonal.

Classic style Aesthetically restrained, adhering to traditional forms and practical applications.

Contrast fabric A secondary fabric used in a design, usually less fabric than the main, "self" fabric.

Corset A support undergarment characterized by boning and lacing.

Cowl A length of fabric that has been adjusted inward to create extra fullness and folds in the center.

Crossgrain The weft thread of a fabric.

Crystal wash A type of dyeing technique that results in crisper edges than a standard ombré.

Ease The extra fabric that is purposefully left in the fit of a garment for comfort and also sometimes for style purposes.

Embellishment Any type of ornamentation that is added to a design.

Ergonomics The study of fit and movement.

Face The right side of a fabric.

Faggotting A specialty stitching technique that is characterized by a series of threads which hold two pieces of fabric together decoratively. Usually quite narrow, ¼".

Filament In fashion terms, a nylon thread that is inserted into a hem to make it stand out.

Flat sketches Two-dimensional sketches used to chart proportions, seam positions, and construction details.

Flounce A straight or circular piece, usually sewn on to the edge of a skirt or blouse, but can also be placed on a diagonal.

Foundation A boned corset that is meant to be sewn into the inner construction of a garment, such as evening wear.

French seam A delicate seam finish made by first stitching two fabrics together at a seam, next trimming that seam allowance to a very narrow measurement, and then turning those narrowly cut seam allowances to the inside and stitching again to enclose the raw edges inside the second stitch line.

Fusible (interlining) A support fabric that has glue crystals which adhere to a fabric with heat.

Garment dyeing A dye technique that involves submerging an entire garment after it is sewn, rather than dyeing the fabric or cut pieces.

Gerber system A computer pattern-making system (see CAD).

Godet A triangular inset added for fullness or style usually at a hem.

Grainline The direction of the warp and weft threads. Warp is lengthgrain, and weft is crossgrain.

Hakama Wide leg, pleated pant of Japanese origin.

Heirloom A precious artifact handed down from generation to generation; in clothing, one that is meant to last indefinitely.

Horsehair braid A type of crinoline netting used as a support material, most often for hems, but also for hats, sleeve edges or wherever a specific shape is needed.

Ikebana The Japanese spiritual practice of flower arranging.

Inseam The seam that runs from crotch to hem on trousers.

Kamishimo Everyday formalwear worn by samurai warriors; this two piece outfit consists of the upper garment, the *kataginu*, which is tucked into the trousers, or *hakama*.

Kataginu Historically worn by the Japanese samurai, it is a vest-like garment with wide, wing-shaped shoulders, narrow front panels and a wide panel falling down the back. Currently worn as ceremonial costume by Japan's imperial family, or in kabuki theatre.

Lengthgrain The warp thread of a fabric.

Lettuce-leaf hem Reminiscent of the curling, twisting shape of the edges of lettuce leaves, this type of hem is formed by pulling slightly on a baby hem while stitching it, or inserting a filament into the hem which causes it to curl and roll.

Mock-up A trial technique used to show an example of how you want a finished product to look.

Mood The emotional state created by tone.

Muslin A plain weave cotton fabric made in a variety of weights, commonly used for draping and to construct fitting "toiles."

Nap (fabric) Velvets or corduroys are examples of fabrics with "nap," meaning there are raised fibers in the woven cloth which fall in a certain direction. In construction, a fabric with nap must have pieces that are cut in the same direction, or they will have a different type of shade or shine.

Obi A Japanese style of belt, usually very wide and stiff.

Ombré dyeing A classic dye technique of a gradual light to dark shading.

Origami The Japanese are of paper folding.

Ornamentation An addition to a fabric or garment—either two-dimensional with paint or printing, or three-dimensional with a treatment or embellishment.

Peignoir A light dressing gown or negligee.

Petersham ribbon A corded ribbon in varying widths of cotton, rayon, or viscose. It does not have the finishing edge thread of a grosgrain ribbon and so can be shaped with an iron, and has many uses in construction. It is characterized by a slightly uneven edge, sometimes called "mouse's teeth."

Planned obsolescence In fashion, clothing that is meant to wear out after a certain number of washings.

Princess seam/princessline The seam that runs approximately halfway between side seam and center front seam.

Romantic style Following the power of the instinctual and intuitive.

Sandwash A method of softening a fabric and changing the texture by washing it with gravel or any material that abrases the surface of the fabric.

Self-fabric The main fabric of a garment, the one that uses the most yardage.

Slow fashion A movement that addresses the ethical concerns of sustainability in the fashion industry.

Sublimation printing A method of printing fabric using heat and ink, transferring a design from paper onto fabric.

Tailor tacking Commonly used in tailoring and couture, they are hand-sewn threads used to mark darts or pattern lines when other, easier methods are unsuitable because of the delicacy or thickness of a fabric.

Tap pants Full cut shorts, usually with slits up the sides.

Tear-away A construction material that is pinned or basted onto a fabric to keep it from stretching during sewing. It is solid enough to hold during sewing, but light enough to then "tear-away" from the seam after stitching it.

Template Here, a timeless design that is standard and classic enough to be used as a block.

Thread tracing A light, widely spaced stitch similar to a hand-baste, used to mark a grainline, sew line, or other needed construction indications.

Toile (fitting sample) Traditionally made of muslin, the fitting toile is used to check the fit and style of a design, ideally on a model, but sometimes on a dress form. It is used to check for corrections in the truing up process, which can then be transferred to the pattern before the final garment is cut and sewn.

Tone Level and pitch of intensity, which creates the mood.

Topstitching Stitching that is done after the joining stitches either to hold a seam in one direction or help to flatten a seam, or which is added as a decorative accent.

Treatment A type of ornamentation

added to a garment that is usually made of the self-fabric trench coat.

Underlining (flat-lining) A support fabric that protects an outer fabric from damage at stress points, hides construction details, and sometimes changes the hand of the fabric with extra weight or loft.

Underpress Pressing that is done during the construction process, such as pressing seams open or to one side.

Walk ("walking the seams") In pattern drafting, each seam must match the seam to which it is to be sewn. "Walking the seam" means to check that all the seams meant to be sewn together match in length.

Warp The lengthgrain thread of a fabric weave—usually, but not always, the stronger thread.

Weft The crossgrain thread of a fabric weave—usually, but not always, the weaker thread.

Yoke A section of a garment, such as the top part of a blouse or skirt which supports another, usually fuller section of fabric.

Videos

Scan these QR codes using your smartphone to view the videos in which Karolyn Kiisel demonstrates different draping techniques and skills.

Contents

Chapter 1: Experimental Draping
Getting to Know Your Fabrics

Chapter 2: Inspirational Draping
Upcycle Study
pages 68—70

Chapter 3: The Block-to-Drape Method
Block-to-Drape: the Tailored Jacket
pages 96—103

Chapter 4: Draping on the Half-Scale Form
Modernizing the Cut of a Tradition Ethnic Design
pages 110—13
(see also Chapter 2 video for example of draping on the half-scale form)

Chapter 5: Draping from an Illustration
Draping from a Costume Design
pages 133—36

Chapter 6: Draping with the Use of Two-Dimensional Surface Design
Ombré, Airbrushing and the Use of Novelty Airbrushing Techniques
page 152—53

Chapter 7: Draping with the Use of Three-Dimensional Embellishment
Embellishment Mock-Up Tests
pages 174—79

Chapter 8: Draping for Costume Design
The Minuet Dancer Costume
pages 200—09
(see also Chapter 5 video for example of draping for costume design)

Chapter 9: Draping the Heirloom Design
Heirloom Design Development
pages 225—27

Credits
Featuring **Karolyn Kiisel**
Directed and edited by **Kyle Titterton**

Production coordination by **Kirsten Taylor**
Additional art direction by **Claire Fraser and Kirsten Taylor**
Production assistance by **Linda Aguirre**
Hair and makeup by **Naomi Camille**
Karolyn's wardrobe by **Michele and Magid Bernard**

Resources

Books

Color
Nina Ashby, *Color Therapy, Plain and Simple*. Newburyport, MA: Hampton Roads Publishing Company, 2018.

David Hornung, *Colour: A workshop for designers and artists* (3rd edition).. London: Laurence King Publishing, 2020.

Dyeing
Betsy Blumenthal and Kathryn Kreider, *Hands on Dyeing*. Loveland, CO: Interweave Press, 1988.

Illustrating and flat sketching
Michele Wesen Bryant, *Fashion Drawing: Illustration techniques for Fashion Designers* (2nd edition). London: Laurence King Publishing, 2016.

Kathryn Hagen, *Fashion Illustration for Designers* (2nd edition). Upper Saddle River, NJ: Prentice Hall, 2005.

Basia Szkutnicka, *Flats: Technical Drawing for Fashion—a complete guide*. London: Laurence King Publishing, 2017.

Ornamentation (treatments and embellishments)
Ellen Miller, *Creating Couture Embellishment*. London: Laurence King Publishing, 2017.

Colette Wolff, *The Art of Manipulating Fabric* (2nd edition). Iola, WI: Krause Publications, 2003.

Patternmaking and draping
Helen Joseph Armstrong, *Patternmaking for Fashion Design* (5th edition). Upper Saddle River, NJ: Prentice Hall, 2013.

Dennic Chunman Lo, *Pattern Cutting*, (2nd edition). London: Laurence King Publishing, 2021.

Karolyn Kiisel, *Draping: The Complete Course* (2nd edition). London: Laurence King Publishing, 2020.

Research and inspiration
Harold Koda et al., *Charles James: Beyond Fashion*. New Haven, CT: Yale University Press, 2014.

Ezinma Mbeledogu, *Fashion Design Research* (2nd edition). London: Laurence King Publishing, 2022.

Max Tilke, *Costume Patterns and Designs*. New York: Rizzoli International Publications, 1990.

Slow fashion
Peggy Blum, *Circular Fashion: Making the Fashion Industry Sustainable*. London: Laurence King Publishing, 2021.

Kate Fletcher and Lynda Grose, *Fashion & Sustainability: Design for Change*. London: Laurence King Publishing, 2012.

Sass Brown, *ReFashioned: Cutting-Edge Clothing from Upcycled Materials*. London: Laurence King Publishing, 2013.

Stitching
Natalie Chanin and Sun Young Park, *The Geometry of Hand-Sewing*. New York: Abrams, 2017.

Anette Fischer, *Sewing for Fashion Designers*. London: Laurence King Publishing, 2015.

Claire Shaeffer, *Couture Tailoring: A Construction Guide for Women's Jackets*. London: Laurence King Publishing, 2021.

Charles Germain de Saint-Aubin, *Art of the Embroiderer*. The Los Angeles County Museum of Art, 1983.

Textiles
Clive Hallett and Amanda Johnston, *Fabric for fashion: The Complete Guide* (2nd edition). London: Laurence King Publishing, 2022.

Clive Hallett and Amanda Johnston, *Fabric for Fashion: The Swatch Book* (2nd edition revised). London: Laurence King Publishing, 2021.

Supplies
School of Making, Natalie Chanin
alabamachanin.com/the-school-of-making.com

Dharma Trading Company
dharmatrading.com

Richard the Thread
richardthethread.com

Farthingales
farthingalescorsetmakingsupplies.com

Bohemian Crystals
bohemiancrystal.com

B. Black & Sons
bblackandsons.com

Britex Fabrics
britexfabrics.com

Park Pleating
parkpleating.com

Dress forms
Kennett & Lindsell Ltd (UK)
kennettlindsell.com

Morplan (UK)
morplan.com

Siegel & Stockman (Paris)
siegel-stockman.com

Wolf Dress Forms (US)
wolfform.com

Patterns
Karolyn Kiisel
karolynkiisel.com

Patterns for all designs in *Advanced Creative Draping* and *Draping: The Complete Course* (2nd edition) are available to purchase; specific sizes on request. Order by page number and title of design.

Please note: Websites were accessed and URLs were correct at time of writing.

Index

Page numbers in *italics* indicate
   illustration captions.

A

AALTO 13
Ackermann, Haider 9
African textiles 148, *148*
airbrushing 152–3
Alabama Sewers 20
Albaz, Elber 118, 130, 174
Amati, Ludovica 223
appliqué 167, *167*, *168*
Araujo, Barbara *200*, *210*
art 16–17
Art Deco 15, 131
Art Nouveau 15, 131
artisans 166, 223
assessment 59
   block-to-drape method 85, 89, 93,
      103
   costume design 208, 209, 212, 216
   fabrics 36, 39, 40, 41
   half-scale form draping 113, 117,
      119, 125
   heirloom design 227, 244
   illustration 132, 136, 142, 145
   improvisational draping 65, 75
   protocols 59
   three-dimensional embellishment
      173, 179, 187
   two-dimensional surface design 156,
      161
Atonement 29
authenticity 222
avant-garde 14–15

B

Bacall, Lauren 157, 161
balance 59
Barrère, Hubert 221, *228*, 230, 238,
   239, 243, 244
beading 169
Beatles 16, *16*
Beaumarchais, Pierre 192
Beyoncé *191*
Bjork 17
block-to-drape method 77, 78
   bodice block 86–9
   costume design 191
   draping a block from a reference
      garment 81–5
   draping and drafting methods 80
   pant block 90–3
   recognizing templates for blocks 79,
      228
   tailored jacket 96–103
   two-piece sleeve block 94–5
   using reference garments 80

blouse, Dubarry pattern, 1930s 86–9
Blume, Guy 64
bodice block 86–9
bodice variations 60
   adding repeated shapes 61
   adding sleeve 61
   Origami bodice 62–3
   use of contrasting fabrics 61
   working with negative space 61
bomber jackets 79, *79*
bouclé 43, *43*
Bowie, David 14, *14*
Bratis, Angelos 118, *118*
brocade opera cloak 154–6
Burke, J. T. *Beautiful Mask 50*
burn tests *134*, *135*
bustiers 138, 139, 143, 202

C

Capote, Truman 17
Carm Goode *17*
cascades 44, 45
Chalayan, Hussein 16, *57*, 121
Chanel *18*, 79, *129*, *170*, *184*, 221,
   224
   Chanel, Coco 22, 26, 169
Chanin, Natalie 'Alabama' 20, *20*,
   167–8, *168*
cheongsams 12
Chloé 129, *129*, *232*, 234
Cirque du Soleil 156, *190*, 214, 216
classical style 57
Clifford+Challey 223
close-fitting drapes 35
coat, Sikh prince 110–13
color 150, *150*
   testing color for surface design when
      draping 150
construction quality 59
construction testing 46–7
corrections 92, 143, 212
corsets 202
costume design 189, 190
   base/rehearsal pieces pieces 201–7,
      211–12
   Beaumarchais Costume 192, 196,
      198, 210–17
   building a costume 190–1, 201
   building the overpieces 213–16
   costume design illustration 133–6
   costume fitting guidelines 207
   costumes of quality 191
   creating authenticity in period
      costumes 193
   design development 194
   experimental draping 196–7
   final design illustrations 199, 200
   fittings 208–9, 212, 216

Ghost costume 197
   half-scale design development 195
   improvisational draping 198–9
   Minuet Dancer costume 192, 196,
      200–9
   ornamentation for communication 195
   stages of costume design 192–4
   Sybilla Costume 196, 199
   synchronizing the vision with the
      director 194
cotton 43, *43*
Courrèges, André 16
couture 10
   couture details 244
   Ten Essentials of Couture 21, 59, 97,
      132, 143, 144, 216, 220, 228
cowls 44
   draping a "half-lock" cowl 44
craftsmanship 10, 22, 170, 191
   fabric choices 31
   superior decorative craftsmanship
      224
cultural ancestral gravitas 224
cultural appropriation or appreciation?
   12
cultural references 62
cutting, zero-waste 118–19

D

Dacquoise 114–17
Dark Radiance 9, 32, 52, 157
   Cosmos skirt 71–5
   Galaxy jacket 152–3, 171–3
   improvisational drapes 65–7
darts 42, 43
De Vic, Robin *154*
design 59, 145, 149
   Designer's Aims and Aspirations 10,
      170, 191, 220
   draping to test design elements
      42–5
   fabric choices 31
   Ten Principles of Good Design 17,
      106, 108, 115, 132, 220, 228
digital printing 157–61, 235–8
Dior 221
   Dior, Christian 18
documenting your work 50, 121
drafting methods 80
draping 6
   draping and drafting methods 80
   draping preparation 58–9
   draping with a mirror 116
   draping with muslin 7, 60
   eye, hand, and heart 7
draping tape 37
   taping for general guidelines 175
dress form preparation 58, 62, 72, 82,

87, 91, 94, 99
costume design 201, 210
half-scale form draping 111, 115, 118
illustration 132, 134, 138
three-dimensional embellishment 175
two-dimensional surface design 158
dress, 1940s 81–5
dress, digital print 157–9
digitizing pattern and print 161
fitting toile 160
marking and truing 160
print scaling tests 160
dress, flower 163, 174–9
dress, Ikebana 64
dress, Saints Descend to Earth 221, 228–33, 243–4
correcting the fitting toile 234
digital printing steps 235–8
embroidery and embellishment at Maison Lesage 239–43
marking and truing 233
Duquette, Tony 194
Durran, Jacqueline 29
dyeing 148
ombré, airbrushing and novelty dyeing techniques 152–3

E
Earth's Heritage 11, 32, 53
improvisational drapes 60–1
Edelkoort, Li 58, 222
Edzard, Christine 193
embellishments 49, 59, 164, 239–43
categories of embellishment 167–9
communicating with your artisans 166
purpose and origin of embellishment 165–6
see also three-dimensional embellishment
embroidery 167, 168, 221
embroidery and embellishment at Maison Lesage 239–43
ergonomics 10, 18, 59, 170, 191
fabric choices 31
Erté (Romain de Tirtoff) 15, 131
experimental draping 25, 26–31
construction testing 46–7
costume design 191, 196–7
experimental draping from inspiration boards 50–3
first impressions 32–5
special effects and embellishments 48–9
studying grainlines 36–41
testing design elements 42–5

F
fabrics 26, 149
beginning a collection 30–1
block-to-drape method 90
controlling hand and surface textures 46–7
creating your own fabrics 214
draping from an illustration 132, 133, 134, 138
editorial fabric research 114
evoking mood and tone 29
experimental draping 32–5
fabric evaluation checklist 28, 137
"face" preference 42
half-scale form draping 114, 118, 120
handling 32
heirloom design 225, 230
improvisational draping 58, 59, 60, 62, 64, 65, 66, 71
observation and assessment 36
special effects and embellishments 48–9
testing design elements 42–5
three-dimensional embellishment 171, 175
two-dimensional surface design 153, 154, 157, 158
understanding fabric qualities 39
use of contrasting fabrics 61
visualization 27, 114
fashion 16–17
fashion illustration 131
draping from a fashion illustration 137–45
feathers 164, 169, 185
Ferretti, Alberta 163, 174
flower dress 174–9
film noir 157
fittings, professional 144, 207
flat sketches 58, 65, 71, 81, 87, 90, 110, 118, 120, 133, 138
heirloom design 231
draping from a costume design illustration and flat sketch 133–6, 204
technical flat sketches 132
three-dimensional embellishment 175
two-dimensional surface design 153, 155, 158
flounces 44, 45
flowers 169
focus 8–9, 10
costume design 191
embellishments 170
fabric choices 31
foundations 202

four-ply silk crepe 67
Fraser, Claire 179
fusing 46

G
Gallay, Charles 97
gathers 42
Gaultier, Jean-Paul 16, 165
Ghost costume 197
Givenchy 13
grainlines 26, 36, 81
bias grainline 38
grainline direction 38–41
locating 36
marking 37
setting mood and tone 39–41
Sikh prince coat 111
studying drape 37–9
Greffulhe, Countess 17
Grès, Madame (Alix Grès) 7, 107

H
half-scale form draping 105, 106–7
costume design 191, 195
crafting stuffed arms for the half-scale form 107
design development on the half-scale form 120–5
draping on the half-scale form with final design fabrics 118
experimental draping to evaluate fabric and grainline choices 121
full-scale drape 113
improvisational draping 108–9, 114–17
mathematical draft method to scale up to a full size pattern 112–13
modernising the cut of a traditional ethnic design 110–13
re-drape method for scaling up 117, 124
scan and tile method of scaling up 123
techniques to take half-scale drapes to full size 106
zero-waste cutting 118–19
Harley-Davidson jacket 79
Harlow, Jean 137
Hayworth, Rita 137
Healey, Peter Wing 133, 133, 154, 192–4, 206
see Spell of Tradition, The
heirloom design 23, 23, 219, 220
draping the modern heirloom design 228–38, 243–4
embroidery and embellishment at Maison Lesage 239–43
heirloom design development 225–7

modern heirloom garments 221–4
qualities of an heirloom garment 220
hem finishes 47
historical references 62
Hollywood 137, 157

I
Ikebana *10, 32, 51*
Ikebana dress 64
improvisational drapes 62–3
illustrations 127, 128
checking proportions 135
costume design 191
design sketches 129–30
draping from a costume design illustration and flat sketch 133–6
draping from a fashion illustration 137–45
fashion illustration 131
technical flat sketches 132
improvisational draping 55, 56
Cosmos skirt project 71–5
costume design 191, 198–9, 212
draping preparation 58–9
self-awareness 57
studies from inspiration boards 60–7
upcycle study 68–70
working intuitively 57
inherited clothing or textiles 223
inspiration 8, 58, 60, 62, 64, 65, 66, 67, 71, 149
block-to-drape method 86, 90, 94
costume design *192, 193*
draping from an illustration 132, 133, 137
half-scale form draping 114, 118, 120
heirloom design 225, 229
three-dimensional embellishment 171, 174, 180
two-dimensional surface design 152, 154, 157
inspiration boards 8, 59
Dark Radiance *9, 32, 52, 157*
Earth's Heritage *11, 32, 53*
experimental draping from inspiration boards 50–3
Ikebana *10, 32, 51*
Saints Descend to Earth 236
intuition 57

J
Jacaranda *166, 168*
jacket, equestrian 94–5
jacket, Galaxy 152–3, 171–3
two-dimensional application on the drape 153
jacket, tailored 96–103

James, Charles 17
Joyce, James 56

K
Kahlo, Frieda 17
Kawakubo, Rei 16, 18
Kiisel, Karolyn *30, 168, 219, 223*
Kiisel, Valentina Marie 167, *167*
Knightley, Keira 29
Koché 108–9
Kocher, Christelle 16, 163
embellishment development 180–7
from half-scale drape to runway 108–9
Lemarié for Christelle Kocher 169

L
Lacroix, Christian *27, 129*
Lady Gaga 17, 33
Lagerfeld, Karl 16, *22*, 129, *129*, 166, *166, 183*, 221
Lanvin 130
layering fabrics 48
Lemarié *164, 166, 166*, 180, *180, 181, 182–6*, 224
Lemieux, Dominique 67, 156, *190*, 214, 216
Lesage *20, 147, 151*, 166, *219*, 221, 224, 229, 238
embroidery and embellishment at Maison Lesage 239–43
Libertine 16
linen 42, *43*
Lopez, Antonio 131
Louis Vuitton 13, 221

M
Maharishi Mahesh Yogi 16
marking the drape 74, 85, 103, 142, 160, 233
Marras, Antonio *30, 30*
Matreyek, Mira 171, *171*
McLaren, Malcolm 16
McQueen, Alexander *8*, 16, *78*
tailored jacket 96–103
Merikosi, Tuomas 13
mirrors 116
Miyake, Issey 18
mock-up techniques 151, 174
embellishment mock-up tests 174–9
Monae, Jonelle *16*
Monroe, Marilyn 137
mood 29, 52
draping to capture a mood 134
setting mood with grainline direction 39–41
Moschino *149*
Moya, Eddie 205

muses 67
music 67
muslins 7, 60
block-to-drape method 82, 87, 90–1, 94, 98
costume design 201, 208, 210
draping from an illustration 132, 134, 138
embellishment mock-ups on muslin drape 178
fitting sample with embellishment mock-ups 179
half-scale form draping 111, 115, 118, 120
heirloom design 226, 231
improvisational drapes 58, 60, 62, 64, 65, 66, 72
patching muslin while draping 176
three-dimensional embellishment 175
two-dimensional surface design 153, 154, 158

N
Nakamura, Hiroki 224, *224*
"Napa Valley Almond Blossoms in the Rain" 120–5
Native American symbolism 165, *165*
needlework embellishments 167–8
negative space 61

O
ombré *151, 152*, 152–3
opera cloak, brocade 154–6
two-dimensional application on the drape 155–6
Organic Cotton Plus *20*
Orientalism 15
Origami bodice 62–3
originality 14
overview 59
Owens, Rick 9, 56, *56*

P
pant, high-waisted, fitted 90–3
Park Pleating 166, *168*, 205, *205*
past and present 11–12
pattern measurement conversion chart 202
Pei, Guo 169, *169*
peignoir, bustier and tap pant set 137–42
assessment 145
conducting a professional fitting 144
corrections 143
final sample 144
final touches 145

first assessment 142
"good design" 145
marking and truing 142
preparing a fitting toile 144
perspective 59
pick-and-pull method 36
pinning 176
pattern correction technique when
pinning at a seam is difficult 92
pleats 42, 205
inverted pleats 43
pleating embellishments 168
Poiret, Paul 15, *15*
Powell, Anthony 194
preparation 58, 156
block-to-drape method 81–2, 86–7,
90–1, 94, 96–9
costume design 201, 210
detailed analysis 59
draping from an illustration 132,
133–4, 137–8
first impressions 59
half-scale form draping 110–11,
114–15, 118, 120
heirloom design 225, 229
improvisational draping 60, 62, 64,
65–7, 68, 71–2
three-dimensional embellishment
171, 174–5
Pugh, Gareth *18*
Punk 16

Q
quilting *167*, 167–8

R
Rabanne, Paco 16
recording your work 32, 50, 121
reference garments 80, 191, 193
draping a block from a reference
garment 81–5
repeated shapes 61
research 10–17
block-to-drape method 86, 90, 96–7
costume design 191, 193
draping from an illustration 132,
133, 137
editorial fabric research 114
embellishments 170
fabric choices 31
half-scale form draping 114, 118,
120
heirloom design 225, 229
improvisational design research 56,
58, 62, 64, 66, 67, 71
research methods 11
three-dimensional embellishment
171, 174, 181

two-dimensional surface design 152,
154, 157
Rey, Bastide 7, 67, 130, 134, 137
Rodarte *148*
Rolland, Stéphane 28, 67, 130, *131*
romantic style 57
Ross, Jillian *133*
rough sketches 71, 115

S
Saab, Ellie *152*
Saint-Aubin, Charles Germain de
Designer to the King 169
Saint-Martin, Jean 107
Saints Descend to Earth dress 221,
228–38, 243–4
embroidery and embellishment at
Maison Lesage 239–43
Sami *12*, 13
scale 32
Schiaparelli, Elsa 221
Scott, Jeremy *149*
seam finishes 47
self awareness 13–14, 57
sequin work 169, *184*
silk charmeuse 34
silk chiffon 32–3
silk matelassé 34, 35
silk peau de soie 33
silk satin organza 33
Siriano, Christine *16*
sketches 230, *230*
design sketches 129–30
see flat sketches; rough sketches
skirt, Cosmos 71–3
assessing finish 75
marking and truing the drape 74
sleeves 61
sleeve draping order 84
two-piece sleeve block 94–5
slow fashion 10, 19–20, 170, 191, 221
fabric choices 31
socio-political statements 16
specialty stitching 168
Spell of Tradition, The 133, *133*, 154,
192–4, 206
Beaumarchais Costume 192,
210–17
Minuet Dancer costume 192, 200–9
stability 59
Stanwyck, Barbara 157
stitching tests 47
Strauss, Levi 26
support elements 47
sustainability 19–20
Sybilla Costume 196, 199
symbolism and spirituality 165, *165*,
223

T
technology, integration of in clothing
171–3
templates 79
tension of fabric, testing 36
Thomas, Dylan 56
thread-tracing 37
three-dimensional embellishment 163,
164
costume design 191
creative draping and developing
embellishments 170
embellishment development 180–7
embellishment development mini
exercise 181
embellishment mock-up tests 174–9
integration of technology in draping
171–3
see also embellishments
Tilke, Max Karl *110*, *224*
timeless cuts 222
toiles 21, *147*, *151*
block-to-drape method 81, 92–3
fitting toiles 144, 160, 208, 234
Toledo, Ruben 128, *128*, 129
tone 29, 52
setting tone with grainline direction
39–41
treatments 49, 167
fabric treatments 168
trims 59, 114, 118, 120, 132, 133,
138, 153, 154, 157, 171, 175, 225
trousseau lingerie 137–45
truing the drape 74, 85, 103, 142, 160,
213, 233
tucking 168
testing tucks 43
tunic, Shibori and shells 225–7
two-dimensional surface design 147,
148
artisan-crafted two-dimensional
design 154–6
costume design 191
creative draping techniques to use
with two-dimensional surface design
151
draping using a digital print 157–61
maximising the impact of a two-
dimensional surface design 149
ombré, airbrushing and novelty
dyeing techniques 152–3
understanding the power of colour
150

U
underlining 46
Ungaro, Emmanuel 90, *90*
upcycle study 68–70

V

Valentino 221
Van Herpen, Iris 14, *14*
Viktor & Rolf 16
Vionnet, Madeleine 15, *106*, 107, 118,
    221
visualization 27, 114
visvim WMV 224
volume 32

W

Walsh, Gerard *Tiger Lily 51*
Ward, Nari *We the People* 180, *180*,
    187
wash tests 46–7
Waterhouse, John William *The Danaïdes*
    29
Watnick, Rita 22
Westwood, Vivienne 16
wool 42, *43*
Worth, Charles Frederick 221

Y

Yamamoto, Kansai *14*, 18
Yves Saint Laurent 221

Z

zero-waste cutting 118–19

Credits

Pleating; 169 Richard Bord/ GettyImages for Mac Cosmetics; 171 Miwa Matreyek; 172 Electronics designed by Christopher Brown; 173 Model: Claire Fraser; 174 Catwalking. com; 179 two-dimensional and three-dimensional embellishment mock-up by Claire Fraser; 180 (bottom) Courtesy the artist and Lehmann Maupin, New York, Hong Kong, Seoul, and London; 183 (bottom left and right) Sylvain Novelli at Lemarié with flower press; 184 (middle left) Eleonore Stoll at Lemarié with flower petal; 184 (middle right) Eximé-Destin Erlande at Lemarié with metal shaping ball; 185: Julie Bastart at Lemarié sewing feathers; 187 Model: Laia Bonastre; 190 illustration by Dominique Lemieux; 191 Larry Busacca/Getty Images for Coachella; 192 Mood board created by Anita Rinaldi-Harnden and Karolyn Kiisel; 193 (top left) Public domain; 193 (top middle) Max Tilke, *Costume Patterns and Designs*; 193 (top right) Public domain; 193 (bottom right) Public domain; 193 (bottom middle) Public domain; 193 (bottom right) Donna Ward/Getty Images; 194 (top) Mood board created by Anita Rinaldi-Harnden; 194 (bottom) Tony Duquette, Inc; 196 Model: Li Liu; 197 (bottom): 1930s' style hat design, Christopher Brown; 199 Model: Karen Hogel-Brown; 199 (bottom) Model: Karen Hogel-Brown, photo by Gerard Walsh; 200 Illustration by Barbra Araujo; 201 Performer: Liza Barskaya; 205 Pleating samples by Park Pleating; 208 Performer: Liza Barskaya; 209 Performer: Liza Barskaya; 210 (top) Illustration by Barbra Araujo; 212 Model: Gerard Walsh; 214 Hand-painted embellishment by Georgette Arison; 216 Performer Anthony Jensen;

216 Hair and makeup: Naomi Craig; 217 Performers Anthony Jensen, Liza Barskaya; 217 Hair and makeup: Naomi Craig; 217 Minuet Dancer and Beaumarchais costumes co-designer: Anita Rinaldi-Harnden; 223 CLIFFORD+CHALLEY; 224 (top right) Max Tilke, *Costume Patterns and Designs*; 228 (bottom) Photo by Karolyn Kiisel; 224 (bottom right) Hiroki Nakamura/ visvim; 229 (bottom) Karolyn Kiisel and Hubert Barrère at Lesage; 230 (top left) Karolyn Kiisel; 232 (bottom) Estrop/ Getty Images; 235 (top left) Alamy Stock Photo; 236 (top right and bottom) digital print work by Jianren Wang; 239 Dominique Dufour and Hubert Barrère at Lesage; 240 Dominique Dufour at Lesage; 241 Luc Darribère at Lesage; 243 (top) Photo by Sky & Olga Photography, Karolyn Kiisel; 245 Model: Soleil Ife, Hair and makeup: Naomi Craig.

Commissioned photography

Gerard Walsh: 4–5, 9, 10, 11, 26, 31, 35, 38 (top far left), 38 (top middle left), 40–1, 43–5, 46 (middle), 47–9, 50 (left), 51–3, 55, 58, 60–6, 68–70, 71 (middle), 71 (bottom), 72–6, 79 (bottom left), 79 (bottom right), 81, 83–5, 86 (left), 87 (bottom left), 87 (bottom right), 88–93, 94 (bottom), 95, 97–104, 111–14, 116–17, 119–26, 134–6, 139–45, 150, 151 (right), 152 (top left), 152 (bottom right), 153–4, 156, 157, 158–62, 167, 168 (bottom left), 168 (bottom right), 172–3, 175–9, 188, 192, 194 (top), 195, 196 (top right), 196 (top left), 196 (bottom left), 197–8, 199 (top left), 199 (bottom right) 201–2, 203 (bottom), 204–10, 213–15, 222, 223 (right), 223 (far right), 225–7, 232 (top left), 232 (top middle),

232 (top right), 233–4, 235 (top right cluster), 235 (bottom), 237, 238 (top), 243 (bottom), 244–5.

Sia Aryai: 24, 32–4, 36–7, 38 (top middle right), 38 (top middle left), 38 (bottom left), 38 (bottom right), 39, 46 (top left), 46 (top right), 46 (bottom left), 46 (bottom right), 67 (bottom), 155, 196 (bottom right), 199 (top right), 203 (top), 203 (middle), 211–12, 237 (top left).

Rowan Morgan: 21, 22, 108, 146, 151, 164, 166, 170, 180 (top), 181–7, 218–21, 224 (top left), 229, 230 (top right), 230 (bottom), 238 (bottom), 239–42.

Line art

Barbara Araujo: 34, 40, 42, 58, 68, 74, 79, 87 (top), 107, 120, 133, 136, 139–41, 155, 175, 199, 200, 207, 210, 226.

Saeyoung Chang-Gagnon: 80, 81, 90, 92, 94, 96, 110, 153, 158, 231.

Selina Sanders: 87 (bottom).

Acknowledgments

Over the last several years, it has taken the efforts of many of my professional colleagues, friends, and family to bring this book to fruition. My heartfelt thanks to:

Sophie Wise and Charlotte Selby, my outstanding editors at Laurence King Publishing, for their wise counsel and endless forbearance.

Helene Gustavsson, for her creativity and resourcefulness in bringing me the exciting copyright images, and her great patience and perspicacity for seeing it all the way through to perfection.

Vanessa Green, for her superb skill in book design, for crafting it in such a cohesive and artistic way, and for actually making all of it fit despite starting out with 30 extra pages.

Jared Gold, for all of his inspiring ideas, and for instilling in me the courage to write about couture and the importance of craftsmanship and research.

Jory Weitz, for encouraging me to see the book as a personal, documentary-style journey by adding my own personal reflections and experiences, and for securing for me the many fascinating interviews with all of the talented designers I spoke with.

Christelle Kocher, for inspiring the chapters on Draping on the Half-Scale Form and Draping with the use of Three-Dimensional Embellishment, and for allowing me to document her design process.

Hubert Barrère, for his talent, expertise, and humor during the work on our Saints Descend to Earth dress; a final project that feels like the crowning glory of the book.

Saeyoung Chang-Gagnon and Jianren Wang, for their work on the Saints Descend to Earth digital print.

Sebastian Oxlaj, for his ability to execute the highest quality of couture techniques, and wrangling Chapter 8's costumes into shape.

Donna Lobato, for her patience and pattern-drafting expertise.

Barbara Araujo, for jumping in at the last minute to draw the flat sketches, and doing the beautiful illustrations for Chapter 8: Draping for Costume Design.

My colleagues at LACC Theater Academy, Eddie Bledsoe and Christopher Brown, who provided the digital print for the Film Noir dress, and the technology for the Galaxy jacket.

My student interns, especially the very talented Linda Aguirre.

Gerard Dislaire, for his limitless support and transcendent understanding of the complex world of fashion.

Lisa McCaskill, for her early draft organizational skills, and for her take on the contemporary definition of the Classic vs. Romantic styles.

Naomi Camille, makeup and hair artist extraordinaire, for her work on the videos and models.

Peter Wing Healey, composer of the opera *The Spell of Tradition*, for inspiring the beautiful costumes in Chapter 8, and for his ongoing support and many words of wisdom.

Anita Rinaldi-Harnden, for reining me in or cheering me on as needed, and always steering me in the right direction with her unerring eye for good design. Always a joy to work with, she co-designed and was an indispensable part of the construction of the Film Noir dress and the costumes for the Minuet Dancer and Beaumarchais.

Kyle Titterton, who elevated the tone of the videos by taking an authentic interest in the subject of draping, infused it with his love of filmmaking, and made the difficult process of filming the videos into a month of laughs and adventure.

Gerard Walsh, for his professionalism and astonishing talent.

Kirsten Taylor, my hard working, multitalented, tech-wizard assistant, for her dedication, unfailing energy, and amazing sense of artistry on so many of the projects.

My daughters Claire and Ellen Iona, for their loving support and constant feedback on what appeals to a younger generation, and to Claire for her beautiful hand-painting on the Ferretti gown, for modeling the Galaxy Jacket, and for all of her work on the inspiration boards.

My husband Scott, whose cogent comments toward the end helped bring it in for landing just in time.